What They Are Saying

In the history of soccer in the United States, there will be a before and after Alan Rothenberg. He will be remembered as the man who changed soccer forever in our country, both on and off the field. He organized the greatest World Cup in FIFA's history, which led to the creation of Major League Soccer. He is one of the greatest leaders and builders our sport ever had.

—Legendary Univision sportscaster Andrés Cantor
("Goaaaallllllllllllllllllll!!")

Alan was a visionary. He could see the potential of women's soccer before a lot of other people. Because of his vision and risk-taking, the 1999 Women's World Cup could happen in the big way that it did. No one had seen crowds like that for women's sports. The success of the 1999 Women's World Cup transformed not just women's soccer, but women's sports globally.

—Former U.S. midfielder Julie Foudy,
a two-time World Cup champion

The roots of the soccer culture that is currently being experienced in the United States—around MLS and NWSL teams, viewership of FIFA World Cups and Women's World Cups, and even the tremendous interest in the English Premier League—can all be attributed to the work of one man, Alan Rothenberg. Rothenberg made the 1984 Olympic Soccer Tournament a huge and unexpected success, which led to his taking over U.S. Soccer and the 1994 FIFA World Cup in the early 1990s. His work professionalizing U.S. Soccer and staging a wildly successful FIFA World Cup led to the founding of Major League Soccer, the burgeoning interest in international professional soccer, and the reimagined and also wildly successful 1999 FIFA Women's World Cup. The success of the FIFA Women's World Cup, in turn, led to the continuing interest in the U.S. women's national team program, women's professional soccer, and eventually the NWSL. Truly, it all starts with Alan Rothenberg.

—Marla Messing, former CEO,
National Women's Soccer League

Alan is a doer. He gets stuff done. Plenty of people talk a lot, but things fall to the wayside. Alan had to educate the masses that weren't within the soccer world about what the World Cup was and what it meant. Alan made the World Cup an event that you needed to be part of, that you were going to regret if you missed out. He did an amazing job of selling that to people.

—Hall of Fame former U.S. midfielder Cobi Jones

My lifelong dream was to play for the German national team. Alan Rothenberg couldn't make that happen, but as honorary chairman of the World Cup board I worked with him, and I had a front-row seat watching as he transformed soccer in this country.

—Former U.S. Secretary of State Henry Kissinger

We'd gotten to a point where the game was ready to take another huge leap, but it was missing someone like Alan Rothenberg. Even though soccer was growing, the situation was pretty bleak. Alan brought us out of the Dark Ages into an era that has gone further than any of us could have imagined back in the late 1980s and early 1990s.

—Mike Woitalla, executive editor, *Soccer America*

He's the leading figure in bringing U.S. soccer into the world soccer community. He was very respected by FIFA and elevated the status of U.S. soccer. We were third-class citizens until Alan came along and brought the World Cup in 1994.

—Former U.S. men's national team coach Bruce Arena

THE BIG BOUNCE

THE SURGE THAT SHAPED THE FUTURE OF U.S. SOCCER

ALAN ROTHENBERG

Library of Congress Cataloging-in-Publication Data available upon request.

This book is available in quantity at special discounts for your group or organization. For further information, contact:

Triumph Books LLC
814 North Franklin Street
Chicago, Illinois 60610
(312) 337-0747
www.triumphbooks.com

Printed in U.S.A.
ISBN: 978-1-63727-761-4
Design and page production by Nord Compo
Photos courtesy of Daniel Rothenberg unless otherwise indicated

To my wife, Georgina, and sons, Brad, Richie, and Danny, for sharing this journey with me. I couldn't have done it without your loving support and contributions.

CONTENTS

FOREWORD

EACH AND EVERY DAY that I get up and work and live in the world of American soccer in the 2020s and see what the sport has become, I know it's because of people like Alan Rothenberg. He was an incredible visionary. Like any true visionary, he had the ability to look around corners and peer into the future and see things that others didn't. American soccer is a labor of love, but it's still a labor. I know sometimes we kick ourselves for what we haven't done as a soccer nation. We also have to pat ourselves on the back and recognize how far we've come in a relatively short period of time. If you look back at when Alan first came to soccer, what it was then and what it is now, it's pretty amazing.

Alan was just what soccer needed in the 1990s. As a person, Alan could be incredibly thoughtful and kind, but as a businessman he was a bulldog. He recognized early on that he needed to have that tenacity in order to be successful. When he took over as president of U.S. Soccer in 1990, it caused a stir. Here was a leader who took the tools and skills of other businesses and applied them to moving soccer forward, ultimately making it much more progressive and evolved.

For a lot of us, who up to then had been stuck in a kind of Wild West, mom-and-pop type of existence for soccer, it was incredibly refreshing to have somebody who approached our sport with a business mind and a business strategy and recognized soccer's potential and how to capitalize on it. So even though kicking the ball might have been foreign to Alan, he found hidden value in soccer as a business and was able to foster it. I remember a lot of us on the national team at the time really appreciated having someone like Alan leading the charge. His skills, passion, and vision all came together in his work organizing the 1994 World Cup and showing what the World Cup could bring not only in the moment, but more importantly longer term, including paving the way to establish Major League Soccer as a thriving professional league.

One of the proudest moments of my life was getting on a plane in Italy after playing in Serie A—the first American to play in the greatest league in the world with all the best players and the best money and all the prestige—and flying home to the United States to start Major League Soccer in 1996. You don't get to start things from the very beginning very often in your life. So, I remain incredibly proud of being part of everything that was done to start that. There were some really trying times. As Alan will tell you, we had countless difficulties and challenges along the way, as you can imagine. But Alan always had a belief and a vision as to what he wanted it to be and what it could be, and ultimately has been proven right in terms of the success of the game both on and off the field.

Alan and I both grew up in Michigan, and there was something about being from Detroit that forged a bond between us right away. Especially for someone in soccer who grew up in the '70s and '80s, to meet somebody else from Michigan in the soccer world, especially someone of that stature, was a rarity for me. Having Detroit and Detroit sports in common connected us immediately. Whether it's something in the water or growing up in that sports environment, or maybe more importantly what the city once was or is still attempting to return to, I think all of that played into it. Detroit's proximity to Canada—I grew up going to the Windsor Ballet—and obviously everything that came with Motown, the industry and the music and the culture that exists and has existed there, all of that makes it a pretty unique and interesting and fun city to come from. And I think it produces people with, I guess for lack of a better word, perspective. They take what they do seriously, but they don't take themselves too seriously. That was Alan to a T.

In sports there is always kind of a separation between the suits and the players, but Alan was always incredibly comfortable going back and forth. This was not somebody with a traditional soccer background, or any soccer background at all for that matter, but none of that mattered. He was gregarious and sociable, and you enjoyed talking to him. Even in the midst of negotiating, there was always a sense of, *wow, there might be sides taken, but this was for the greater good of building something that was going to last well beyond our careers and lifetimes if it was done correctly.* Alan respected that he needed the players in order to do what he wanted to accomplish with soccer. He had dreams and aspirations relative to the game that coincided with many of ours, but the question was: How are you going to make it happen? By having people that are smart, people that are driven, and people that believe that this can be something bigger. Alan embodied all those qualities.

Alan recognized that, whether you were on the field kicking the ball or off the field, there was an element of being a soccer pioneer and an element of spreading the gospel. Thankfully, multiple generations of men and women have seized that mantle and looked at it as their responsibility and part of that job. When I see all these players that are playing different places around the world, and I see MLS going into its 30th year, or I walk the streets and I see people wearing U.S. men's and women's national team jerseys or MLS jerseys, whether it's the NWSL, the Women's League, the USL, or other leagues, it's come about because of the fertilization of the American soccer landscape. If you look back in history, there are seminal moments in the evolution of the game. MLS doesn't happen without the '94 World Cup. And so, the '94 World Cup was huge. The '99 Women's World Cup was huge. The arrival of David Beckham and now the arrival of Lionel Messi. But the flag that can be planted with the 2026 World Cup hosted by North America is incredible. This ramp that we have up to 2026—we can't afford to waste it on and off the field. The tent that is soccer gets bigger when a World Cup comes, but when the circus does leave town, are people converted? Do they stay? That's where the opportunity lies.

As I get older, I am asked a lot about the history and the evolution of this game. There is the tendency to think that there should be gratitude and respect relative to everything that's come before. But let's be honest, we've all stood on the shoulders of previous generations. And I think the greatest legacy that Alan Rothenberg leaves is that when a young kid in America wakes up today and looks at the opportunities and the pathways and the options that they have at their disposal playing soccer, it is dramatically different than when Alan came on the scene. This whole generation that does wake up today knows nothing of the Wild West and the challenges and the difficulties that faced everyone on and off the field. I consider that a win.

I'm incredibly proud of the difference my generation made. We'll tell the stories, and they should be told. People should be celebrated and respected for all the work that has gone into bringing the sport forward. Right at the top of that list is Alan Rothenberg for everything that he did. Those boys and girls that do wake up and have this on their soccer plate in front of them, and don't know it's because of everything that has been done before.... Guess what? They hopefully will go on and pass it along to another generation, and hopefully there will be more Alan Rothenbergs that recognize the potential and work their ass off to realize it and reap the benefits, and then pass it along to that next generation.

—Hall of Fame former
U.S. defender Alexi Lalas

CHAPTER 1

THINKING BIG: THE 1984 OLYMPICS

PETER UEBERROTH CHANGED MY LIFE—and set in motion the events that truly launched soccer in the United States as a major sport. I first met Peter in late 1980 when he called me to his office in Century City to talk about his work organizing the 1984 Olympics in Los Angeles. I had been hearing good things about the moves Ueberroth was making. If you were in the sports business world in Southern California, you heard plenty of informed speculation about how these Olympics would be a bust, financially at least. There was fear and panic in some quarters. But not from Peter. He was considered and shrewd in his preparations for the Olympics, among other things coming up with a clever plan to get established people to work for him basically for free. All it took was giving them a cool title, "commissioner," each charged with overseeing a sport or a venue.

I was inclined to say yes to his offer to become one of his 23 Olympic commissioners and join the large-scale effort, unprecedented in scale and innovation, he was marshalling. It made sense, as a patriotic American who wanted the Olympics to be a big hit, and also to do Los Angeles proud. The question was: Which sport? Basketball would have made sense, given my background with the Los Angeles Lakers as vice president and counsel, working out trades and in many ways running the sports business on behalf of its owner Jack Kent Cooke, for some years even sitting on the NBA Board of Governors. (An interesting aside: at one point well before my friend David Stern took over, I narrowly missed being selected as the next NBA commissioner, which would have been quite the interesting journey.)

Peter surprised me by asking if I might be interested in being commissioner of soccer for the Los Angeles Olympics. He knew that in the 1970s I'd been part owner of the Los Angeles Aztecs, a team in the old North American Soccer League, and before that, in the late 1960s, I'd served as general manager of the Los Angeles Wolves. Peter assumed with that background I must know a lot about soccer. That was wrong, but I didn't try too hard to convince him otherwise. The truth was, I had absolutely no ongoing involvement with soccer and little interest. I had never played soccer, never coached soccer, and had never seen a soccer match until the Wolves came to Los Angeles.

My main concern at the time was my law practice. I was managing partner of my rapidly growing law firm, Manatt, Phelps and Rothenberg, heading our litigation department. At that time I was still a young, aggressive, ambitious lawyer trying to establish my own reputation and that of my firm. My thought process was simple: soccer was the best organized sport in the world, as I saw it, thus I assumed there would be less of a burden on me as commissioner of soccer, compared to the other, more chaotically directed sports. So, I accepted

Peter's offer. A fateful decision for me—and also, as it turned out, for the sport.

Peter had a lot of good ideas and getting people like me involved as commissioners was one of them. The thought was that busy, engaged, successful people in mid-career couldn't give up two or three years of their life to work full time helping organize the Olympics—and as a matter of fact, he didn't have the budget to pay them for full-time work even if they'd wanted to take that on. So instead, we would in effect be super volunteers. Peter wanted to tap our Rolodexes and networks of contacts (our databases, in today's terminology) and also tap our brains, and he wanted to get us talking up the Olympics and generating buzz. He would pay us something, a nominal annual fee of $1,000. You can't fire a volunteer, but you can fire somebody you pay, so Peter was smart to set it up that way. If he had any issues with any of the commissioners, he had options. Basically: *If I don't like what you're doing, I can fire ya.* And he did, as a matter of fact, fire a couple commissioners when that became glaringly necessary. Ten years later as CEO of the 1994 FIFA World Cup, I unhappily was compelled to terminate one such "volunteer," someone with a high local profile. Quieting criticism, John C. Argue, the prominent Los Angeles business leader who led the effort to bring the Olympics to Los Angeles, said, "If you're making an omelette, you have to break some eggs."

Even before I met Ueberroth, I was intrigued by what I'd heard about his energy and vision. Born in Illinois, he grew up in Northern California and studied business at San Jose State on an athletic scholarship, starring on the water polo team and just missing a spot on the U.S. Olympic water polo team in 1956. He was a good enough amateur golfer to be one of three

Americans who took part in a four-round amateur tournament in Taipei in 1976. As a high school student, Ueberroth had a lot of entrepreneurial energy and was financially self-sufficient while still a teenager. He was also, like me, always family oriented. Soon after graduation he was married in 1959, with his younger brother John as best man. He and his bride, Ginny—they're still married, more than 65 years later—relocated to Hawaii, where Ueberroth worked as Honolulu manager for Trans International Airlines. He learned the travel business and founded First Travel, which grew into the second-largest travel company in the United States by the time he sold it in 1980.

I discovered that at First Travel, Ueberroth had developed a philosophy of trying to attract a critical mass of bright, innovative people whose ideas would complement each other, a management trait I shared as I was building our law firm and one I have consistently followed throughout my career. I knew Peter was the kind of energetic visionary I would learn a lot from working together on a major project—I just didn't understand quite how major.

I was always a big sports fan, growing up in Michigan, but never thought I'd work in sports. It probably started when, on my sixth birthday, my father took me to Briggs Stadium to watch Hank Greenberg, the great slugger beloved by the fans of Detroit. My dad was a pharmacist and owned a drugstore in Detroit where I would help out from the time I was nine years old.

At the University of Michigan, I loved all-night gin rummy games with my fraternity brothers from Sigma Alpha Mu (the "Sammies") and going to Michigan basketball, football, and hockey games. Sports were fun, I thought, but not real life. For me, real life began when I married Georgina Silverman in August 1960 and started Michigan Law School. Until then, I'm the first to say, I was a screw-off: a massive under-achiever. I was admitted into the University of Michigan and its law school based on my test scores and because I was a Michigan resident. Thankfully, times were different then. My focus after that was on working hard, earning a living, and building a family.

I excelled in law school, finishing in the top of my class, which qualified me to serve as an editor of the *Michigan Law Review*. I was also a finalist in the moot court competition and the recipient of various honors and scholarships. As a result, I had numerous job opportunities. I was invited to visit a number of Los Angeles law firms. Georgina and I immediately fell in love with the Golden State, which it truly was then. I accepted a job with O'Melveny & Myers, then the largest, oldest, and most prestigious law firm in Los Angeles and one of the first to begin hiring young Jewish lawyers. I was actually one of the first Jewish lawyers the firm had hired in its entire history, going back to 1885. (To put the realities of the time into context, Georgina and I actually would have preferred to move to San Francisco. That was the cool city, as far as we were concerned. The top San Francisco law firms would not even give top young Jewish law school graduates interviews in those days, let alone hire them.)

L.A. it was. We settled in the San Fernando Valley, initially in an apartment and soon thereafter in our first house.

Besides raising our three sons, Georgina worked as a substitute teacher, volunteered for the Anti-Defamation League, and—moved by the assassinations of Martin Luther King Jr. and Bobby Kennedy in spring 1968—got involved in working with a friend for social change by creating and running an interracial intercultural day camp for eight years. She also began taking sculpture classes, and her artistic talent and love for creativity led to a successful career as a sculptor and jewelry designer.

Like a lot of young guys just out of law school, I was confident in those days, maybe too confident. I left O'Melveny in 1966 to join a small firm set up in the San Fernando Valley by two young former O'Melveny attorneys, Chuck Manatt and Tom Phelps. Chuck and Tom had known each other growing up in Iowa and kept taking me to lunch to recruit me until I finally said yes. Chuck was always politically active and politically ambitious, a former national chairman of Young Democrats of America. A junior partner warned me Chuck might leave the firm to run for office. That sounded fine to me, since I figured that would only give the firm more clout.

Chuck never did run for office, but he built the firm into a powerhouse and, in the 1980s, served as chairman of the Democratic National Committee. Before that, soon after Jimmy Carter was elected in November 1976, he reached out to another of my politically active partners, Mickey Kantor, and asked him to organize a business trip to Cuba to help open up U.S.-Cuban relations. I was looking forward to meeting Fidel Castro, but at the last minute some urgent Aztecs business came up that forced me to stay behind in Los Angeles. Georgina made that trip to Havana in March 1978 without me, met Castro, presented him with an Aztecs jersey, and invited the Cuban national team to come play our team—the Aztecs—in California. "Georgina Rothenberg of the Los Angeles Aztecs," the Associated Press reported from Havana, "said Castro approved sending a Cuban soccer team to Los Angeles." Another report dubbed her "the Kissinger of Sports." Relations took a downturn shortly afterward, but Castro honored his commitment, and the Cubans came and played the Aztecs in the Rose Bowl. That was the only business deal resulting from the mission. (Twenty-five years later, the president of the Cuban Soccer Federation approached me and introduced himself and told me he had played in that match at the Rose Bowl.)

One year after I joined Chuck and Tom at the new firm, I received an interesting phone call from Clyde Tritt, a partner at O'Melveny who had taken an almost paternal interest in me. Tritt told me that one of the firm's more important clients, though also notoriously difficult, sports and media mogul Jack Kent Cooke, was looking to hire someone to work as in-house counsel and right-hand man. Tritt asked me if I'd be interested. I had some hesitation, fearing a man like Cooke with a mercurial temper might well chew me up and spit me out in relatively short order. I heard he could really be very difficult to work for.

I also felt loyal to Chuck and Tom. But they encouraged me to follow the opportunity—and, critically, Georgina also advised me to give working for Cooke a try. Actually, her first reaction was more like panic: *What? I wanted to give up a good job at a new, exciting firm to take a chance on something different?* Then she called her father and asked his advice. His immediate opinion: "Jack Kent Cooke? Are you kidding? Alan should jump on that opportunity!" We agreed it was better to take a chance and have a little fun going for it, rather than looking over my shoulder the rest of my life and asking myself, "What if?" A friend called when he heard the news to get all the details and Georgina, up to that point never much of a sports fan, told him, "Make it quick, I'm in the middle of reading the new issue of *Sports Illustrated* and want to get back to it." Another friend called and asked me how much I paid to get the job.

I was drawn to the work. It was exciting and demanding in a way I loved. The *Los Angeles Times* interviewed Georgina in September 1984 and quoted her as follows: "He just loves working in sports law. He finds it challenging. There's a tremendous number of lawyers who would love to do what Alan does." She emphasized that I always made time for family. "A friend of ours put it best," she said. "'Some people have hobbies like sculpting or art or stamp collecting. Alan's hobby is his family.' Any moment he's not working, he spends with us. Plus, he tries to incorporate us into his work. When he was soccer commissioner, he got (volunteer) jobs at the Rose Bowl for all of us so we could be together."

Cooke was a man who did not like to be told no. Born in Canada, he'd started out selling encyclopedias door to door in Western Canada during the Depression. His family couldn't afford to send him to college. He went on to become the leading national salesperson for Procter and Gamble and then built an empire of radio stations and publications in partnership with Roy Thomson, who later purchased the *London Times*, moved to London, and was ultimately known as "Baron Thomson of Fleet." Cooke, in 1951, became owner of the minor league Toronto Maple Leafs baseball team and promoted the team so colorfully he was sometimes called the Canadian Bill Veeck, brash and always nattily dressed.

I'd first heard of Cooke—who would have as much influence on me as anyone in my life, other than my parents and Georgina—when he tried to buy the Detroit Tigers from the estate of longtime owner Walter Briggs in 1956, offering the then unheard-of sum of $5.6 million, but the estate wanted to keep the team in Michigan and Cooke wanted to relocate the franchise to Toronto. Cooke was a principal in the proposed Continental League, scheduled to be owner of the Toronto franchise, which was stillborn when Major League Baseball created the expansion New York Mets to fill the void left in 1957 when the Dodgers and Giants departed New York for the West Coast. He also tried unsuccessfully to buy the Philadelphia Athletics and the St. Louis Browns but got nowhere.

Cooke moved into basketball and bought the Los Angeles Lakers in 1965 for the then record sum of $5.175 million and was also awarded an expansion franchise by the National Hockey League, the Los Angeles Kings, which began play in 1967. Cooke moved to Southern California in the early 1960s and put together a network of highly lucrative cable-television franchises.

But my favorite Cooke story was about his ownership of the Washington Redskins starting in 1960. Before then, famous sportscaster Harry Wismer—who had played football at Michigan State until a knee injury cut his career short—owned 25 percent of the Redskins. Wismer had an opportunity to own the New York Titans of the American Football League (AFL), which began play in 1960, but he had two problems: one, he needed to find the money to buy the Titans and two, he was legally blocked from owning both an AFL team and an interest in an NFL team. So Wismer sold his 25 percent share in the Redskins to Cooke for $350,000. Over the years, Cooke ended up owning 100 percent of the Redskins by exercising his right of first refusal when other owners decided to sell. He never invested another dollar of his own money, as he financed the additional purchases with distributions from the Redskins. On the other hand, Wismer couldn't continue to finance the cost of running the Titans and lost the team in a bankruptcy in 1965. (The next year the NFL/AFL merger occurred, and the New York Titans emerged as the New York Jets, a franchise that as of 2024 is valued at $6.9 billion.)

Cooke engaged in a massive legal fight with the Los Angeles Memorial Coliseum Commission, which operated the newly opened Sports Arena, inaugurated with the 1960 Democratic National Convention that nominated John F. Kennedy as president. Despite knowing that Cooke was building his own privately financed arena—the Forum—the commission required him to post a huge financial guarantee and promise to play all his games at the Sports Arena, even though the Forum would be ready at midseason.

In June 1967, on my first day working for Cooke, in our offices in front of the Beverly Hilton Hotel, he dropped the thick "Coliseum Commission" file on my desk with a resounding thud. He wanted out of his contract obligating both the Lakers and Kings to play all their games at the Los Angeles Memorial Sports Arena.

"There hasn't been a contract written yet that can't be broken," Cooke barked. "You're my brilliant Michigan Law School grad, No. 1 in your class! You get me out of this!"

I wasn't No. 1 in my class, and would never say I was, but in Cooke's world you were either the best or the worst, nothing in between.

Cooke bolted out of my office and left me in stunned silence. I was shaken, nearly in tears. I feared my dream job might be over after only one day. I dug through the file and came up with a creative solution, arguing that Cooke had been "under economic duress" when he signed the contract. The argument was: If he didn't sign it, he'd have no place for his teams to play and would be jeopardizing two major league franchises. Therefore, it was not binding.

On the day the Forum opened, December 30, 1967, we filed a lawsuit against the Coliseum Commission, moved the teams to the Forum, and announced that we were refusing to pay the large guarantee. Ultimately, the Coliseum Commission, having been blistered in the press for losing two major league franchises, backed down. We never paid them one cent! I'd dodged a bullet. Cooke seemed willing to trust me after that with more and more responsibility.

I was a sports lawyer before there were sports lawyers. In those days, when I went to work for Cooke, the business side of sports was run by ex-jocks. They played, they coached, and then they became general managers. They knew the sport, but as the dollar signs started to pick up and contracts grew more complicated—we started getting into TV contracts and collective bargaining with the leagues and players and building arenas and stadiums—it changed dramatically. New skill sets were required, and in an influx of talent analogous to the wave of PhDs that would later infuse Major League Baseball in the post-*Moneyball* era, sports teams brought in lawyers, CPAs, and MBAs, throwing them into the nitty-gritty of running a team. That's what Cooke did with me. He basically turned over much of the running of the business side of the Lakers to me, and it was just a remarkable opportunity.

My first month working for him, we flew to Montreal for the NHL Expansion Draft. As a huge hockey fan who had grown up in "Hockey Town USA," as Detroit was known, I was thrilled, especially when the Kings took former Red Wing goalkeeper Terry Sawchuk with the first pick of the draft and named Red Kelly as coach, both future Hall of Famers—and both personal heroes of mine. As the draft was taking place, we were all closely following the much more important and dramatic events in the Middle East, what would come to be called the Six-Day War, a stunning, David-and-Goliath victory for Israel.

I worked for Cooke two years and loved the challenge, but also chafed at being a "kept man." I wanted more autonomy. I decided to rejoin my former firm, now named Manatt, Phelps, & Rothenberg. Cooke was not bitter about my move. Far from it. Entrepreneur that he was, he understood. A week after I left, he called me to his office at the Forum to make me an offer. He wanted me to take over all his legal work from my previous firm, O'Melveny. I was thrilled but mortified. I went to see Clyde Tritt to let him know I was extremely uneasy, eager to make clear that I had not done anything to take business away from O'Melveny.

"Clyde, I want you to know…" I began, a little awkwardly.

"Alan," he stopped me short. "This is something between the firm and Jack, and we can't represent him anymore. If we can't represent him, there's no one else I'd rather see doing it." What a gentleman!

I loved working in sports, but the fan in me soon found it wasn't always as fun as people might imagine. Long before actor Jack Nicholson and other celebrities turned sitting courtside at Lakers games into a thing, I would sit with Cooke at most games. Sitting courtside is amazing. You see everything, and you hear everything, including what the players say to each other—or the officials—and all sounds of the game, like sneakers skidding on the wood floor and the swish sound of a ball hitting nothing but net. But often you yourself have to stay quiet! That for me was hard.

If something amazing happens, I like to jump up and cheer. Or if one of the players is just not getting it done, you want to yell a little. Sometimes you want to boo. You can't do that when you're sitting with management. You had to be measured in your reactions. What if you happened at the time to be in the middle of difficult negotiations? If a player did something great, inwardly you might be thinking: *That's going to cost us.* And if he did something bad, disappointing as that was for the team, you might be thinking: *That'll save us some money.* You were also constantly looking around. How do the sponsor ads look? Are the ushers all doing their jobs? The word "fan" is a derivative of "fanatic," and it was hard to be a fanatic when your job was to be all business (although some, like Steve Ballmer and Mark Cuban, are unrestrained in their enthusiasm).

Later, Cooke had me serving on the NBA Board of Governors as the Lakers' representative, and there was a lot going on in those years. I was deeply involved, for example, leading a rump group of owners, including colorful Warriors owner Franklin Mieuli, to negotiate a new TV contract for the NBA. The TV talks dragged on, and I also worked closely with

Bill Alverson of the Bucks, who was in many ways my opposite number. A Milwaukee lawyer who represented Bucks owner Wes Pavalon, Bill served as president of the team and alternate governor on the NBA Board of Governors, similar to my role with the Lakers. Bill and I had developed a special relationship. (As part of the never-ending tension between clubs and the league, at that time the NBA TV contract was heavily loaded with games featuring the Lakers, Celtics, Knicks, Bucks, and Warriors—negatively impacting those teams' local TV contracts, which were more lucrative than their respective shares of the NBA contract. When our group of "rump owners" took over negotiations, the resulting contract was very beneficial to the clubs but hurt the value of the NBA TV contract.)

It sounds a little unbelievable in retrospect, but in 1974 I was considered a leading candidate to replace NBA commissioner Walter Kennedy when he stepped down the following year. In June '74, the Board of Governors had a nine-hour meeting to decide between me and Henry Steinman, also a Los Angeles–based attorney, but neither of us could clear a majority. The job ultimately went to Larry O'Brien, who was a key force in getting John F. Kennedy elected to the Senate and, in 1960, as president, and was a close White House advisor who was with Kennedy in Dallas the day he was killed.

Here was how *Sports Illustrated*, probably the highest authority in sports at that time, put that chapter into the history books, in a 1976 article: "Typical of the NBA's disordered state was the 21-month search for Kennedy's successor," Ray Kennedy wrote. "At one point in 1974, a vote was taken on a pair of candidates, Alan Rothenberg and Henry Steinman, both West Coast lawyers with ties to NBA teams. The owners split into two hopelessly deadlocked factions. 'The feeling was,' says Milwaukee's Alverson, 'that each group was trying to shove their man down the other's throat. We were probably all wrong, but it shows you the kind of suspicion that prevailed.' Enter O'Brien, who at the time headed his own management consulting firm in New York. 'Things were going along rather well financially, but quite frankly I was bored,' he says. 'I'd get up each morning, light a cigarette and say to myself, 'Well, what do I do today? Have a long lunch with a friend?'"

The kicker to that story of Steinman and me both being up for NBA commissioner: 15 years later, I joined Steinman as a partner at Latham & Watkins.

Cooke also had me negotiating trades. That was a tough assignment. If Cooke was happy, you could exhale. If he wasn't, you had to watch out. I'll never forget when he tasked me with helping to negotiate with the Milwaukee Bucks to try to land Kareem Abdul-Jabbar, one of the greatest players ever.

In May 1975, I flew to Stapleton Airport in Denver, joined by general manager Pete Newell and Jim Lacher, our treasurer, for a long meeting to hash out the details of the trade with the Milwaukee Bucks, who were represented by their general manager, 6′8″ Wayne Embry, an NBA Hall of Famer and the first Black general manager in the NBA, and my friend Bill Alverson. That meeting in the United Red Carpet Lounge lasted more than five hours. I would step away from time to time to make a call and update Cooke on what progress we were making, which wasn't much. We were ready to put together a package of four players, Elmore Smith and Brian Winters as well as highly valuable draft picks in the NBA draft coming one month away—the second and eighth picks overall. In return we needed more from the Bucks than just the big prize, Abdul-Jabbar.

We agreed that Milwaukee would tell us whom to draft (as it turned out: Dave Meyers and Junior Bridgeman), and it was the Lakers' responsibility to sign the players to contracts below an agreed-upon ceiling. If we exceeded the ceiling on either player, anything over that amount would be the responsibility of the Lakers. But no matter how hard I tried, we couldn't agree on another Bucks player to add to the trade package.

Finally, Pete and Jim headed off to catch a flight back to L.A., and I was trying to call Cooke with another update when I put the phone down and ran after Embry and Alverson before they could fly to Chicago. I knew how much Cooke wanted this deal, and I couldn't let them out of my sight.

"I'm going to Chicago!" I yelled to Newell and Lacher, whose gate for their flight to L.A. was nearby.

On the flight to Chicago with Embry and Alverson, we were drinking up a storm for a couple hours, but they wouldn't budge. I got an idea.

"You guys like me, right?" I pleaded with them.

They agreed they liked me.

"You know Cooke," I continued. "He'll kill me if I took this flight from Denver to Chicago and came back empty-handed. He won't pay me for my time, and he won't even pay me for the airplane ticket. You can't do that to me. You've got to give me something."

They were laughing by then, but I was dead serious.

"Just go to the very bottom of your roster and let me pick a couple of players," I said.

"Okay, fine," they finally agreed. "We don't want you to get in trouble with Cooke. Here's the list."

That was how we added Walt Wesley and an option on "Jungle Jim" Loscutoff to the deal, and made it happen—but we weren't out of the woods yet. We had to keep the trade secret before we announced it in mid-June, which wasn't easy. Kareem arrived early in Los Angeles, and was spotted playing tennis, which made the papers and fueled much speculation. "Abdul-Jabbar, the super center," wrote Ted Green in the *L.A. Times*, "has been here for a few days, visiting friends and playing tennis and backgammon with the Lakers' Lucius Allen, a former teammate at UCLA." A Laker spokesman was quoted saying no trade was imminent, but Jack Kent Cooke told the *Times* the idea was "titillating."

We also had to sign the two players we'd drafted, at their direction. Dave Meyers was represented by Larry Fleisher, the very competent longtime head of the NBA Players Association. Fleisher had learned the amount that had been designated for Meyers' contract and came to the Forum to tell Cooke he wasn't going to fool around on this. He'd agree to that number.

Bridgeman, on the other hand, was represented by Chicago lawyer Arthur Morse, who also represented the owners of the Chicago Blackhawks, the Wirtz family. Morse was well known to Cooke. As expected, he came to us with an outrageous demand, and Cooke let him know how outrageous he found it. In fact, he physically escorted Morse right out of his office. I was stunned. I couldn't believe we were about to blow the biggest trade in NBA history.

"What just happened?" I said, clearly aghast, when Cooke came back into the office.

"Don't worry," Cooke said. "Before he gets as far as LAX, he'll turn around and come back."

Sure enough, not 10 minutes passed before Morse called to say he was coming back to the office. We soon wrapped up the deal.

In early June, I attended a Board of Governors meeting and found myself in an awkward position. Red Auerbach of the Boston Celtics was pushing for a change in the rules. Their center, Dave Cowens, was only 6′9″, and Auerbach wanted to change the rule requiring a center jump ball at the start of every quarter. Knowing we were about to get Kareem, that was the last thing we wanted to see, but I couldn't make that public, so I argued against Auerbach's proposal with an impassioned—and vague—speech on the traditions of the game.

"Red Auerbach has never proposed a rules change that didn't help the Celtics," I insisted.

My arguments failed completely, and no one ever put two and two together on that until the trade was made public.

THE BUCK STOPS HERE; JABBAR'S A LAKER ran the banner headline in the *Los Angeles Times* on June 17, 1975.

"Last season the Lakers didn't get off the ground," Ted Green wrote in the accompanying article. "So, now they've reached for the sky by sending four players to the Milwaukee Bucks for pro basketball's best center, Kareem Abdul-Jabbar. The announcement, which ended weeks of speculation, came Monday at an elaborately staged, carnival-like press conference at the Forum."

That led ultimately to the Showtime Lakers Era when the Lakers added Magic Johnson with a draft choice I had obtained in a trade with New Orleans, and it was a lot of fun to be a part of that. Incidentally, the decision to draft Magic is a reminder that in this data-driven, post-*Moneyball* era, judgment remains vital. Laker scouts rated Sidney Moncrief ahead of Magic in three of the five skills they valued. Ignoring that, new Laker owner Jerry Buss said, "Magic just won the NCAA Final Four! He's a winner—plus he has a great smile."

For more than a decade, I went through an incredible period during which, in many respects, I became Cooke's alter ego. The exposure I was fortunate to receive elevated my profile and enhanced my reputation in the legal community and especially in the world of sports. Cooke was not one to dispense with much praise. His biggest compliment was "Atta boy, Alan!" But his insights and observations made me a whole lot smarter. He loved sports because of its unpredictability and the glimpses it offered into how people really are.

Cooke contrasted sports and entertainment. "A great performance in theater is zero mistakes," he used to say. "You don't create. You follow the script. In sports, what's so exciting is it doesn't follow the script. Sometimes it's an amazing, horrible mistake that leads up to the winning goal or shot. Somebody might come out of nowhere and do something miraculous or never expected. You never know."

That's how it was at the Memorial Coliseum in July 1967 for the championship game of the United Soccer Association, a battle between the Washington Whips and Cooke's team, the Los Angeles Wolves, featuring players on loan from England. No one in the crowd of 17,824 was going to complain about this one not having enough action. It was tied at 5–5 after regulation and went into sudden-death overtime—and the Wolves won on an own goal. As the *Los Angeles Evening News-Citizen* described the action, "a ball accidentally kicked backward by Ally Shewan of the Washington Whips scooted its heartbreaking way into his own net for the goal that gave the Los Angeles Wolves a highly sensational 6–5 triple overtime victory."

One day that year, Cooke visited my office with an interesting news flash.

"You're in charge of the soccer team now," he told me.

In February 1968, the news hit the local papers: at age 28, I was named general manager of the Los Angeles Wolves, who were due to open play in the new North American Soccer League that April against Baltimore. Another round of articles at the end of that month quoted me announcing the Wolves would play all 16 home games at the Rose Bowl in Pasadena. "The Rose Bowl is the finest facility for watching soccer in Southern California," I told the Associated Press, sounding very authoritative for a man who had never seen a soccer game until 1967, nor ever even played the game.

That was the start of the Rose Bowl as one of the top venues for soccer in the country, but in truth it wasn't even our first choice. Given the war with the Coliseum Commission, the Los Angeles Memorial Coliseum was a nonstarter. Cooke had sent me to visit Los Angeles Dodgers owner Walter O'Malley to see if he might rent Dodger Stadium to us. O'Malley had worked closely with architect Emil Praeger on designs for the gleaming 56,000-seat baseball palace in Chavez Ravine, which had opened five years earlier at that point, in April 1962. As Matt Jaffe later wrote in *Los Angeles Magazine*, "Dodger Stadium is where the majors went modern."

Unlike in recent years, Dodger Stadium in the beginning was seldom used for events besides baseball. O'Malley had been scarred by the experience of hosting the featherweight championship of the world at Dodger Stadium in March 1963, featuring 29-year-old champ Davey Moore against 21-year-old challenger Sugar Ramos, a Cuban exile. Moore, knocked down in the 10th round, hit his neck on the ropes—and was dead in 75 hours. The accidental death unleashed a torrent of negative attention from California Governor Pat Brown to

L.A. Times columnist Jim Murray to Bob Dylan, whose 1963 song "Who Killed Davey Moore?" mercifully did not mention Dodger Stadium.

Cooke and O'Malley were in many ways kindred spirits, private entrepreneurs who had each built a stadium and an arena and fought city hall along the way, but O'Malley still said no. Those Dodger teams won on defense and pitching, behind all-time greats like Sandy Koufax, Don Drysdale, and Maury Wills.

"If one ball hits a divot created by a soccer game and takes a bad hop over Maury Wills and causes us to lose a game, no amount of rent would be worth it," O'Malley told me.

Cooke believed in generating excitement, and we did our best with the Wolves. That August, we earned a headline in the *San Bernardino Sun*, reading PONY GIVEN OUT AT SOCCER GAME. "A live pony and numerous other prizes will be given away tomorrow as a prelude to the Los Angeles Wolves–Oakland Clippers soccer clash for the California State Governor's Cup in the Rose Bowl," the article read. "Wolves General Manager Alan Rothenberg said bicycles and soccer balls, in addition to the pony, would be given away."

I was always bullish on soccer's growth potential in the United States. All you had to do was look around the world at all the countries where it was the No. 1 sport or at the sports fields of the United States, where growing numbers of kids—girls and boys—were playing youth soccer. Looking to bring soccer back to L.A., I headed up an investment group that bought the Los Angeles Aztecs in 1977 along with a group of limited partners that included friends, family, and the law firm. We were just sure we were on the ground floor of a tremendous growth opportunity, assuming soccer was ready to keep growing dramatically in popularity in the U.S.

Attendance had surged around the country after the New York Cosmos made a splash in 1975, signing the world's greatest player, Pelé, a telegenic Brazilian who was an ideal ambassador of the sport, and the rapidly growing league also adding other international stars, including Carlos Alberto of Brazil and Franz Beckenbauer of West Germany. Pelé's arrival with the Cosmos was an event like the Beatles arriving for their first U.S. tour. Tens of thousands of fans had to be turned away. Even his fellow players were awestruck. "I remember the first practice," his coach at the time, Gordon Bradley, later told the *Guardian*. "A cross went behind Pelé's head, and he was running toward the goal. He jumped up in the air and did a bicycle kick and scored. The press couldn't believe it. I ended the practice right then."

My fellow investors and I thought we were like early NFL owners that paid paltry sums, starting at $25,000, for a franchise and watched their values soar. We were ahead of our time. WAY AHEAD! If the Cosmos could take off behind the star power of Pelé, we had our answer in George Best of Northern Ireland, an insanely gifted dribbler and goal-scorer who, come to think of it, looked like one of the Beatles. Unfortunately, as we soon discovered, he couldn't handle his fame. He partied too wildly, drinking way too much and experimenting with recreational drugs. Later, forced to declare bankruptcy, he was asked where all that money he earned had gone. "Booze, birds, and fast cars, and the rest I squandered," he said.

We immediately realized we had to trade Best and did. With the Cosmos selling out the Meadowlands with their team studded with international stars, we knew we had to follow suit to have a chance to make it in L.A. We set our sights on signing the Dutch great Johan Cruyff. Amazingly, he'd won the Ballon d'Or, awarded to the best player in the world, three times already: 1971, 1973, and 1974. Cruyff and his coach, Rinus Michels, were proponents of Total Football, a revolutionary innovation based on having players with multiple skills who could play interchangeable positions, to this day the prevailing tactic. Cruyff, a master of the style, led the Netherlands to the Finals of the 1974 World Cup, but lost to Beckenbauer and West Germany.

The Cosmos were after Cruyff as well, but we were able to sign him in May 1979. The world press was a bit surprised we'd been able to land him. London's *Sunday People* newspaper called Cruyff's decision to sign with us "baffling," and mentioned me, saying I'd "admitted" I'd never heard of Cruyff until months before, but quoted Cruyff on his decision: "I feel I owe something to football," he said. "This is the best place for me to pay that debt.…My job is on this coast. It makes me sad that the biggest sport in the world isn't known very well here. I want to do something to change that."

Cruyff was absolutely sensational. Despite a reputation for being uncooperative at times, he worked tirelessly for us off the pitch promoting the team throughout the greater Los Angeles area. We loved having him and his family over to our house for a swim and dinner with our family. And attendance did pick up—but not enough. That was the time of an energy crisis with continuous oil boycotts following the Yom Kippur War in 1973 and culminating with the Iranian Revolution. In Southern California, drivers could only fill up every other day.

The economics were just too tough. By the end of that season, we were ready to sell and found a buyer in Televisa, the

Mexican media behemoth. But there was a catch: they would have no interest in assuming Cruyff's contract, since they wanted stars who would be popular in Spanish-language media. We had to sweat that one out, worried we'd have to eat his enormous contract. Then we got lucky. Talent agent Sonny Werblin, who made his reputation creating Joe Namath's "Broadway Joe" persona, was general manager of the Washington Diplomats and wanted a star.

He took over Cruyff's contract—and we could all exhale. My gamble on the Aztecs had cost me big, and I spent years working to pay back the money I'd borrowed to make the deal. I can only imagine how much more I would have had to struggle if Werblin had not solved our Cruyff guaranteed contract obligation.

Punishing as the Aztecs venture was, it brought me to Peter Ueberroth's attention and helped entice him to ask me to join the Olympics organizing effort as soccer commissioner. The 1984 Olympics were unique in many ways. Fearing a financial disaster, as previous host cities had faced following past Olympic Games, L.A. voters passed a referendum that stipulated the city could host the Olympics only if no tax burden or other liability were involved. The organizing committee was run as a nonprofit, and Ueberroth came in committed to tight budgetary discipline.

I'd taken on the role of soccer commissioner in part because I saw FIFA as a well-run federation and figured that would make my job easier, which was true. The qualifying tournaments were conducted by the various geographic confederations within FIFA, so everything was set up so an intact group of teams would qualify for the Olympic tournament and show up in the United States a couple of weeks before the Games. At that point, I'd have to back off my legal work completely and devote myself full-time to my duties as commissioner for at least six weeks, moving my family with me to Pasadena so we would be near the Rose Bowl.

I needed to watch a lot of soccer! Georgina and I traveled to Spain for the 1982 World Cup, my introduction to the spectacular event, and I had my eyes opened. The first match we attended in Barcelona was Italy against Brazil, in which Italy shocked Brazil led by a hat trick from Paolo Rossi, the best player in Europe, just returning to the team following a two-year suspension for gambling. We were taken aback seeing the stadium with the fans separated from the pitch by a barbwire fence guarded by Spanish soldiers with drawn bayonets; we'd never seen anything like that. The action on the pitch was enthralling and, in some cases, brutal. FIFA later had to institute rules changes to crack down on the kind of nonstop fouling Italian defender Claudio Gentile inflicted on the great Diego Maradona of Argentina. In the spectacular semifinal match between France and West Germany, it was knotted up 1–1 in the second half, and French defender Patrick Battiston sprinted in toward the German goal, trying to run down the ball, and ended up taking a brutal hit from German goalkeeper Harald Schumacher. Battiston was knocked unconscious, lost two teeth and broke his jaw, and had to be carried away on a stretcher. France went up 3–1, but in the closing minutes the Germans scored twice to tie it up—and won the match on a penalty-kick shootout.

I cheered when Italy upset West Germany in the Final, cruising to a 3–1 victory. Georgina and I traveled throughout Spain and elsewhere in Europe that June and July. We were amazed to see how in every empty space—in the streets, in alleys, in empty lots, in parks, on any surface, cement, dirt, sand, gravel, or grass—kids were playing soccer. After the Final we drove to Italy and everywhere we went, we saw parades of cars flying the Italian flag, honking and cheering, singing songs seemingly without end. The passion of the fans of all countries was exhilarating. No matter how frenzied American sports fans would become in support of their teams, I'd never witnessed anything like what I observed in 1982. I was hooked on the power and potential of World Cup soccer.

Given the U.S. boycott of the Moscow Olympics in 1980, following the Soviet Union's invasion of Afghanistan, we knew going into the 1984 Olympics that a tit-for-tat response might be in the offing. The Soviet Union announced in May 1984 that it would be boycotting, joined soon by Bulgaria, East Germany, and other Soviet bloc satellite states. One year earlier, President Ronald Reagan had delivered his "Evil Empire" speech, calling the Soviets "the focus of evil in the modern world." We should remember that.

TASS, the Soviet propaganda agency, put out a statement in justification of the boycott hitting at the "arrogant, hegemonistic course" of Reagan's foreign policy, which it termed "at odds with the noble ideals of the Olympic movement." Bulgaria's statement was curiouser, warning vaguely of "an abnormal situation in this American city." And East Germany seemed almost to be attacking our Organizing Committee personally, or so it felt at the time, with its bizarre suggestion that "the American government and games organizers have destroyed the basis" for participation. Games organizers? You want to say that to my face, Comrade? The return-boycott meant we lost three of the 16 teams that had qualified: Czechoslovakia, East Germany, and the USSR itself. These three were replaced with Italy, Norway, and West Germany.

Although the Russians boycotted those Olympics, some of their sports officials were still involved. At that time, really the height of the Cold War in some ways, with Ronald Reagan as president and the Soviet Union led by a feeble functionary named Konstantin Chernenko, the Soviets arriving in L.A. acted in some ways as if they'd come from another planet. Each of the Soviet IOC officials, including Slava Koloskov, a Soviet sports official about my age, maybe a couple years younger, designated by FIFA as their soccer representative, came with his own interpreter and only spoke Russian with us. We were briefed to assume these "interpreters" were all KGB agents. Be careful, we were told.

We invited Koloskov to have lunch at UCLA, where visiting athletes were housed during the Olympics. His interpreter, Lev, was there with him the whole the time. We ate at the cafeteria and as we went through the line, at every station Koloskov and his interpreter just scooped up whatever was there and piled it up on their plates. Their trays really were overflowing by the end.

"This is a lot of food," they said.

"Looks like you guys don't know how to handle free choice," I remarked, but I think the remark sailed right over the heads.

Pete Siracusa, our Olympic commissioner for cycling, lived down in Newport Beach and threw a party, inviting commissioners, IOC people, and of course his Soviet counterpart. Pete had gone through the same rigmarole of his IOC representative only speaking Russian and having the interpreter translate and assuming he was KGB. At one point they went out for a dip in the ocean, and it turned out the interpreter couldn't swim, so he just stayed next to shore. Pete and the IOC representative swam out past the breakwater. They were just floating out there.

"Quite a nice spread you have here, Pete," the Russian said in fluent English.

Pete took a mouth full of water and almost drowned, he was so surprised. And he was a former lifeguard there at Newport Beach! For two years this man had spoken only Russian in his presence. We'd been right about the representatives and interpreters all being KGB. They'd been playing us the whole time.

I wanted to think big, as everyone involved in Olympic organizing was thinking big. That meant, of course, showcasing the historic Rose Bowl in Pasadena, where we'd negotiated to have the Los Angeles Wolves play two decades earlier. I'd told the Associated Press in 1968 that the Rose Bowl was the finest facility for soccer in Southern California, and I still felt that way. The Rose Bowl also had Olympic history, having hosted cycling events during the 1932 Los Angeles Games—which, by the way, did not include a soccer competition.

We wanted to excite Americans throughout the country, not just Angelenos, and decided to play matches in additional locations. In Northern California, we'd have games at picturesque Stanford Stadium in Palo Alto near San Francisco Bay. Beyond those two natural California choices, we wanted sites on the East Coast to broaden interest. We were going to have to get creative finding other venues around the country where other games could be hosted.

One option was Harvard Stadium in Boston, which had a capacity of 30,000. But there were some issues we would have to finesse. The field was too narrow. FIFA had very strict rules about the dimensions of the playing field, it went without saying, although we knew there were cases in Europe where FIFA had looked the other way for some group-stage matches. As part of the approval process, we knew we'd have to deal with someone sent by FIFA walking the field and measuring.

Walter Gagg, FIFA's technical director, who was Swiss and known to be very exacting, flew in to inspect the stadium. It was a snowy winter day in the Northeast. My deputy commissioner, Scott LeTellier, a Los Angeles attorney who ran our day-to-day activities, joined me on the field in Boston to walk with Gagg as he carefully paced off the perimeter of the field; he saw no need for a tape measure. We were friendly and talkative and made it look very casual when we "accidentally" bumped into him midway, knocking him off stride, so he would have to start all over again. We were hoping, given the snowy and freezing conditions, he'd call it a day and leave it at that. Fat chance we'd get off that easily! Gagg was Swiss and very determined. He dutifully walked off the dimensions again. We made another effort to disrupt him, but he finished the job—and, as it had before, FIFA looked the other way. (One city bidding to host the '94 World Cup had a stadium that was too narrow; so they took out a tape measure, cut six feet out of the middle, and stitched it back together. That was a clever way to deal with the width problem; who would know?!)

It was at Harvard Stadium that I first met Hank Steinbrecher, then acting as the venue director, whom I later hired to be the general secretary of U.S. Soccer, where he became an integral part of the team of people who helped grow soccer in the 1990s.

For the fourth site, we chose Memorial Stadium in Annapolis, Maryland, home field for Navy football games, located near the Naval Academy campus. Officially, it's called Navy-Marine Corps Memorial Stadium and, taking a walk around the facility, you immediately know it. The names of major battles of the U.S. Navy and Marines ring the upper deck of the stadium: Belleau Wood, Pearl Harbor, Java Sea, Wake, Coral Sea, Midway, Eastern Solomons, Guadalcanal. As a 1984 *Washington Post* article explained, each seat in the stadium is "marked with a plaque to memorialize individual seafarers, from Medal of Honor recipients to less-heralded servicemen."

FIFA came and inspected Memorial Stadium, and it all checked out—except one little thing. We were informed that there was an issue with the words and images throughout the stadium. For the Olympic Games, the requirement was for a "clean stadium" to protect the exclusivity of their sponsors. Oblivious to the markings' patriotic messages, FIFA asked us to cover them up. Can you imagine? Being the one to order "Guadalcanal" or "Pearl Harbor" be covered up? Needless to say, the games went on without our covering up any historical references.

Palo Alto was a great setting, but Stanford Stadium needed work. We had to build a press box and a "Tribune of Honor," an area at midfield to house FIFA "big wigs," assorted public officials, and various other dignitaries and celebrities. Stanford embarked on a $2.2 million renovation that also included new locker rooms. We didn't have that money budgeted. Luckily, it worked out well for us: Super Bowl XVII would be held at

Stanford Stadium in January 1985, so the NFL paid for the construction of the new press box, large enough to handle 400 members of the print media on the first two levels as well as radio and TV on the third.

The Rose Bowl was, in a way, like a champagne glass: it looked best when it was full. We'd learned with the Los Angeles Wolves that, for all its dignified beauty and majestic lines, the Rose Bowl could be very unforgiving of small crowds, which had a somewhat disturbing effect of mocking the site's potential for giving sports an almost mythic feel. Pack in 106,869 giddy, amped-up fans, like on New Year's Day 1973 for a tense contest between top-ranked, undefeated USC and No. 3 Ohio State, and the magic of the place comes through unforgettably—that's the stadium record. Super Bowl XIV in January 1980, the Los Angeles Rams versus the defending champion Pittsburgh Steelers, pulled in an NFL postseason-record 103,985. But given its contours and size, the Rose Bowl could make even decent-sized crowds look puny, like the 35,000 who showed up for the 1934 Rose Bowl pitting Stanford against Columbia.

The Rose Bowl was constructed in 1922 as a permanent home for the annual college football game, the Rose Bowl, which launched in 1902 as a way to help offset costs of the annual New Year's Day Tournament of Roses Parade along Colorado Boulevard in Pasadena, first held in 1890. Architect Myron Hunt, born in Massachusetts in 1868, moved to Los Angeles in 1903 and made a name for his work designing various local universities; the landmark Mission Inn in Riverside; and, in Los Angeles, the Ambassador Hotel, opened in 1921, which later became infamous as the site of the Robert F. Kennedy assassination in 1968.

On Sunday, October 8, 1922, all six columns of the front page of the *Los Angeles Times*, over the fold, were given over to a large picture of the nearly complete stadium—PANORAMIC VIEW OF IMMENSE OVAL WHICH WILL SEAT TENS OF THOUSANDS, just over a headline: CECIL DE MILLE OFFERS FAT PRIZE FOR REAL NOTION FOR NEXT FILM. Originally horseshoe-shaped with 57,000 seats, the stadium was planned so that "its seating capacity can readily be enlarged at any time it is found desirable," the *Times* reported. "Though the Arroyo Seco, flanked by foothills and with mountains in the distance, is the most beautiful setting imaginable for the stadium, it was found to have some practical disadvantages. One of them was a lack of roads and the other was the danger that the stadium would be damaged by water during the winter rains."

Another disadvantage, if you were holding events at the Rose Bowl and didn't know how many fans to expect, was the headache of printing up—and organizing—so many tickets. Back then there were only hard tickets, not yet electronic tickets. I was always optimistic we'd get a strong turnout, but in the battle for media attention, soccer at that time was perpetually an also-ran—and the truth was, we really didn't know what kind of turnout to expect. There weren't many advance sales. Going into the first game at the Rose Bowl, Italy against Egypt on July 29, we obviously weren't going to print up 103,300 tickets and assume a sellout. You could have a lot of unused tickets in that scenario, taking up a lot of space and demanding a lot of time. We printed up about 30,000 tickets and hoped they'd all move.

The afternoon of the match, which started at 7:30 PM, we could see a lot of fans streaming into the stadium. We were flooded. People were coming. I was wondering what was going to happen if we ran out of tickets. We wanted to avoid a riot. If we started telling people they couldn't come inside and would have to go home, we'd have had a riot on our hands. So, we hurried down into the bowels of the Rose Bowl and found old rolls of tickets, like what you used to see at old movie theaters. It was time to improvise. They would do. I'm sure some ticket-takers made a fortune that day, because they were getting cash, and we had no record of what they were selling. Official attendance for the game, which Italy won 1–0, was 37,430, though I'm sure the actual number on hand was easily 50,000 or more.

For our second game at the Rose Bowl, Brazil against Saudi Arabia on July 30, we came up with a new plan. About an hour before the gates were going to open before the 7:30 PM start, we helicoptered in our full batch of tickets. That surprised everyone. Brazil won 3–1 and the crowd was 40,799.

The deeper we got into the Olympic tournament, the better we were feeling about all our work organizing. Our big attendance numbers were one of the surprise stories of the Olympics, and we knew the crowd for the gold-medal game at the Rose Bowl would be tremendous. The week before that game, we let off a little steam by taking to a soccer field outside the Rose Bowl itself. That year was the one time in my life I ever played soccer. It was our organizing committee team against the FIFA organizing team.

"I'll play defense," I said.

One sport I *had* played was American football. I figured I'd just play like a linebacker. Basically: *If anyone comes near me, I'll knock 'em down. And if, God forbid, the ball comes anywhere near me, I'll kick it to someone else or out of touch as quickly as I can.* And that was pretty much what I did.

Two days later, we decided to play another game—this time in the Rose Bowl, with music and cheerleaders and the whole thing. This was Walter Mitty stuff. I started out the game with the same approach as before, then thought to myself: *Wait a minute, I'm the boss, I can do what I want.* I decided I'd try to jump into the action and see if I could maybe score a goal. I'd play forward. Of course, by that time the word was out on me. The FIFA people knew I had no idea how to play soccer. So, they left me unmarked. All of a sudden, a teammate crossed a perfect ball.

Visions flashed in my head of diving valiantly and sending a perfect header into the net for a goal! Except for one small problem. I had no idea what I was doing. I figured if I tried that, I'd look ridiculous and miss, ending up in a face-plant. So, I kept it simple. I turned and belly-flopped the ball, and it went right into the net! You know how in soccer your teammates all jump on you when you score a goal? My teammates couldn't do that, because they were all on the ground laughing so hard.

"There's nothing to this sport," I said, walking off the field. That was the extent of my soccer career.

Those were wonderful weeks for us as a family. We moved into the historic Huntington Hotel in Pasadena to be nearby, and it was kind of a funny story. Ueberroth, despite by that time the evident success, was still emphasizing to everyone how Spartan these Games had to be run, everyone watching pennies, and of course that meant we should have modest hotel accommodations. Now, the only other Olympic event in the Pasadena area was the equestrian competition at Santa Anita Park, a racetrack, and its president was Princess Anne of England, sister of Prince—now King—Charles, who had participated in the 1976 Olympics in Montreal, riding the Queen's horse. As I was checking in to the hotel, I found out that equestrian was given one of the two penthouses in the swank hotel, so I asked—only half-seriously—for a penthouse as well, and that's where they put us.

That was our family home base for six weeks. Georgina accompanied me everywhere. Our youngest son, Danny, drove a three-wheel vehicle around the Rose Bowl, doing chores. Our middle son, Richie, volunteered to work in the locker room, where he learned a lesson in the value of speaking other languages. When France won the Final, Richie, speaking French, was able to talk his way into commandeering a French uniform and even a faux gold medal, and paraded around in those. On Georgina's birthday, we had a postgame party in the hospitality tent. We brought out a great, large Olympic poster, and a Magic Marker was given to Prince Philip, the Duke of Edinburgh and father of Princess Anne, and he handed it to João Havelange, FIFA president, who signed the poster, "Havelange." Then Prince Philip signed, "Philip." Then the pen was handed to our oldest son, Brad, home after his sophomore year at Brown University, who, with a dramatic flourish imitating Havelange and Prince Phillip, signed it, "Bradford."

Just as we were approaching the beginning of the Olympics, an urgent matter in my law practice diverted my attention. Donald Sterling, whom I dubbed "the Howard Hughes of the NBA" in one article, tried to move the San Diego Clippers to Los Angeles without NBA permission soon after he bought the team in 1981; the league enjoined the move. He also was chronically late paying players and publicly pronounced that he wanted the team to lose all its games in order to get the No. 1 draft choice. The NBA commenced proceedings to revoke his franchise. NBA Commissioner David Stern urged—okay, really he ordered—Sterling to retain me to straighten out management of the team. In early 1984, the United States 9th Circuit Court of Appeals decided that the NFL's attempt to block the Oakland Raiders' move to Los Angeles without NFL approval violated the antitrust laws. Knowing Sterling's desire to move to Los Angeles, I advised him that the Circuit Court ruling gave him an opportunity. Since NBA bylaws were identical to the NFL's bylaws, which the Court had held violated antitrust laws, Sterling now had the opportunity to move the team without NBA approval, if he hurried. We'd have to move with alacrity before the NBA could amend its bylaws to comply with the Court's finding. It was now or never. We hastily and in complete confidence made all the arrangements to move, including a lease at the Los Angeles Sports Arena. In May it was a done deal. The team became—and remains—the Los Angeles Clippers. (Interestingly, notwithstanding my defying the NBA, David Stern and I remained friends and colleagues for the rest of his life. As a fellow lawyer, he understood that I was performing my duties as a lawyer acting in the best interests of my client.)

When I think back on those Olympics, what jumps out in my memory is constantly worrying about the state of the playing field. We played seven games in nine days at the Rose Bowl, which would be hell on any turf. The situation was compounded by the fact that the last event they'd had at the Rose Bowl before they turned it over to us was a two-day motocross event in early June. What were the odds? As the *L.A. Times* reported that July, "the Rose Bowl will be used for only 44 events this year—far less than most stadiums," but given its capacity would still be profitable. And they had to squeeze in motocross as we were in our final preparations, leaving huge mounds of dirt on the field, which, naturally enough, killed the grass.

As the *Daily Breeze* wrote on June 24, "Olympic soccer games are scheduled to begin July 29 in the Rose Bowl. They would be playing on dirt if they had to play there today."

Ueberroth had to address the grim situation at a June 23 press conference after touring 17 different Olympics facilities with International Amateur Athletic Federation president Primo Nebiolo.

"It was shocking for him to see the field at the Rose Bowl," Ueberroth said. "That's the one stadium we're going to use that is without a field right now. But I've assured him it will be ready for the games."

In other words: *Alan! Get to work!*

We flew in the nation's premier expert on turf, George Toma, groundskeeper for both the Kansas City Royals and Kansas City Chiefs (and, previously, the Kansas City Athletics). Toma is a genius, widely celebrated as the "Sodfather" and "God of Sod." (As of this writing, he's still alive—95 years old, one of the few to personally attend every Super Bowl from 1967 to 2023). We toured the ravaged field and Toma told us there was no way to grow enough fresh grass in the time frame we had. Better to bring in giant rolls of sod and lay those down. (In an interesting footnote, Toma's home field in Kansas City was AstroTurf, not grass, but as he liked to say, AstroTurf requires maintenance, too.)

We lived up to Ueberroth's word. By the time the tournament started, the field looked great. The field looked beautiful to spectators on hand and on TV—but we were on borrowed time and knew it. By the Final, the field was so ripped up, the grass had really been thinned out. We thought we were real smart. We took green spray paint and sprayed the surface green, which looked just fine until the first slide tackle. Green dirt flew into the air, and we were exposed.

Before the Final match, there was a bomb scare. A nightmare! Now keep in mind, 1984 was 17 years before 9/11 changed everything about how we went about security precautions. It was, I guess you could say, a more innocent time, though it's worth remembering that no one who lived through it would ever forget the horror of the Munich Olympics in 1972, when terrorists infiltrated the Olympic Village and killed 11 Israeli athletes. In 1977, theaters across the U.S. showed a John Frankenheimer film called *Black Sunday*, based on a Thomas Harris novel. In the movie, terrorists are on the verge of exploding a bomb loaded with a quarter-million steel projectiles in the carriage of the Goodyear Blimp as it flies over a packed stadium a lot like the Rose Bowl. It was just a movie, but it made you think.

We had a full house at the Rose Bowl for the Olympic Final in 1984, more than 100,000 people, much like in the movie, though of course at the time I couldn't think about that. It was my job to decide what to do. Order an evacuation? Ride it out? Figure out a third option? I try to stay cool in a crisis situation and listen to everyone, then weigh my options and make a choice and move on. That day was no different. I was in the Rose Bowl press box, surrounded by top-notch law-enforcement people, FBI, state police, Pasadena police, and Los Angeles County sheriffs. They carefully briefed me on the sweep of the Rose Bowl and surrounding areas that had been conducted.

"Sir, we've come up with nothing," I was told. "We see no evidence of any explosive devices. But you're the commissioner. It's your call."

Yes, it was my call, and it weighed heavily. I carefully considered the options. Based on the reports from law enforcement, I was fairly certain it was a hoax. I shuddered at the notion of giving the word to announce over the loudspeakers: "Don't panic, but please exit in an orderly fashion!" The vomitories at the Rose Bowl were long and narrow. Thousands of people could have been trampled. Hundreds could have died and many more seriously injured. Panic was just what we would have had.

"Let's play," I said.

And we did—and thankfully no bombs went off.

After the game, we let loose with a massive fireworks show, one I'd had to make happen with a little low-key skullduggery. As I mentioned before, Peter was really running a tight ship, even though by that time it was clear the Olympics would be financially successful. He had a strict limitation: you couldn't have a purchase order of more than $10,000 without approval from headquarters. There was also another rule that no individual sport was to put on any kind of closing ceremony, because he didn't want to detract from the Olympic Closing Ceremony itself and its over-the-top fireworks show orchestrated by maestro Tommy Walker, who was on the team that had helped Walt Disney develop the Disneyland theme park in Southern California leading up to its July 1955 opening.

My attitude was: *damn it!* Soccer at that point was always forgotten and overlooked. I felt we'd been dissed. And we'd had such an amazing success, blowing past anybody's wildest expectations of how many tickets we'd sell for our games. We ended up selling more tickets than any other sport including track and field, which even I didn't expect. Nobody expected that.

We were news. The *Los Angeles Times* posed the question on the morning of August 14: "What was the most popular sport at the Olympics?" Funny you should ask. Just the question we wanted out there. "If you judge by attendance, it was soccer. In the Final at the Rose Bowl, 101,799 fans saw France beat Brazil 2–0, a record attendance at a soccer match in the U.S. In all, the Olympic soccer tournaments games drew 1,421,627 spectators. Track and field was the next most popular event, with 1,129,465. Total attendance, not including the last day: 5,652.111." It would go down in the books as the record, 5,797,923 in total attendance, including the opening and closing ceremonies, easily surpassing the previous Olympic attendance record of 4.4 million set at the 1972 Olympics in Munich.

People all over the country were giddy about what a success the L.A. Games had been. "These were the American Games," columnist Dick Connor wrote in the *Rocky Mountain News.* "Artistically, athletically, any way you want to measure, it was the United States versus the world, and the United States won. The crowds were beyond belief.... They drew 101,000 to the Rose Bowl for a France-Brazil soccer Final."

Soccer had earned a celebration, and as the commissioner I was going to give us one. So, I signed ten $9,999 purchase orders to pay for a $100,000 fireworks display. It was magnificent and ended with the FIFA logo interlocked with the Olympic logo, all in multi-colors. People were just sitting there with their eyes wide open and their jaws agape. Among the fans of that fireworks display were FIFA President João Havelange of Brazil and Sepp Blatter, then general secretary of FIFA, who were sitting near me. They loved seeing the FIFA logo in the fireworks display and loved the success of our tournament. They also were in awe of "The Wave," which first began at the Olympics. They thought I must be some kind of genius. Who was I to tell them otherwise? The FIFA hierarchy saw the mighty Rose Bowl filled with cheering fans, 100,000 strong, and for the first time ever felt confident thinking ahead to bringing world soccer's crown jewel, the World Cup, to the United States. Havelange never forgot how impressed he was by what he saw, emphasizing later, "I sensed the enthusiasm when I was there at the Olympics in 1984."

When the '84 experience was over and our family was having breakfast the next morning, our son Danny put it best. "I wish I could press rewind," he said.

The 1984 L.A. Olympics, under Peter Ueberroth's leadership, were considered to have been so successful, they saved the Olympic Games and left behind a massive surplus that is still funding sports programs in Southern California to this day. Those Olympics also turned out to be the launching pad for the explosion of soccer in the United States—with me unexpectedly thrust front and center.

CHAPTER 2

A CELEBRATION SO PURE: THE WOMEN'S FIRST WORLD CUP IN 1991

WHO CAN FORGET THE THRILL of Brandi Chastain in the Rose Bowl scoring the winning goal in the 1999 Women's World Cup Final against China? Waving her jersey in the air and clenching her fists in a timeless gesture of triumph and empowerment? It was a long road for the U.S. women's team to get to that point—a long and bumpy road—and the women who made it happen are a great American success story.

Jack Kent Cooke was right about sports. It's not about the numbers, it's not about what you plan or cook up ahead of time, it's about the drama and wonder and twists and turns you never see coming. It's about people and character and the surprises that reveal so much about both—and thrill us along the way. For U.S. sports fans in recent decades, the ultimate embodiment of the greatness of sports, the ultimate proof of its power to move us and inspire us, and even make a difference, has clearly been the skill and grace and amazing dominance of the U.S. women's soccer team from the 1990s on. So many great athletes, great competitors, and great champions, from Michelle Akers and Mia Hamm in the 1980s to Julie Foudy and Briana Scurry in the 1990s to Abby Wambach and Hope Solo in the 2000s to Megan Rapinoe, Carli Lloyd, and Alex Morgan in the 2010s. So many unforgettable moments.

Looking back, it's amazing that I played even a small part in helping set this remarkable story in motion at a time when women in U.S. soccer received basically no support. You won't believe the details. I was no visionary. I was just doing what I think any sensible person in my shoes would have done. Our great women athletes in soccer deserved a chance to show what they could do, and they took that chance and ran with it, capturing the hearts of the country and burying many an opponent along the way, both on and off the field. It really all started with the U.S. women's victory in the first Women's World Championship in China—which FIFA wouldn't even let be called a "World Cup" at that time—and a celebration afterward that was as joyous and heartfelt and natural as any I've ever personally experienced in sports. I was lucky enough to be there in China to cheer on our women and whoop it up that night at the team hotel.

The ball got rolling in 1990, the same year I was surprisingly elected president of the U.S. Soccer Federation. I say surprisingly because it all took place quickly and unexpectedly. It was never a job I sought out, but others had ideas for me. Following the success of the 1984 Olympics, which showed FIFA and the world that the United States could host great soccer events, I knew it was only a matter of time before the U.S. earned the ultimate honor of hosting a World Cup, and I wanted to be involved. João Havelange and Sepp Blatter wanted me involved, too. I'd planted that seed in 1984, when they stood near me at the Rose Bowl and took in the electricity of the 100,000-strong crowd, the FIFA logo glittering overhead in firework finery. I turned back to my law practice, but my work for soccer had not been forgotten. FIFA smelled money in the U.S. market, the way U.S. sports leagues have coveted money in China and the Middle East in recent decades. We were the backwater being opened up as a new market.

Blatter and I had exchanged a few calls after the 1984 Olympics and kicked ideas around for how a U.S.-hosted World Cup could be organized. Given the success of those Olympics, run by a private company, I threw out the idea that we could organize a U.S. World Cup in the same manner. That way, the concerns we both had about whether the U.S. Soccer Federation, an underfunded volunteer grassroots entity, would be up to the organizational challenge might be allayed. Blatter didn't disagree that such an approach had many advantages, as we had shown organizing the Los Angeles Olympics that way. But for soccer it just wouldn't fly. The idea was abandoned. There was just no way FIFA could make an exception and organize a World Cup along those lines, since it would have undermined the authority of all the other national soccer federations and destroyed the viability of the entire FIFA international organizing structure.

In early July 1988, members of FIFA's Executive Committee gathered in Zurich, Switzerland, to make a final decision between the three candidates for the 1994 men's World Cup: Brazil, Morocco, and the United States. Whatever the political undercurrents, the Rose Bowl lesson was not lost on FIFA. The U.S. had an edge in pre-existing infrastructure with an assortment of competition-ready stadiums, starting with the Rose Bowl and Stanford Stadium. Fittingly enough, the vote came on the Fourth of July—and it was a win for the United States. We would host the World Cup for the first time ever.

And I read the news in the paper the next morning like everyone else, having no advance knowledge. (I'm a lifelong reader of the sports section. What was it former California governor and U.S. Chief Justice Earl Warren said? "I always turn to the sports pages first, which record people's accomplishments. The front page has nothing but man's failures.")

Around the world, news of the United States hosting a World Cup earned a few Bronx cheers. Concerns were raised about the powers that be in the U.S. soccer establishment, and Blatter and Havelange shared those concerns. They wanted new leadership. When they saw no signs that it was forthcoming, they played hardball and threatened the U.S. Soccer Federation that it was in danger of having FIFA renege on its commitment to host the 1994 World Cup on U.S. soil.

FIFA eventually got the new blood it wanted: in 1990, at the behest of FIFA, I was approached through my former '84 Olympics colleague, Chuck Cale, about organizing the World Cup, and I was open to taking on the massive challenge. It sounded exciting to me. I knew Georgina and the boys would all like it, too. But there was a catch.

"To do that," I was told, "you have to become president of the U.S. Soccer Federation."

I wasn't even a member of the Federation but learned that the bylaws didn't explicitly require that. So, I ran for president of the Federation. FIFA had set one condition of awarding the World Cup, which was that the United States needed a new professional men's soccer league and backers of the current indoor professional league came together in support of my candidacy. There was the usual politicking and back-room bickering before it came to a vote in Orlando, Florida, in August 1990.

I remember in Orlando, Rick Davis, then the best-known American player—the Landon Donovan of the 1970s—urged me to meet Sunil Gulati, with whom I would work with closely for years to come and who would play a unique role in building soccer in this country as the longtime president of the U.S. Soccer Federation. Back then, Sunil was very close to Werner Fricker, the president at the time, who was my opponent in the race for president. When Sunil and I were introduced in Orlando, it was a very short meeting. I don't think I even shook his hand. He was in the rival camp, serving as basically Fricker's campaign manager and aide-de-camp, and I was there to find votes. What point was there in wasting time on pleasantries?

"I met Alan at Rick's insistence, and he spent two seconds and then walked off," Sunil remembers. "I told Rick, 'This wasn't just anybody he was meeting. I'm kind of the secretary of state for Werner Fricker and he blew me off.' Alan explained it later. He said, 'Listen, I wasn't going to spend much time with you, because I knew I wasn't going to get your vote,' which made perfect sense."

The voting strength was distributed one third to thc youth organization, one-third to the adult organization, and one-third to the professional leagues, and I was told that Fricker was somewhat controversial, so the youth and adult votes would be split. A significant number would vote for anyone other than Fricker. If I could get the professional vote, I could prevail, and fortunately I had some useful contacts. I knew Earl Foreman, the commissioner of the Major Indoor Soccer League, from my NBA days. The lawyer for the Kansas City team was my college fraternity brother, law school classmate, and longtime close friend, Herb Kohn, who was also married to Georgina's college roommate. The general manager of the San Diego Sockers, the most successful team in MISL, was my friend Randy Bernstein, who had worked with me at the Clippers.

I was such an outsider that I knew virtually no one in the youth and adult soccer community but was told to call Marty Mankamyer, the chair of the United States Youth Soccer Association starting in 1984, whom I didn't know, but who knew everyone in the grassroots and could gather those votes. I placed the call, and when a woman answered, I asked to speak to Marty. She replied, "I'm Marty."

The meeting itself was like a high school student council meeting with posters, flyers (including a "hit piece" against me that was slipped under every member's hotel room door), and speeches. One speaker on my behalf was Charles Marshall from the Oregon Youth Soccer Association, whom I had never met (although subsequently we became close colleagues and he was instrumental in guiding the finances of the U.S. Soccer Foundation, formed with the more than $50 million surplus earned from the 1994 World Cup). The other was Ricky Davis, to whom I had been introduced shortly before he spoke on my behalf. In the midst of the meeting FIFA executive Guido Tognoni called an officer of the USSF, who promptly took the mic and declared that the Federation was in the midst of a "hostile takeover by a foreign entity: FIFA."

Despite the shenanigans, we prevailed handily. I was elected with 59 percent of the vote to 29 percent for Fricker, with just 12 percent for Paul Stiehl, the treasurer who had received the "hostile takeover" call from FIFA. Ridge Mahoney, writing in the *Washington Post*, saw my election as good news. "The country known around the world as the sleeping giant of soccer may have opened one eye today when attorney Alan Rothenberg, 54, scored a stunning victory in the presidential election of the U.S. Soccer Federation.... He swept into office on a wave of discontent with incumbent Werner Fricker and promises of injecting sound business practices into an organization plagued by ineptitude."

There was a famous scene in a 1972 movie with Robert Redford called *The Candidate* where at the end, the newly elected senator played by Redford pulls an aide aside, and plaintively asks, "'What do we do now?" I felt a little like Redford as the newly elected president of the U.S. Soccer Federation, but there was no time to figure it out. I'd been elected for one reason—to organize the '94 World Cup—but the job held other duties.

I walked out of that meeting electing me president and straight into another meeting: a board meeting, led, ostensibly, by me, their new president, although I knew nothing about the operations of the Federation. To my tremendous surprise, I was informed that there was no transition period. None at all. The truth was, I'd been elected but knew almost nothing about what the job entailed.

To underline my ignorance, at that first meeting, Bob Palmeiro, our director of adult soccer in the Northeast, made what sounded like a reasonable motion, moving that we allocate $400,000 for the women's national soccer team to hold a training camp in preparation for the 1991 world championships. Up to that moment, I had no idea there even *was* a women's team. Few others did, either. Hard as it might be for contemporary fans to fathom, women's soccer had a long way to go in this country. They had no training camps, no per diems. Great athletes competing for their country were asked to do it on the cheap and do it basically all on their own, along with whatever support their amazing and talented coach, Anson Dorrance, could provide. Naturally I supported Bob Palmeiro's motion to find $400,000 for the women's team, money coming from the dwindling coffers of the almost-bankrupt federation. Once I found out that we had a women's team, and they had been playing for nothing, I quickly embraced the cause.

I had by then established myself in various posts as an advocate for women. As the managing partner of my law firm, I was a pioneer in the hiring—and promotion—of qualified women, and the firm was the better for it. When I ran for president of the California State Bar Association (and won), I received the endorsement of the California Women Lawyers association and was proud to have it. We dropped out of a prestigious private club in Los Angeles at the time because I was going to take an oath pledging that I didn't belong to any club or association that discriminated against women. At the time that club didn't allow women to be members, so I resigned. The club subsequently opened up to women, as they should have done years earlier.

I grew up with a strong sense of respect for women. My mother and her six sisters, as well as my own three sisters, made sure I had respect! It wasn't like I was reading Simone de Beauvoir, whose major feminist book *The Second Sex* came out in 1949 when I was 10, or Betty Friedan, whose landmark book *The Feminine Mystique* was published in 1963, when I was in law school, but in the mid-'80s we were asked to host an event for Betty Friedan at our home, which we were proud to do.

"No longer will we be shackled," Friedan said theatrically, standing on the steps leading down to our living room. "We used to wear girdles, but no longer! We're free to be strong women."

I applauded her talk along with everyone else. Georgina was a strong woman who didn't spend much time worrying about labels such as feminism, and she didn't march, but we raised our three sons to take women's equality seriously. Georgina was forever amazing me. Though a devoted wife and mother, she was always a truly independent woman. I had so much respect for her energy and the constant organizing she did in fulfillment of social responsibility, and I knew how smart she was. It did put me in a mind-set to look for ways to give more opportunities to women. When I look back on people whom I selected for key roles I'm proud that so many were women; two of the four members of my World Executive Committee were women, Marla Messing and Eli Primrose-Smith. There was also Vice President of Government Relations and Protocol Karen Bybee and our general counsel was Leah Tuffanelli. Donna de Varona was honorary chair of the 1999 Women's World Cup and Kathy Carter started with us in 1994, ultimately becoming MLS' head of marketing and running Soccer United Marketing. And there were many others. I guess as a classic liberal I just instinctively and intuitively knew it was the right thing.

"From Day One Alan was open to change," Julie Foudy said in an interview for this book. "There were people at the Federation saying, 'You're missing the boat on women's soccer, we have an untapped market and have to do more around it,' and Alan would always be the one who got that. I used to say, 'Alan, I don't care where people fall on the spectrum of loving or hating women's soccer, the fact is we are not tapping into any of this potential in revenue. We're leaving money on the table. You have all these people that want to get in, you have all these girls playing, and yet we're not marketing it. We're not showcasing it.' He got all those things."

From that first U.S. Soccer board meeting, I knew I would work on behalf of women in soccer, but I had only a very vague idea back then of what that might entail. We were looking ahead to the next year's world championships, to be held in November 1991 in Guangzhou, China, but FIFA would not let them be called the "Women's World Cup." Keep in mind, at that point, we'd never had a Women's World Cup. The name of this tournament, ludicrously enough, was to be the FIFA World Championship for Women's Football for the M&M's Cup. FIFA had lined up Mars candy as the sole sponsor and Mars wanted it called the M&M's Cup, so that's what it was called.

Naturally, the athletes hated that. As Brandi Chastain, a young reserve on that 1991 team, remembers now: "Of course it was annoying! So annoying! You can't just call it what it is? Just be brave enough to do that! It's not like you're ruining men's soccer by having a Women's World Cup. It was kind of laughable, but we were also very grateful to represent the U.S. at such a big and important tournament. That felt to all of us like such a tremendous gift."

"FIFA officials were deeply ambivalent about the whole endeavor and weren't ready to confer their precious World Cup brand on a bunch of girls knocking a ball around, which seems to be how it was widely viewed," Wayne Coffey later wrote in the *New York Daily News*.

Sepp Blatter, president of FIFA from 1998 to 2015, when his run of leadership ended in scandal, never established himself as an advocate for women in the game. Publicly he proclaimed, "The future of football is feminine," but honestly those were words only. Blatter once famously commented to the Swiss newspaper *SonntagsBlick* in a 2004 interview that women's soccer would be more popular if they could "get women to play in different and more feminine garb than the men." Short skirts? "No, but in tighter shorts, for example. In volleyball, women wear different clothes from the men. Beautiful women play football nowadays, excuse me for saying so."

Bob Palmeiro's motion to fund a full-time camp for the women's national team as it prepared to go to China was a good one and ground-breaking not just for the United States but for women's programs all over the world, as it turned out. That wasn't just another era, it might as well have been two or three eras into the past. There had only been a U.S. Women's National Soccer Team since 1985, when it played its first game, and the athletes received almost no support. These were women with jobs and college students, who at that time received no compensation at all. If they were given practice uniforms at all, they tended to be oversized men's T-shirts. There were no sponsorships, no per diems, no nothing, pretty much. We did start offering per diems when I was president, though calling the very modest allowance a "per diem" might be a stretch. It may have been as little as 10 dollars. Not that the athletes complained. It was all so new that they were excited to represent the U.S. and be trailblazers.

"I remember when we first started getting per diems, we were so excited: We could do our laundry and maybe go to a movie!" Brandi Chastain remembers. "It was really small but for us it felt like the icing on top of the cake. We'd already won being selected to be on the team. We were really grateful for this wonderful opportunity to play at this level. We put up with the shiny white sparkly Elvis impersonator sweat suits and the lime green and purple and plum travel jackets that we got. Nothing was really red, white, and blue."

Basically, the women's soccer program at that time *was* Anson Dorrance, the longtime soccer coach at North Carolina. He'd taken over as coach of the U.S. women's national team in 1986 when he was only 35 years old and done a great job, joined by his longtime assistant—and, ultimately, his successor—Tony DiCicco. Anson had lived all over the world growing up and was more worldly than most 35-year-olds. As Tim Crothers wrote in his biography, *The Man Watching*, "Albert Anson Dorrance IV was born in an earthquake. Peggy Dorrance felt the tremors as the car barreled through the narrow streets of Bombay in the middle of the night on the way to the hospital. First, she thought it was just the rumbling in her belly, but these were Mother Nature's contractions."

Anson had made progress with the women's team, but it was time to make the next step. Anson has since gone on to be a Hall of Fame coach, one of the best this country has ever produced in any sport, and even in his mid-twenties, new on the national stage, he was willing to take major risks. The team he took over had a core of hard-nosed veterans he knew could stand up to the pressures of international competition, but needed an influx of raw, young talent.

Anson, a visionary, saw that with some patience and commitment these young players could develop quickly and add both athleticism and talent. He was looking to turn the U.S. women into the fittest, most athletic team in international soccer. So, in 1987, he started adding teenage players from the U.S. under-19 team, including midfielders Julie Foudy, Kris Lilly, and Mia Hamm, and defender Joy Biefeld. Soon this group was known as "The Babies." Their talent was evident, and they would soon anchor the team, but with only a fledgling program, it was difficult to develop them and give them the international seasoning they needed.

Leading up to the world championships in China in '91, we'd come up with the money to fund a proper training camp, even if that just meant putting up the women at a Holiday Inn near the practice facility in Chapel Hill and giving them three meals a day. These women had given up their jobs and put their lives on hold, all with very little support. There wasn't a lot of discussion at the board meeting when it came up. People were mostly focused on the men's team at the time. But we decided to take action and came up with a few hundred thousand dollars to fund a camp for the women in North Carolina.

"It wasn't like the women's game was really supported back then, but Alan Rothenberg gave me the tools to compete and win in China," Anson says now. "He allowed me to literally bring the entire national team into Chapel Hill in the fall of '90. He really wanted to win this first world championship. The athletes were with us for more than a month, which made all the difference. We had a very young team with very few training opportunities. The average number of caps on the

U.S. roster wasn't anywhere near the caps on the top European teams. When Alan paid for it, we were ecstatic."

The team's talent and toughness were not lost on everyone. Filip Bondy, a sharp-eyed correspondent for the *New York Times*, wrote an upbeat assessment of the women's team's prospects in June 1991 under the headline U.S. WOMEN'S TEAM MAY BE WORLD'S BEST. Here was his acerbic opening paragraph: "The ball is round and cannot be touched with the hands. Soccer has another rule, unwritten but tradition-bound: teams from the United States make accommodating doormats for the world's more talented feet. Yet on Sunday at the Yale Bowl in New Haven, local fans will have the chance to see an American squad that is one of the top soccer teams in the world.... The United States women have clinched a berth for the first Women's World Cup this November in China, outscoring Central American and Caribbean teams by 49–0 during qualification matches."

Bondy quoted Michelle Akers-Stahl: "We're on the budget plan, and it can wear a little thin. We handle it very well, we don't complain. We're not here for the frills."

It's doubtful younger sports fans used to how things are now could even believe how little focus there was nationally on the women's national soccer team at that time. Only a few reporters traveled with the team to China to cover the world championship tournament, mainly Roscoe Nance of *USA Today* and Ridge Mahoney of *Soccer America*. Longtime *Los Angeles Times* soccer writer Grahame L. Jones was there, writing not for the *Times*, but for a magazine. And Rick Crow was also in China, reporting for a small regional publication in the Washington, DC, area.

No one read newspapers online back then, this was still the era of paper or nothing, and of course there was no social media to give people updates from China on the games. Hard-core fans in the U.S. would actually drive out to airports to pick up *USA Today* so they could read how the U.S. women were faring in China! To this day, Anson still subscribes to *USA Today* out of loyalty for the newspaper's coverage back then.

I wasn't even sure I was going to make the trip to China for the world championships in November 1991. I was busy with the law firm, with the Federation, the U.S. men's team, and the World Cup Organizing Committee. As much as I wanted to go, and as great as I thought it would be to see China and support our women's team, it was hard to justify being out of commission for two weeks without even having any idea how the U.S. women would fare in that tournament.

We knew the team was talented. We also knew they were young and untested. Anson was confident, but then, Anson is always confident, as he'll be the first to tell you. We knew we had a heck of a team; we just didn't know how they matched up against the competition. I decided I'd commit to being there in China, but only if the women advanced as far as the Finals of the tournament. Up until that point, I'd have to rely on the daily briefs I received as president of U.S. Soccer.

Our team opened play on November 17 against Sweden, one of the other three teams in Group B, and had their hands full. We were up 2–1 on two Carin Jennings goals when 19-year-old Mia Hamm scored in the 62nd minute to push our lead to 3–1. Sweden chipped away with one more goal nine minutes later, but we held on to win 3–2. That turned out to be our closest game before the Final. We breezed past Brazil (5–0) and Japan (3–0) to win our group and advance, then smoked Chinese Taipei 7–0 in our first game in the knockout stage. The American women were not only winning easily, but they were also playing a fierce, exciting style of soccer that turned heads and energized women's soccer.

"We didn't sit back," Anson says now. "No, no, we reached out and grabbed them by the freaking throat and tried to squeeze the life out of every team in the world. We were very aggressive in how we assaulted this World Cup. We were going to go in as the fittest, the most athletic, and just beat them to death."

That's what they were doing in China! We were all thrilled, needless to say, but it wasn't as if the nation was riveted. The *New York Times* to that point, for example, had not covered the competition in China, except on what's called the agate page, Results Plus.

USA Today was on the scene and Roscoe Nance reported on what an impression the marauding young American team was making on the host Chinese. "The USA's veteran frontline of Michelle Akers-Stahl, April Heinrichs, and Carin Jennings is the heart and soul of the team that is two victories away from winning the inaugural FIFA Women's Soccer World Championship, the equivalent of the men's World Cup," he wrote. "They are the leading scorers for the USA, 4–0 going into Wednesday's semifinal with Germany. The Chinese have dubbed them The Three-edged Knife—you might avoid being cut by two, but not all three."

The Chinese fans were unbelievable. They fell in love with the U.S. team. They loved the blonde ponytails of our athletes and their youth and intensity. "After the first U.S. game, throngs of Chinese fans came to U.S. practices to take pictures and get autographs," Ridge Mahoney of *Soccer America* remembers. "They were there just about every day if they knew where the U.S. was training. The players were like rock stars. One day the fans stayed until the bus driver threatened to leave the players there."

Next up was Germany, the European champions, in a match on November 27. You always took the Germans very seriously. They were a great soccer country and knew how to win. But we were on a roll at that point and cruised to a 5–2 win. Jennings had a natural hat trick—three goals in a row—before the Germans even scored.

We were earning respect within soccer. The legendary Brazilian Pelé, the best ever until Lionel Messi, was there in China at the tournament, and he was enthusiastic about the talent on display, especially from Michelle Akers-Stahl. He called her a great player. "And she wears No. 10, like I did!" he added with a smile.

"That was very cool, a great moment for her and the team," Ridge Mahoney of *Soccer America* remembers.

Michelle was known in later years as the Pelé of women's soccer. Many claim she was the greatest women's soccer player in history—arguably even better than Mia, Julie, Carli, or Marta.

Once we reached the Final, we did see more media coverage. For example, the *Washington Post* and the *New York Times* had not sent sports reporters to the competition, but did have their foreign desks mobilize and send one of their Asia foreign correspondents, Lena Sun for the *Post* and Barbara Basler for the *Times*. Looking ahead to the game against Norway, which had defeated the U.S. women the last two times they played, Basler wrote about the impact our team was having.

"The United States women's team, which has played aggressive, entertaining, high-scoring soccer throughout the competition here, has 'captured the attention of even the old stodgies here,' said one soccer official, referring to some of the officials of FIFA, the organization governing world soccer, who are attending the event," she wrote.

So, in other words, maybe FIFA could have called it the World Cup after all, which after the fact they did. The team's success gave direction to a trend going back to the 1970s, when youth soccer for both boys and girls took off in the United States, dramatically boosted by the implementation of Title IX, passed in 1972, which required equal rights for women in colleges receiving federal funds: "No person in the United States shall, on the basis of sex, be excluded from participation in, be denied the benefits of, or be subjected to discrimination under any education program or activity receiving Federal financial assistance."

The impact of Title IX goes beyond sports. I remember telling a story in the early '70s. I was managing partner of my law firm and had a meeting with our office manager. When he left my office, my secretary came in and asked how I could tolerate that boring, unfriendly man. I said, "I'm the coach of this football team and not everyone can be a triple-threat back. I need pulling guards, tight ends, etc. Everyone has a role." She burst into tears, saying, "That's why we women will never succeed, because we've never had that team sports playing experience."

No more!

Taken together over time, these trends helped soccer to gain more acceptance, but that took years. As Caitlin Murray wrote in her book *The National Team: The Inside Story of the Women Who Changed Soccer*, the barriers against women in soccer were enormous. "In England, the country that invented the modern game of soccer, women were effectively banned by the English federation until 1971," she wrote, adding that in soccer-mad Brazil, "it was illegal for women to play soccer until 1979. In Germany, women were finally allowed to play soccer in 1970, and even then, they were required to play shorter games, just 60 minutes instead of 90, with a lighter ball."

Now, finally, women's soccer was getting the international showcase it deserved, and our American women were dominating. They'd buried Mexico 12–0. In China, the U.S. women won every game, and outscored opponents over their six games by a combined 25–5.

We were excited for our athletes. I was home in Los Angeles with Georgina, our three sons, and other family members and friends gathered for Thanksgiving dinner, after which I drove over to LAX to catch a flight up to San Francisco for my long connecting flight to Hong Kong. From there it was a six-hour train ride up Guangzhou, and I arrived in town a few hours before the Final started.

As a veteran of high-level sports, I had no issues feeling that I belonged. I knew my background on the sports business side and my contacts could help move soccer forward. At the same time, I was caught up in the excitement. How could you not be? I'd been hoping to get a chance to make this trip to China, and now here I was, greeting the team hours before the match with Norway.

"The thing I loved about Alan is he didn't pretend to know anything about the game, and he left me alone," Anson says now. "He never told me who to play or how to handle anything. He didn't pretend to be a soccer junky. He never wore a track suit, which all of us were used to seeing when people were trying to ingratiate themselves to us. He was our president and our leader, and he behaved that way. When he came to see us, he was in full lawyer regalia with an expensive tie. I was brought up with a silver spoon in my mouth, so I recognize expensive clothes. Alan came as himself. He came as a high-priced lawyer, and he looked like it."

That Final against Norway was a nail-biter. The Norwegians had built a confident, disciplined team. We took an early lead on a goal from Michelle Akers-Stahl, who would win the tournament's Golden Shoe Award as the leading scorer with 10 total goals, but Norway equalized just before the 30-minute mark and for most of the game that's how it stood, 1–1. Then, in the 78th minute, Akers-Stahl connected again, and we won 2–1, a great moment for U.S. sports—our women's team placing a marker before the world by winning the first Women's World Cup.

A FIFA protocol officer had given our athletes strict instructions about how to behave—and not behave—at the end of a game. They were told not to swarm onto the field and celebrate "like hyenas," as Anson remembers it. Alas, those instructions were not strictly adhered to. It was pandemonium! And I loved it.

"America won its first international soccer championship tonight when the United States defeated Norway 2–1 to take the first World Cup trophy for women," Basler reported for the *New York Times*. "At the end of the game, 12 Chinese motorcyclists carrying the flags of the tournament's 12 competing nations zoomed onto the field, and a float draped in tinsel and flashing lights with a model of the trophy set in a lotus flower was moved to the center of the field. Amid a huge shower of fireworks, with a Chinese pop song blaring from stadium loudspeakers, the 18 jubilant Americans received their championship medals and big bouquets of flowers, as friends and parents in the stands cheered hoarsely and waved small American flags."

I went downstairs after the game to see the team, and to this day that's probably the most joyful, authentic reaction I've ever seen. I equated it to my kids' junior high school basketball championship: it was so pure. There were no agents. There were no sponsors. It was all about soccer and competing to prove something to themselves, a group of women who had committed their lives to this effort.

"We weren't little kids, but it *felt* like we were little kids," Brandi Chastain says now.

These women had been killing themselves for nothing other than love of what they were doing, and now they were celebrating like the happiest people on earth. They were loving it and partied well into the morning. First was the long bus ride back to their hotel. "We were in traffic with lots of people on motorcycles all around us, and we were at the windows of the bus handing out our signature cards," Brandi remembers. "We'd never had anyone to hand those out to before! The players were super excited, and horns were honking. It was such an amazing moment and most of the world didn't even hear about it."

The team was staying at the White Swan Hotel, a sprawling place along the Pearl River on Shamian Island, where there were a lot of embassies. The hotel had a huge indoor waterfall and a pond stocked with carp. The celebration party raged there until well in the morning.

"That was definitely one of the best parties I'd ever been to," Ridge Mahoney of *Soccer America* remembers. "It was a real barnburner."

Anson was keeping a low profile up in his room on the eighth floor, but the players sent up his favorite player, Joy Biefeld, to tell him he couldn't make himself so scarce.

"We're so happy, you have to come down," Joy told him. "Our team poet, Amy Allman, has a written a poem, and you have to hear what she has to say."

The poem got him down there. I remember at about 2 AM or so, not like I had much sense of time, having just flown from California, one of the players dragging me out onto the dance floor. It was Brandi Chastain. Here she was, this young, blonde woman, 23 years old at the time, and I was this 52-year-old guy. It was a little like: *What the hell is going on here?* But everyone was smiling and enjoying themselves and that's how a celebration goes. The next morning, I caught a train and reversed my whole trip and was home a day later and could revel in what the team had accomplished for our women's soccer program.

"It gave us credibility," Anson remembers. "Obviously before then the United States had no credibility to compete against the world in the world's game. We also showed the rest of the world what you could do in a women's sport. The world gave us the game. We showed the world what we could do in this gender with this game. You treat your women well, you give them respect, you teach them to compete. In the years ahead other countries would try to learn from us and from what we were doing."

Years later, in 2007, when I was inducted into the U.S. Soccer Hall of Fame along with Mia Hamm and Julie Foudy, I referenced the accomplishments of the 1991 U.S. women's team that won the first Women's World Cup in China. I was delighted to receive a card afterward from Coach Dorrance. "Just a short note to congratulate you on your induction and to thank you for the wonderfully gracious words you shared about the 1991 world champions," Anson wrote. "I was sitting next to Laurie Gregg, my assistant in 1991, and we agreed with everything you shared about that unjaded, unspoiled first championship team. Laurie also related to me the joyous champagne bath you took at the hands of our girls in the locker room following the victory. I feel very good that the United States' first World Championship in soccer came during your watch *and* that we gave it to you. You have been our greatest president and have transformed our game on both sides of the gender divide, and it was an honor to serve you."

And an honor to work with *you*, Anson!

That victory in China was a start, but only a start. Michelle Akers-Stahl later told Grant Wahl of *Sports Illustrated* about her flight home from China after the sweet U.S. victory.

"A little old lady sitting next to her on the plane asked where Akers had been," Wahl reported. "She explained that she had just played in the world championship soccer tournament."

"How'd you do?" Akers-Stahl was asked.

"We won," she said.

"That's nice," the little old lady told her.

Nice! Nice? As Wahl wrote, "The win was more than just nice. The 2–1 victory over Norway in the Final gave U.S. soccer its first world championship since 1862, when the first team was organized in the U.S. Whereas the U.S. men's team has struggled for the past century merely to be competitive in most international games, the women's team became a power soon after the women's game went worldwide in the mid-1980s."

They were true pioneers. Everyone at U.S. Soccer was trying anything we could think of back then to get more attention for the game, so we decided to contact the White House to see about a visit. The first President George Bush, Herbert Walker Bush, had actually played soccer at Yale, center forward on the 1945 team, as well as baseball. In fact, he'd been captain of both the soccer team and the baseball team at Yale. Everyone knew he was a big sports fan. So, after the victory in China, we were invited to the White House to meet President Bush on January 23, 1992.

There were a lot of smiles all around. The president was behind schedule, so when he was introduced—"the president of the United States"—and came in and started shaking the hands of the women on the team, there was a rush of excitement. I was the sixth or seventh to shake his hand, but I was mostly doing my best to stay out of the way and keep my head down. I think that was the day I heard President Bush tell the story about when he played on the Yale soccer team and scored three goals, then called his mother to tell her about his big game. "But how did the *team* do?" his mother asked. "Did they win?"

"Let me just say that it's great to join you in honoring a group of women who reflect a favorite American pastime; it's known as *winning*," Bush said at his press conference with us. "Leave it to an American team to win the first FIFA world championship—*world* championship, I emphasize. And leave it to an American women's team to win our first world soccer championship ever.... Someone once said that sport was the first great separator of the sexes. For the sake of the male ego, I hope the men start catching up." To this day, that remains the case!

Standing near President Bush up front, I nodded and grinned at that line, then clapped along with everyone else. It was funny because it was so true.

The president singled out Michelle for praise, saying, "She scored the winning goal, showing what Hemingway so clearly described as 'grace under pressure.'"

President Bush was having a great time. He was never so comfortable as talking sports and character. "The American spirit is proud, not arrogant, confident, determined, and victorious," he told us. "I remember the day when America's athletic excellence was limited to perhaps baseball and football in the eyes of the world. Well, today, Americans are taking over everywhere from sumo to soccer. And as proof of just how far soccer has come in this country, the U.S. will proudly host the 1994 World Cup championship. So let me just say to today's champions, *world* champions: Your victory is an inspiration, no matter what sport. Your victory is an inspiration to all our athletes, male and female, young and old."

He got a little twinkle and continued, "I get accused in my job of having perhaps too keen an interest in sports. Well, too bad."

That brought a nice round of laughter.

"I think it does a lot for the real spirit of this country," he said, and the coming years would show just how true it was. "Certainly, this team has made a contribution to the real spirit of this country. You've made us very, very proud."

I presented the president with a No. 1 U.S. team jersey with "G. Bush" and "USA" on the back. It was very exciting, and I didn't want to miss out on an opportunity to talk up these amazing women and their triumph in China.

"Thank you very much, Mr. President," I said. "On behalf of the entire U.S. Soccer family, we thank you so much for giving this richly deserved honor to our women's national team, the champions of the world. They really epitomize what sport and what the United States is all about. They won this championship the old-fashioned way: they earned it. I'm not sure if everybody is aware, but these women deferred careers, deferred education, and deferred raising families to win this championship for the United States and they did an admirable job of representing our country on and off the field."

Then, standing behind the podium with the presidential seal, I handed over the jersey.

"It's a beauty!" the president said, holding it up. "It's lovely. USA! No. 1!"

Anson was next, talking about his years abroad growing up as the son of a U.S. oil executive. "The world has a love-hate relationship with the United States," he said. "These women, Mr. President, are among your greatest ambassadors. They play the world's game better than anyone has ever seen."

Our team captain, April Heinrichs, had a soccer ball all the athletes on the team had autographed. Instead of handing it to the president, she was going to have some fun.

"I know in your job, you often have to use your head," she said. "In our sport, we also have to use our heads."

"Shoot it up there!" the president encouraged her.

So, she headed the ball his way, and he put something on it, heading the ball right back—over her head. That got such a good round of applause, she threw the ball to him again and he headed it back. Then, and this was really cool, she tossed it his way, he headed the ball to her, she headed it back, then he headed it back *again*, and she headed it one more time, and he caught it, then did a little behind-the-back pass to give her the ball back. It was an electric moment.

President Bush's people were beside themselves. This was soon after the president had been in Japan for a state dinner and came down with the flu. He'd actually gotten sick at the dinner, and he'd been roughed up in the press over that. So, his people didn't want to take any chances: *He's going to get a bloody nose! They're going to make fun of him.* They were going crazy on us. But the fact is, the evening news picked up a few seconds of that clip of him heading the ball, which was exactly what we'd been hoping for.

That was a plus for President Bush, who looked good, smiling and clearly enjoying himself like the true athlete he was. This was a man who would celebrate his birthdays later in life by jumping out of an airplane with a parachute, right up to his 90th birthday in 2014! The exposure was great for us. We knew that it was through moments like that that you help build a sport. Bush had been eloquent in honoring our accomplishments in soccer to that point and urging us on in the future. A lifelong Democrat, I began to admire George H.W. Bush!

President Bush came through for us in style, giving the sport a nice boost, and the press coverage was extensive. Even *El Nuevo Herald* in Miami, Florida, had fun with the moment, running a big picture of Bush heading the ball, behind the presidential podium, with members of the team looking on.

BUSH DEMUESTRA HABILIDADES FUTBOLISTICAS was the headline, which probably means just about what it sounds like.

The warm glow of exposure had me thinking again about an idea that first occurred to me on that long flight back from China following the women's feel-good victory in the first Women's World Cup. Someday, I started thinking, we were just going to have to find a way to host the Women's World Cup ourselves in the United States. We would have to go all out, making sure that the women played before large, enthusiastic crowds and everything they did was covered by a huge throng of world media. It would be a celebration of soccer, a celebration of our great women athletes, and a celebration of America. It could be epic.

The next step would be hosting a women's soccer tournament as part of the 1996 Olympics in Atlanta. So in April 1992, I wrote a letter to Havelange. "While we have had a number of discussions about adding women's soccer to the Olympic Games in 1996, I am not sure whether any formal request has ever been made to FIFA to seek that approval from the International Olympic Committee. Because of that, please deem this correspondence to be the formal request by the United States Soccer Federation that women's soccer be added to the Olympic Games in 1996." It was that simple. We were on our way.

The 1991 triumph launched a 30-year period of domination unequalled in soccer history—men's or women's—during which the U.S. women's national team won four FIFA World Cups and four Olympic tournaments. But first, we would have to pull off the daunting task of organizing the men's World Cup in 1994 and demonstrating to the world that the Olympic soccer tournament I'd overseen in 1984 was a mere warmup. We were now ready to host the great soccer nations of the world for a memorable time, beamed out to millions of people around the world through live satellite TV coverage, so that any mistake would be magnified. The world was watching to see how we'd handle the challenge.

CHAPTER 3

HOSTING THE WORLD'S BIGGEST PARTY: THE 1994 MEN'S WORLD CUP

THE CALL FROM THE WHITE HOUSE—if it really *was* the White House—came over the Christmas 1992 holidays, just before New Year's Eve. We had closed the World Cup office in the Washington, DC, area until the New Year, celebrating a year of hard work with a lively office Christmas party, and people had dispersed. I was back in our office in L.A. when the phone rang. Someone on the other end claimed to be calling from the White House. The White House? In the middle of the holidays, the last week of the year?

"The president is about to leave for Riyadh," someone was telling me. "From Saudi Arabia, he'll travel on to stops in Mogadishu and Sochi on the Black Sea, where he and Boris Yeltsin will sign the START II treaty. This is his last foreign trip as president."

I had not forgotten the way President Bush had reveled in welcoming the women's national team to the White House after their victory in China in the first World Cup. We had all bonded over soccer, and I'd had the honor of presenting Bush with a team jersey, which he loved. Given the way Bush had come through, heading the ball back to April Heinrichs, it made sense he would have positive associations. And he clearly liked soccer memorabilia. He wanted more!

Apparently, as the caller from the White House was explaining, Bush was going to be meeting with King Fahd of Saudi Arabia on December 31. One thing they had in common was they were both huge soccer fans.

"The president would like to give the king something from the U.S. team," I was told. "Can you help?"

"Of course we can help!" I said instantly, trying to sound convincing.

Actually, I had no idea, none whatsoever, if we could help. How could we quickly get our hands on something appropriate for a king with the offices closed for the holidays? There was no texting back then. No one used email. I started working my way down the list of everyone who worked in the DC office, starting at the top, calling everyone at home. It wasn't going well. First, I tried Scott LeTellier, chief operating officer of the U.S. World Cup Organizing Committee, whom I'd known since we worked together on the L.A. Olympics when he'd been my right-hand man. No answer. Karen Bybee, chief government and protocol officer, also did not pick up. Randy Bernstein, head of marketing and sponsorships, unavailable. I was so desperate I tried the number for a young guy just out of college who had started working for us days before, Tim Larkin, who was working with Karen. He had actually played some professional soccer, two years as a midfielder for the Dallas Sidekicks of Major Indoor Soccer League, and was maybe 25 or 26 at the time.

I called the number I had, and someone answered who was not Tim. I could hear a TV in the background, and muffled conversation.

"Tim!" a voice yelled. "Tim, there's a Mr. Rothenberg on the phone for you."

When Tim picked up, he sounded doubtful.

"I assumed one of my buddies was playing a joke on me," Tim says now. "Why would Alan Rothenberg call me at my home? Even when I got to the phone and said hello, I still expected a voice that was fake, that wasn't Mr. Rothenberg, but it was him."

I explained the situation.

"Can you go down to the World Cup offices for me? Please get there ASAP."

He said he would.

"Just go into the Protocol Office and pick out an assortment of gifts," I told him. "I've already left messages for Randy, Karen, and Scott. Just go grab enough things that you think would offer the president an opportunity to bring something over. And then call this phone number, it's for Robin McClain, staff assistant to the president. She will take it from there."

Tim drove to the offices, but guess what? He didn't have a key to the Protocol Office. So, he just grabbed what he could off Karen's, Scott's, and Randy's desks, including a large World Cup '94 T-shirt he hoped would fit the president. He drove to the White House gate, where he was instructed to enter and parked, made it through security, and was escorted by Robin McClain upstairs to the White House residence. She asked him to lay out the stuff he'd brought on a table, which she looked over uncertainly.

"Well, I can't decide," she said. "We'll just let him decide."

Tim was expecting a chief of staff–type to make the call, but in walked President Bush, who ignored Tim and surveyed the items. As he was looking them over, the First Lady, Barbara

Bush, came in with her dog, Millie. It was morning and she was still in her robe.

"Hi, I'm Barbara," she said to Tim.

"Yes, ma'am, I know who you are," he said.

"George," she said, turning to her husband, "I need you to sign this poster."

"Honey, I will in a moment, I'm doing this right now," he said.

"George," she repeated, "would you please sign this?"

So, he signed the poster, and she left with Millie, the dog.

"Is this stuff from the State Department?" the president asked his aide.

"No," she said, "this nice young man here to my right came in from the World Cup '94 office and brought these things with him for you to choose."

Bush greeted Tim with a quick smile, but he was on a tight schedule and picked through the things on the table, choosing a replica World Cup soccer ball, called the Questra, with a USA '94 flag. "It probably cost ten bucks or something, but that was what he chose to bring with him," Tim remembers.

An aide entered the room and told Bush, "Mr. President, you have a meeting in 25 seconds," and handed him a tie and sport coat, which he quickly put on as he thanked Tim and left the room.

"We understand the president likes to run and we have this T-shirt for him as well if he'd like it," Tim told the aide, who was still there.

"Oh, he'd love it," she said, so we gave him that as well.

Tim told me he was so shaken up from his experience that on his way out of the White House parking lot, he drove his car up over a curb and almost hit a light post.

Air Force One was soon en route to the Middle East, arriving on December 30, and Bush met briefly with King Fahd, presenting the gift, before flying on to visit U.S. troops in Somalia. Apparently, the king was pleased, which for us at the World Cup offices felt both surreal and scary. We knew the eyes of the world would be on us, and we had a lot of work to do to make sure that we proved to everyone that the United States could host a World Cup and make it a rip-roaring success.

Now, I do want to clear up one misconception that sometimes gets repeated. For the record, I was not the one to bring the World Cup to the United States. I want to make that point very clearly: despite many headlines referring to me as "the person who brought the World Cup to the United States," I did not. That distinction belongs to my predecessor as president of the U.S. Soccer Federation, Werner Fricker. Full credit to Werner and his team for all the work they did in landing the big one with all the prestige that entailed. Fricker loved soccer and cared so much about moving the sport forward in this country, he helped finance the U.S. World Cup bid by taking out a mortgage on his own house. That is serious commitment. That is putting yourself on the line.

Born in Yugoslavia to a German-speaking family in 1936, Fricker came to the United States with his family in 1952, showed up in papers by 1955 for his play with the German-Hungarian soccer team of Philadelphia, and played on the U.S. team during qualifying rounds for the 1964 Olympics. He served as a vice president of U.S. Soccer for 10 years until 1984, when he was named president. "Werner was a self-made man," says Sunil Gulati, who met Fricker when he was vice president. "He had a construction business, played in our national team program, and ran a club in Horsham, Pennsylvania, called the United German Hungarian Club."

Following Fricker's 2001 death after a fight with cancer, the *Philadelphia Inquirer* wrote, "Bringing the World Cup here, Mr. Fricker said in a 1994 interview, was a means to improve soccer in the United States. That mission came after his own playing experience in '64, when the United States failed to qualify for the Olympics after losing to Suriname. 'That's when I found out how disorganized everything was in this country. I told my wife, in 1964, that someday I would work to change that,' Mr. Fricker said in 1994."

The program came a long way under Fricker and one of his best moves was giving Sunil a bigger role. Chuck Blazer, vice president under Fricker, asked Sunil to run a national team camp in Colorado Springs for younger players. "The camp was a mess," Sunil says now. "Sprinklers went off during the games, we were buying balls at Kmart on a Sunday morning, and so on." The next time Sunil saw Fricker, he told him about the chaos.

"Hey, your national team program's a mess," Sunil said.

"Well send me a note, but don't go sending me a 17-page memo," Fricker said.

So, Sunil, being Sunil, sent Fricker a 17-page memo. He was in after that, one of the key figures in U.S. soccer—but when I took over, I felt like it was time for widespread change.

I had a lot of high-level support in running for president—even Pelé sent in a letter of support on my behalf—but there was shock in some quarters when I won. "When I heard that Rothenberg had been elected, I thought the man who was calling to tell me must have been smoking something funny," said former Fleet Street sportswriter Clive Toye, the architect of the New York Cosmos' plan to add Pelé, Beckenbauer, and Carlos Alberto, which lit the match that started the growth of soccer in the United States. Toye told the *London Observer* in June 1991: "It is hard to exaggerate how much of an achievement it was to come out of the blue and beat the old guard as he did."

I did not see being elected as such an achievement. The achievement, if it could be pulled off, would be organizing the 1994 World Cup into a major success in all senses: first of all, as a great celebration of soccer, one with robust attendance and media interest, and finally, of course, as a commercial success. Very early on, I stipulated to the Federation board that if the World Cup turned any kind of profit, the funds would roll over into a nonprofit foundation, as millions left over from the 1984 Los Angeles Olympics were used to start a foundation—still extant, and used primarily to support, among other things, youth sport in Southern California.

When I brought up the idea, no one said too much, certainly not in opposition, since at that point all anyone could think about was their worry that we'd run into serious problems and drive the Federation into bankruptcy. I'm sure if they'd known we would end up with a more than $50 million surplus, they would never have approved the creation of the foundation, and that surplus would have quickly dissipated without any lasting benefit to the sport. I was confident we'd pull this off, but there was only one way to make that happen and that was through a lot of hard work. "One reason for our success with soccer at the Olympics was that we worked our tails off. We mean to do that again," I told the *Observer.*

"With a mandate for change, Rothenberg went to work," the *L.A. Weekly* wrote in a 1994 cover piece. "A site-selection process spread the tourney's preliminary games among nine U.S. cities, all of which are major media markets with strong grassroots soccer support." As was the case with the women in 1999, FIFA expected us to be in small stadiums and we had to persuade them, as well as some of the bidding cities, that we could fill large stadiums. "Rothenberg began enlisting corporate sponsors to sign on (at a cost of up to $20 million each) and started negotiating domestic TV contracts," the *Weekly* continued. "Rothenberg's most sweeping changes came in the structure of his new organization, which resembles a classic top-down corporate model."

Yes, that was accurate enough. We were intent on putting in place good business practices to promote efficiency and accountability. I recruited and melded together soccer aficionados without business experience, including some veterans of the 1984 Olympics, and more talented and experienced businesspeople who knew little about soccer (e.g., Joe Smith, a prominent music industry executive; Michael Weisman, an Emmy Award–winning TV producer; and Lester Wintz, an advertising guru).

We benefitted from the counsel and leadership of an incredibly distinguished and high-powered board of directors, including Howard Allen (CEO of SoCal Edison); Chuck Cale (attorney); Donna De Verona (Olympic gold medalist and co-founder of the Women's Sports Foundation); Marion Wright Edelman (prominent civil rights leader); Ahmet Ertegun (chairman, Atlantic Records, and former president of the NY Cosmos); Werner Fricker (past president of USSF); Lamar Hunt (owner of the Kansas City Chiefs and co-founder of the AFL); Henry Kissinger (former Secretary of State and national security advisor), who served as honorary chairman of World Cup 1994; Bruce Nordstrom (chairman, Nordstrom department store chain); Jay Pritzker (chairman, Hyatt Hotels and prominent Chicago business leader); Richard Rosenberg (CEO, Bank of America); Steve Ross (chairman of Warner Communications, owner of the NY Cosmos); William Simon (former Treasury Secretary); and Peter Uebberoth (CEO 1984 Olympics, former commissioner, Major League Baseball).

Additionally, we recruited and oversaw thousands of volunteers to manage the effort. One of the legacies of 1994 I'm extraordinarily proud of is the hundreds, probably thousands, of people who worked with us and then went on to successful careers in sports and event management and the media.

"The idea was to make U.S. Soccer operate more like IBM and less like the PTA," one U.S. Soccer official, speaking anonymously, told the *Weekly*. "We weren't a social club anymore, we were a business that would compete internationally, and if you weren't with the program, you were gone. There was a new look, a new feel, a new attitude, and if you reminded anyone of the old days, you were out. I happened to agree with the plan and had no qualms about staying. But I can understand that for a lot of people who had the most to do with the USA winning the right to host the World Cup in the first place, usually without getting much money for their effort, watching this tournament from the outside is going to be a more bitter than sweet experience." We were simultaneously building a World Cup organization and transitioning the U.S. Soccer Federation from a grassroots-run organization to one professionally managed.

We had a lot of work to do on the pitch, though—that was clear in August 1991 when Georgina and I flew to Moscow to attend the U.S. national team's exhibition game against the

Soviet Olympic team at Lenin Stadium on Saturday, August 17. I mention the date because it turned out to be important. We lost 2–1 and it could have been worse. “The score might have been more lopsided if not for the 22-year-old (Tony) Meola who made 10 saves,” the Associated Press reported. Meola, an immediate favorite of mine, was both goalkeeper and team captain. “It was a bad outing,” he said. “Our intensity just wasn’t there.”

On that August 1991 visit to Moscow, they put us up at the Rossiya Hotel, just outside of Red Square, which, with more than 3,000 rooms, had been the largest hotel in the world for a number of years before that. It was amazing because, walking around that hotel, you really realized the corruption of that country, even under the leadership of reformer Mikhail Gorbachev, who had risen to the Soviet leadership in 1985. The players were staying in one wing, and it was like going to the worst summer camp that your kids might have gone to, just filthy, with bunk beds. We’d been told to bring toilet paper since what would be provided was more like sandpaper. We, on the other hand, were in a private wing in a huge suite with our own concierge. It was very luxurious, and I think we might have been the only occupants of this multi-story hotel. Every day they were bringing in caviar, fresh fruit, and brandy. We were sure it was bugged, so we were very careful about what we said.

The day after the match, Georgina and I flew to Leningrad for a quick morning visit and then flew back and the next morning were given a tour of the Kremlin, which was quite impressive. Among other things, we saw a religious service being read—for only the third time inside the Kremlin since the 1917 Revolution, we were told.

Our guide seemed a little edgy. "Something's going on because Gorbachev is down at the Black Sea," he told us, which was apparently out of the ordinary, but we didn't think anything of it. The tour lasted a good four hours, and when we came back outside, the Kremlin was ringed with tanks. We were right in the middle of an attempted coup d'etat against Gorbachev. At first it was pretty off-putting, but in contrast to what had happened in China two years before during the Tiananmen Square massacre, where they sent in the mercenaries, the Soviets had called up the local reserve teenagers, who had no idea what they were doing and were basically there just for show. Normally when we travel, Georgina takes all the photos. This time I took one photo, and it was a classic because it shows her talking through our guide to a young tank operator during the coup and right behind him is Red Square. Through the interpreter Georgina asked the soldier what his orders were. "I had none other than just to show up," he replied. We don't normally send out holiday cards, but that year we sent out a card with that picture and the message "Peace on Earth."

We spent the next day or so dashing around town, frankly, just following the crowds. Men with bullhorns told everyone to move toward the Russian Parliament building, and as we approached, we saw tanks parked to block the bridge. Our guide told us about the rumors that were flying, like "Gorbachev is dead" or "Yeltsin has been arrested."

Boris Yeltsin had been democratically elected president of the Russian federation two months earlier. We actually saw him talking to the crowd, though of course we had no idea what he was saying. That was the day he climbed on top of a tank and gave a speech.

That night we were invited to dinner at the apartment of Slava Koloskov, whom I'd gotten to know during the L.A. Olympics. When the driver dropped us off, he opened his trunk and it was just packed with luxury food items to deliver to Koloskov, further evidence of the kind of corruption that was going on. Ordinary people were scrambling for food and the *nomenklatura* were feasting on caviar and sturgeon. We went up to the apartment and it was lavishly furnished, with expensive artwork and tapestries everywhere, and every type of electronic gear imaginable. Slava and his wife were glued to the radio for updates on the tense situation. Tatyana was the manager of the Lenin Museum and was scared for her life; she'd spent the day hiding all the artwork and other valuable artifacts in the museum's basement.

Flights out of Moscow were halted, but when we were finally able to leave a day later, we had a connection in Frankfurt. Somehow a *Los Angeles Times* reporter caught up with me there for an article published on August 22, asking my observations. I expressed my conclusion that it was hard to believe that Russia was a serious threat to the United States, as its infrastructure was like a Third World country, its corruption was evident, and the dour, unhappy demeanor of its populace was sad to see. "I never thought I'd be so happy to be in Germany," I said.

From the time I was elected president of U.S. Soccer, there were three primary missions. One was the business of building an organization that would create what we saw as the best World Cup event ever. Another was to professionalize Federation management. The other was building a competitive soccer team. If we unleashed a great party, and the U.S. team did not come to play and embarrassed themselves and all of us, believe me, no one working with me was going to feel good about anything we did, even if we ended up with a great event and huge surplus.

As challenging as the organizational work was, building a team on the pitch was an even greater one. It took the U.S. team 40 years to qualify for another World Cup after, in 1950, the U.S. team beat England 1–0 in a mammoth upset. Then, in 1990, the team didn't win anything. Not a very impressive performance, to put it mildly. It was essential that we upgrade the men's national team going into 1994.

Back in 1966, Alastair Reid had written in the *New Yorker*, "Can't somebody tell the Americans that if they were to take soccer seriously and build a national team that could make even a decent showing in something like the World Cup, their world prestige would soar?" It felt, as we prepared for 1994, that we were finally stepping up to that opportunity to connect with the rest of the world.

While hardly a soccer expert, I found it apparent that our national team's style of play, if you dared calling it that, was to kick the ball as far down the field as possible and hope to outrun the opposition to the ball. No string of passes in an offensive buildup, no agile moves by the players. The match reinforced my belief, based on what knowledgeable people had told me, that hiring a new coach was essential—someone much more experienced, preferably a sophisticated international coach.

Bob Gansler, the current coach, had been an American college coach. He felt he'd been given assurances that he'd be the one to coach the team in the next World Cup, but to me and those I talked to it was clear we needed to aim higher. Bob, to his great credit, had taken the U.S. to its first World Cup in 40 years, qualifying for the 1990 World Cup in Italy, but then lost all three matches. Clearly Bob was a good coach. We needed a *great* coach with international experience to take soccer in the United States to the next level—and to me that choice soon became obvious.

In March 1991, we announced we'd hired Bora Milutinović, the Yugoslavian-born coaching genius who'd taken Mexico and then Costa Rica to the second round of recent World Cups. Bora, never lacking for personality, said he was accepting our offer "to show everybody that even Americans know how to play soccer." The job would be a challenge, he said, "not only for me, but I think also for Mr. Rothenberg, for the Federation, for the players, and for the American people."

Like legions of Mexican American soccer fans, I loved Bora. He was delightful—albeit a little infuriating at times. Bora liked to do things his own way. Before the press conference in March 1991 announcing Bora's selection, I asked him please to speak in English, which he spoke well enough. He was fluent in Spanish, but I knew the people who were very displeased that I'd chosen a foreign-born coach would be really angry if he spoke in another language. It'd be like pouring salt into their wounds. Bora told me sure, no problem—then went out and did the press conference mostly in Spanish!

Asked at that press conference if the U.S. team under his leadership would be playing an attacking style of soccer, he laughed and said—in English—"When we have the ball, yes."

He had a sense of what needed to happen before our young U.S. men's team would be ready to make an honorable showing in the World Cup, and he knew it would take time. He considered various styles of play and various formations, answering countless questions from reporters along the way with good-natured calm.

"When you have young people, it is much more important that they understand the basic concepts," he told reporters in February 1994. "Maybe most teams in the world play with a five-man midfield today, but whether it is 4-4-2 or 4-5-1 for my players, the thing to understand is very simple: when we have the ball, keep it; when we don't have the ball, recover it."

Even Yogi Berra couldn't top the wisdom in that one! There was an important message here, which boiled down to: play your game, take care of what you can take care of, and let the rest happen, just as you would in any other contest. Pressure, to Bora, was fiction. "No, the World Cup is not different," he said. "You have to make players understand that it is the same as playing any other game. My experience of the World Cup is that you must enjoy it. You cannot think that it is bigger than anything else. It is the biggest party in the world, so you need to be happy while you're in it. That's different from pressure."

He never had his players practice penalty kicks. It was just: go out there and kick the ball. He felt if you practiced kicks too much, that would only add to the pressure.

Bruce Arena and other great coaches to follow would all talk about concentration and focus, and so did Bora. "One thing is always the same in soccer—it is concentration, not emotion, that is important," he said before our first match. "We must concentrate for the entire 90 minutes. I like America because it is enthusiastic, but we must be under control when we play."

Bora was a master, but the question was whether he would have the building blocks to work his magic. How could we be smart and creative about putting a team together? At that time, the international soccer community had such disrespect for the quality of our players that only a very few even had an opportunity to play for foreign teams. Even then, in most cases it was for a lower-division team. Our player pool primarily consisted of kids still playing in college or, like Tim Larkin, for Major Indoor Soccer League, which was a totally different operation.

Out of necessity, we created a full-time camp. How better to build team unity and cohesion and a higher level of play? How better to turn a bunch of guys into a true *team*? We signed the players that we wanted to contracts for the U.S. national team, a few even before we set up the camp. This was a case where what we did on the business side helped us on the soccer side. The Federation had enough money coming in from World Cup sponsors, which we leveraged to get huge increases for U.S. Soccer to pay for setting up the camp. We brought our players together at the camp in California and sent them together all over the country and the world to play as many matches as they could. We sold tickets to these friendlies and bought in some modest TV revenues. That gave us a budget to sign more players. They weren't humongous contracts, believe me, but it was at least enough that they could come work for us full-time.

The location we found for the camp, at Mission Viejo in Orange County, about 50 miles southeast of L.A., worked out beautifully. It was a friendly community that provided a lot of facilities and services to us at minimal cost and enabled us to build a common soccer culture in the 16 months that team members were there. That's not a lot of time—and we had a lot of work to do.

If you look at the success of various traditional World Cup powers in the world, it's really because there's a true team, bound together with a cohesiveness that runs deep. When Germany was dominant, virtually the entire starting lineup was Bayern Munich players. They knew each other, inside out, and played together all the time. When Spain was dominant, it was virtually all Real Madrid and Barcelona players. They knew each other intimately. The French, when they became dominant, that was because of an academy that the French opened in 1988 in Clairefontaine, which is about 40 miles southwest of Paris. The French academy turned out to one of the great operations of all time, in terms of taking kids from the age of 13 right through the program. They basically borrowed the model the Romanians and other Soviet bloc countries took to building their sports programs in the communist era. So many top French players came up through the academy. Even if they played abroad in other professional leagues, when they came back together for international competition, it was natural for them.

I always believed the talent was there to build a U.S. program; it just had to be developed. We were fortunate leading up to the 1994 World Cup to have a core of young talent we could build a team concept around. The core started with John Harkes, Tab Ramos, and Tony Meola, who had grown up and played together in New Jersey and then played together on the 1990 U.S. World Cup team. So, they had that experience and now they were stepping forward in '94. They were all from Kearny (CAR-nee), New Jersey, only 10 miles from Manhattan, which was sometimes referred to back then as "Soccer Town U.S.A." As Bruce Arena wrote in his book on U.S. soccer, "The Clark Thread Company of Paisley, Scotland, opened a factory near Kearny in 1867, leading thousands of immigrants from Scotland and Ireland to settle in Kearny, bringing with them their love of soccer. The mills hired all the best soccer players arriving from across the Atlantic and every boy dreamed of growing up to be a star. Starting in 1883, Clark Thread Company fielded teams that competed in the American Football Association cups, winning in 1885, 1886, and 1887. Scottish pride and love of sport went hand in hand."

Among the newcomers, Alexi Lalas stood out for me, as he did for most everyone. He came from a great private school near Detroit, the Cranbrook Kingswood School, and even though he had only taken up soccer at age 11, he was named Michigan High School Player of the Year for 1987. Alexi always had such presence on the pitch, almost like a soccer version of Bill Walton in his UCLA and early Portland Trail Blazers days. Alexi was 6′3″, taller than the other players, and he had this long, hippie-like, red hair and red goatee, and also liked to play the guitar. He was just a sharp, fun-loving guy and kept the team nice and loose. He added so much to the color of the team and probably the esprit de corps, because he was someone who could have resisted Bora's teachings but instead embraced them. In fact, he was a Bora fan.

"He was like Yogi Berra and Yoda mixed," Alexi later said to *Sports Illustrated*. "It was incredibly frustrating to a lot of players, depending on where you were in your career and certainly your age. For me, he was huge, because he made me look at the game in a completely different way and asked me to think about my game and the game that I was playing and every moment of the game in ways that I hadn't thought of before. For some older players and players who were further along their career, it could be incredibly frustrating, the type of trainings that we did, the constant testing—not just physical testing but psychological testing."

Alexi formed up a trio of key young players, along with Cobi Jones and Eric Wynalda, Southern California kids who played here at UCLA and San Diego State. Wynalda had played in Italy on the 1990 team, though Jones did not. That triumvirate, if you will, of Lalas, Jones, and Wynalda came in together. You blended those three with Ramos, Harkes, and Meola—our own "Jersey Boys"—as well as Marcelo Balboa, one of the few players with international experience, playing for a Mexican lower-division team, and we really had something. It was a wonderful melding of players.

We knew we had to add quality players however we could, even if it meant getting a little creative. Working with Hank Steinbrecher, a former Boston University soccer coach and our venue director at Harvard during the '84 Olympics, whom I'd named secretary general of the U.S. Soccer Federation in November 1990, we identified players elsewhere in the world who you never would have thought were Americans but qualified for American citizenship.

That was how we found Earnie Stewart. Born in the Netherlands to a father who was a U.S. Air Force airman and a Dutch mother, he was playing professionally for VVV-Venlo in the Netherlands. Because his father held a U.S. passport, Earnie was eligible to play for us and became a key part of our World Cup team.

Tom Dooley—what a great name—also had a father who was a U.S. serviceman. Born to a German mother, he grew up in Germany and played for FC Kaiserslautern in the Bundesliga, which had won both the league title and the DFB-Supercup in 1991. Tom had actually played for the German national team, but not in any major matches, and was eligible to join us. He made his first appearance with the U.S. national team in a friendly against Ireland on May 30, 1993—and would play every minute of the 1994 World Cup.

Jokingly, I suggested that we should send someone to Southeast Asia to look for blond-haired, blue-eyed Vietnamese soccer players.

Roy Wegerle was born and raised in South Africa. He played college soccer in the U.S. and was briefly in the NASL, then made a name for himself as a prominent goal scorer in the Premier League. He was not an American citizen, but he'd married an American, so he was eligible.

It's one thing to identify worthy players who were potentially eligible for citizenship and another to clear all of the legal and bureaucratic steps to make it happen. How could we expedite their path to citizenship? The immigration rules and attitudes then were more favorable than they are now, but there were time-consuming bureaucratic steps that need to be cleared. We didn't have a year to wait. We had a team to build. Fortunately, Hank Steinbrecher somehow identified a friendly judge in the federal courts in Chicago. Stewart and Dooley were moved forward pretty expeditiously, but Wegerle's case was a little more complicated. Without going into all the details, basically we figured out the process would be helped along if Wegerle's wife were shown to be abroad on "essential" work—so we hired her. Problem solved. Her job: bring English tourists to the United States for the World Cup.

For inspiration, the wall of the lobby of our Los Angeles office was emblazoned with these words from poet Robert Browning: "A man's reach should exceed his grasp, or what's a heaven for?" Beneath the quote was a huge digital countdown clock to underscore the urgency of our mission. It was getting closer to the World Cup, literally by the second.

The friendly matches we were hosting became a little less friendly. A lot of strong World Cup teams that had qualified wanted to come and see what it was like in the United States, so they brought over their real teams and not just some B-squad with guys thinking they were coming for a vacation.

To test the readiness of our organization and the team, we had the Federation prepare a tournament in the summer of 1993, which we named the U.S. Cup. We invited England, defending World Cup champion Germany, and the ultimate 1994 World Cup champion, Brazil, to play in the tournament scheduled in some of our large World Cup venues: Foxboro Stadium in Boston, Soldier Field in Chicago, RFK Stadium in DC, and the Pontiac Silverdome in Detroit, where it was played indoors on grass, a first ever. Since Giants Stadium was unavailable, our "New York" venue was the Yale Bowl in New Haven, Connecticut.

On June 9, amazingly enough, we beat England 2–0 on goals from Dooley and Alexi Lalas, in what the *Los Angeles Times* called "the ultimate humiliation for the country that invented the game."

WE CAN'T GET ANY LOWER was the headline in the London *Daily Mirror*.

"English football died of shame last night—and the coffin could be draped with the Stars and Stripes," added the *London Daily Express*, calling the defeat "an abject failure against a third-rate soccer nation."

In all my experiences in team management, I rarely entered the locker room or talked to the players. That could undermine the coach's authority. Before the England match, I made an exception. The team was gathered on the field at Foxboro, while in the press box FIFA officials were meeting. Bora asked me to address the team. I pointed to the press box where FIFA was discussing their "Fair Play" tag line. Channeling my best Al Davis, I pointed to the press box and said, "F—k fair play, just win!" And they did.

People were talking about us, and the players were gaining a confidence we could never have predicted. The Germans won the tournament, led by Jürgen Klinsmann's four goals, and Dooley led us with three, pacing us to a third-place finish. But for us, the competition was already a win, invaluable experience for these young players.

We passed the test with flying colors. The crowds were large and enthusiastic, the matches came off without a significant hitch, and the U.S. team was highly credible, beating England and staying competitive with Germany and Brazil in losses. Needless to say, we were ecstatic—and relieved, confident that we could stage a fantastic World Cup.

For those of us who worked for years organizing the 1994 World Cup, sometimes it felt almost as if we were nightlife impresarios in New York or L.A. with advance knowledge of the next big thing, long before anyone had any notion of what was coming. It was exciting and it was also a little strange. We were already seeing in our minds how sellout crowds at great venues around the country would inject electricity and energy into an event people in every country of the world would be following closely, long before many sports fans even knew the next World Cup would be on U.S. soil—or indeed, even knew what the World Cup was. They would all come to see the light, but it's almost comical to think back to 1991 and the glassy stares we'd see when we started talking about what it meant to host the world's greatest sporting event.

I remember going to New York in January 1992 for the annual Sports Summit, held at the Marriott Marquis in Manhattan. I was one of the featured speakers there, along with Charles Battle Jr., an organizer of the 1996 Summer Olympics in Atlanta. At that time, U.S. sports fans were so focused on the Olympics, I had to jump in when I could to get in a word edgewise about the World Cup, which would be held two years earlier!

The average American sports fan back then didn't even know what a World Cup was. There were a few American soccer aficionados, mostly ethnic immigrants from soccer-loving countries, who knew and cared. How did we break through to the rest? Our feeling was that America loves a big event, and so we had to make this a must-see thing. We surrounded it with as much hoopla as we could, a lot of entertainers, a lot of celebrities. We had our U.S. national team play a lot of friendly games in various places so people would get some introduction to the sport. I'd speak anywhere anybody would have me speak and tried to put in context how big an event this was to the rest of the world. We held glitzy press conferences any time we could: signing a sponsor or a player, announcing another round of ticket sales, signing a celebrity to appear at an event, and whenever we announced a match or visited a venue city. Any excuse!

"There are 209 countries that are members of FIFA, and 209 countries that are members of the United Nations," I would say. "And if you told them they could only be a member of one, all but maybe a half a dozen would choose FIFA, not the United Nations."

I made a similar point to Mayor Richard Daley of Chicago when we were negotiating with him on the city providing security for matches in Chicago. Daley was resisting paying for security outside the venues.

"Mr. Mayor," I said, "when the Pope recently visited Chicago, did you provide security, at the city's expense, through his visit?"

"Of course," Mayor Daley replied.

"With all due respect, Mr. Mayor," I continued, "I know you're a devout Catholic, and I don't want to insult you, but a lot more people around the world care about the World Cup than they do about the Pope, so I expect the same treatment as you provided the Pope."

That got a laugh from the mayor—and we negotiated the details of the arrangements.

More than any other country, the United States is Olympic-centric, so I would talk about how the Olympics are great, an amazing assemblage of top athletes, but tens of thousands of fans don't travel across the world to passionately cheer for their Olympic swimming or sculling team and paint their faces and wave flags. (They actually do that a little bit now, but not back then at all.) Indeed, in our hugely successful 1984 Olympics, over 70 percent of attendees were from Southern California.

"Soccer in the rest of the world is truly war, but without weapons," I'd say. "Wait until you see. Fans are going to come, they're going to have painted faces, they're going to be waving flags, they're going to be singing and dancing everywhere, in the streets, in the bars, and in the stadiums."

All of which happened. I was a salesman for soccer and had to be as visible as I could. How else could we get people excited about the World Cup? At times I may have come across as a little brassy, but even my critics understood strong leadership was required. "Once the United States began preparing in earnest to host the 1994 World Cup Finals, Alan Rothenberg became the perfect leader for soccer in America," the *Washington Post* wrote in June 1994. "His detractors criticize him for being an arrogant, publicity-minded autocratic opportunist who won't bother with detail and has no feeling for soccer. His fans praise him for essentially the same reasons—only they view him as a confident, media-conscious leader with an excellent sense of timing, a brilliant sense of the big picture and a refreshingly innovative outlook on the game."

I vote for the latter!

"Guys like Alan, they're unique individuals," former U.S. World Cup organizing committee managing director Charles Kenny told the *Post*. "He works very, very, very hard. He's a big-time risk-taker. He's a visionary type. Detail guys have some difficulty keeping up with him because he runs so fast, so far ahead. Is that good or bad? He's the kind of person the World Cup needed. Without that kind of energy, I don't think anybody pulls this off."

Randy Bernstein, working in the DC office, remarked: "I'd race to the office to be there by 8 AM in case Alan called, only to find a voice message from him waiting for me, left from him in Los Angeles at 5 AM Pacific Time."

One problem we had was finances. We'd run through most of our line of credit that Scott LeTellier had been able to arrange and had to generate more revenue, so we got creative.

We came up with the idea of having an early Family Ticket Sale, which was basically just opening up a rather small allocation of tickets and making it available to people around the country we had in our Rolodexes, registered players, soccer administrators, and the like. We knew these were people who cared and understood what a big deal it was to be hosting a World Cup. We even persuaded Budweiser to prepay their sponsorship—a deal I closed while lying on the floor for the meeting, since I'd thrown my back out on the flight to St. Louis. My client, Fred Rosen, president of Ticketmaster, said it wouldn't work without advance advertising, which we couldn't afford. Necessity being the mother of invention, we went with the Family Ticket Sale, and it worked.

Almost instantly, these allocations sold out—which was just what we expected, and just what we wanted. We had in mind milking these sales for all the attention we could dredge up. So, rather than holding one big press conference and declaring a sellout, we got creative. This was where some shamelessness came in. We went city by city. One day, we had a press conference in New York to announce that tickets had just sold out. Another day it was: Detroit just sold out. And: Boston just sold out. We basically stretched a one-day story out over two weeks. P.T. Barnum would have approved! We might have been shameless, but we were being strategic. We knew it was going to take good, old-fashioned hype to turn this into a hot ticket and get people excited. And a hot ticket it became. Every time we released another batch of tickets, they sold out instantly.

Fearing a high volume of requests for complimentary tickets, I established a strict "no comps" policy. It was reinforced early when we were having a $1,000-a-plate dinner in New

York. Pelé requested a free ticket. I saw an opportunity and seized it. I told Pelé to send me a check for $1,000, but promised him I wouldn't cash it. I then showed Pelé's check to one and all and declared, "If Pelé pays, everyone pays."

We also wanted to have a really high-priced ticket, because we knew the best ticket locations would sell first and for premium prices, and we really needed the revenue. FIFA said no. They were so concerned about upsetting people and didn't want to take that risk. So, we brainstormed some more.

"All right, we won't sell tickets, but can we sell packages?" we asked.

They agreed to that, with some conditions, like that we didn't advertise them generally. So almost by accident, we created the forerunner of today's hospitality packages, where you pay a huge price and get a ticket and all kinds of extra accommodations and food and beverages and side trips. This basically was: *Okay, we can pull these seats off, they won't show up in a manifest, and nowhere will we look like we're selling tickets*. We created effectively the first premier ticket package, which consisted of a good seat (all that buyers really cared about), a match program, a parking pass, and a hot dog. That was it. But we were able to bring in a fair amount of extra money with that.

Sunil Gulati, whom I'd fired when I first came in since he had been my opponent's right-hand man (but whom, thankfully, I almost immediately hired back), cites that ticket package as one of the most important innovations we made that World Cup cycle. "Alan was an extraordinarily hardworking guy who was thinking big about what the sport could be," he says now. "Alan was not part of getting the World Cup bid. That part is absolutely true, but one of the biggest decisions that Alan made that was in great measure responsible for the success of the World Cup was the whole premier ticket package. FIFA had limits on how much you could charge for tickets. They wanted average people to be able to go. He used something called a Premier Ticket Package, which was a hospitality program. In theory, you could sell a hundred-dollar ticket with a keychain for $5,000. Now, we didn't do that, but frankly, the Premier Ticket Package was a huge part of the financial success of the World Cup for us because we were on risk. It's not like it is now, where FIFA runs everything and you're at no risk. We were on the hook."

When I discussed ticket pricing with our board, Lamar Hunt urged moderate pricing, stating that the Kansas City Chiefs had sellouts for many years with the largest number of people on the waiting list in the NFL, largely because of their friendly pricing policy. I replied that it made sense because the Chiefs were going to be playing perennially and so able to think long range; our World Cup was going to be a one-off and so maximizing revenue, not building long-term good will, was essential.

Another idea that FIFA nixed, overly concerned about the average fans' reaction: I suggested that every seat at the Final in the Rose Bowl be priced at $1,000. I argued with FIFA that the street value of those tickets would be at least that amount. Why should scalpers and third-party ticket brokers realize the ultimate value rather than the rights holder? My arguments fell on deaf ears. FIFA thus lost out on having the prestige of what at that time would have been an unheard-of $100 million gate, cementing the World Cup as the most important sporting event in the world. Really too bad. What a statement it would have made!

It was a given that we'd make the most of the Rose Bowl in Pasadena, which had been my backup plan after Walter O'Malley turned down my request to host L.A. Wolves soccer games in 1984, and it turned out to be so majestic and iconic a setting for great soccer. We had already by that point built up tradition, and you could not top the excitement—and sense of historic moment—that came with having more than 90,000 people on hand for an event. We would pack in 94,194 for the World Cup Final on July 17, and more than 93,000 for games featuring the U.S. team. It was also clear from the beginning that we would once again use Stanford Stadium, another absolute gem, tucked away in a spectacularly beautiful setting, recently refurbished, and with a capacity of more than 84,000.

We needed good geographic dispersal around the country, but after those two plum California locations, our options grew less attractive. When I stepped in, they had no New York venue. They were talking about using the Yale Bowl in New Haven. It was unthinkable for our "New York" venue to be at Hartford—it had to be at the Meadowlands. So, we set our sights instead on Giants Stadium in New Jersey with a capacity of more than 76,000. For whatever reason, my predecessors had been unable to get a meeting with the Giants Stadium people. For help I turned to Bill Simon, the former Treasury Secretary in the Nixon administration, who was on our board. Bill was Mr. New Jersey, a powerful guy who knew everybody.

"I'll get us an appointment," he promised me.

At the time, for my legal practice, I had a legal meeting with the Continental Basketball Association in Iowa. I took a red eye and arrived to find a snowstorm on its way. To get back after the meeting, I had to rent a car and drive as fast as I could to Chicago, and of course in those days we didn't have mobile phones, so I was completely out of touch. There was no way to contact me. At O'Hare Airport before I boarded, I called the office from a pay phone to check in and found out that Bill Simon was frantically trying to reach me and kept calling. He was very agitated. Then I called home, and Georgina told me Simon had been calling her repeatedly in the middle of the night, demanding to know where I was and asking her, "How do you not know where your husband is?"

So, I called Simon, who ranted and raved at me, suggesting I ought to fire my secretary—and even my wife.

"How can you be out of touch?" he yelled. "I've never been anywhere in the world where you can't reach me 24/7."

He went on and on. I finally had to break in, worried I'd miss my flight.

"Okay, I'm really sorry this all happened, but what were you calling about?" I asked him.

"Oh," he said, voice suddenly calm. "I just wanted to tell you I got that appointment for you: it's in two weeks."

Most urgent thing in the world—but the meeting was in two weeks. Later, during the 1992 Olympics in Barcelona, Bill had a cocktail party on his yacht and invited us. There was a separate communications room with gigantic antennas and electronic gear all over the place, and I saw firsthand: of course he could get in touch with anybody anytime!

While Giants Stadium was obviously the appealing option, putting us in the New York media market, the playing field would probably be too narrow. The configuration of most American football stadiums is elliptical, while the soccer field is longer and rectangular, so at that point you're cutting off the corners, unacceptably affecting corner kicks.

As Filip Bondy reported in the *New York Times* on February 27, 1992, just before I flew to Zurich to meet with the FIFA leadership and discuss our options, "With the announcement of 1994 World Cup soccer venues less than a month away, Giants Stadium in East Rutherford, N.J., is at the center of international debate on the geometry of the sport.... The standard international soccer field is from 70 to 80 meters wide (about 76 to 88 yards), although the standard World Cup criterion is 75 meters (about 82 yards). The widest field that Giants Stadium could accommodate, without knocking down retainer walls or building a platform, would be 86 meters wide (about 74 yards)."

So, we knocked down the walls, only to put them back up later, after the competition, obviously. Interestingly, the footprint of Arrowhead Stadium in Kansas City was identical to Giants Stadium, designed by the same architect, but the quote we received to knock down the walls in New Jersey was multiple times higher than the same work would have cost us in Kansas City.

We knew we wanted games in Washington, DC, and RFK Stadium, capacity 53,000, had a track record with soccer. In Boston, games would be at Foxboro Stadium, about the same size, seating more than 54,000. The Citrus Bowl in Orlando could fit more than 60,000, the Cotton Bowl in Dallas had a 90,000-seat capacity, and Soldier Field in Chicago more than 63,000.

The ninth and final city was either going to be Detroit or Columbus, Ohio, and obviously I was drawn to Michigan, where I had been raised, but a far more important factor was that GM, a major sponsor, wanted games in Detroit. The best stadium for us would have been the Big House, in Ann

Arbor, where the University of Michigan, Georgina's and my alma mater, plays its football games. It's the biggest stadium in North America with capacity of more than 107,000. Can you imagine? My eyes lit up.

But I knew it might not be that easy to persuade Michigan to allow us to perform minor cosmetic surgery, fixing the corners, as we were doing at other venues, and bringing in grass to lay over the artificial turf. Also, as a lifelong Michigan fan, I was kind of excited going in for a meeting with Jack Weidenbach, who in 1990 inherited the job of athletic director from Bo Schembechler, Michigan's larger-than-life head football coach from 1969 to 1989. Jack shot us down immediately. He'd called Bo to ask what he thought and came back with a message for us: "Nobody's touching my football field!" Pleas from several very influential alums were to no avail.

Plan B was the Pontiac Silverdome with a capacity of more than 77,000. But again, there were issues: that was a domed stadium with AstroTurf, and FIFA very firmly required that all games be played on grass. We made that deal and a group at Michigan State came up with a program for creating the rolls of grass that we would bring in right before the game and unroll right on top of the AstroTurf. It worked, and now that technique is commonplace. At State Farm Stadium in Arizona, they keep the grass permanently on wheels, so for events where they need grass rather than artificial surface, they just wheel it right in. But the Silverdome in 1994 was the first. Another problem: the Silverdome had been built without air-conditioning, so the matches played there felt like being in a sauna.

The world was going to be watching, we kept reminding people—or they would if we could work out TV rights. Prior to 1994, the World Cup had never been shown live in English. Seriously, though I know that's hard to believe. Earlier World Cups were only available through closed-circuit broadcasts in local arenas, theaters, and selected other venues. In 1990, English-language broadcasts were shown only on tape delay. That all changed forever in 1994. FIFA, as usual, had worked out Spanish-language rights with an international consortium led by Televisa, the Mexico-based behemoth. FIFA agreed to allow our organizing committee to negotiate for an English-language broadcast in the United States.

I approached Dennis Swanson of ABC Sports, whom I knew from his stint in L.A., where he was station manager of KABC starting in 1981. Later he created *The Oprah Winfrey Show*, then succeeded the legendary Roone Arledge as president of ABC Sports in 1986. Dennis had a young No. 2, David Downs, who had played collegiate soccer at Amherst and was a huge soccer fan who became a big advocate for us.

The key issue was how sponsors could get their message onto the broadcasts during the game, which with soccer is much more challenging than with sports that have regular breaks like football, basketball, and baseball. Different ideas were kicked around, including inserting breaks into the matches, which was never going to happen. The matches had to be shown live without interruption. Full stop. End of story. We discussed quick commercial spots, no longer than 10 seconds, which an alert producer could hope to insert in the lull before a goal kick or throw in or free kick. Skilled producers in the UK were able to do that, but the idea was rejected. Other ideas included crawls at the bottom of the screen, split screens, and static display of the sponsor's name unobtrusively placed high up in the upper corner of the screen. We would have accepted any of those options, but to its everlasting credit, ABC chose the least obtrusive option, the sponsor name added up in the corner, and that has been the accepted method ever since. All 52 matches were shown live, without interruption—more than 100 hours of national network television. We made it commercially possible for ABC by bringing three FIFA sponsors, Coca Cola, MasterCard, and Mars, into the broadcasts.

We came up with a pay-per-view plan that would have been a huge revenue generator for us, but required that we audaciously ask for permission to delay as many as six matches on the Spanish language telecasts for eight hours. Not the opening game, any of the semifinals, or, of course, the Final. We'd worked through the numbers over and over and sat down with Seth Abraham of HBO Sports, who knew as much about pay-per-view as anyone, and we knew we could rake it in with pay-per-view broadcasts of games featuring popular teams, especially Hispanic and Latino teams, given the wide interest in the Spanish-speaking community. I concluded that we could gross at least $80 million. However, if those matches were available live on Spanish-language TV, no one would pay to watch those games in English.

I knew that Televisa, controlled by Emilio Azcárraga Jean, considered the most powerful man in Mexico, had world Spanish-language rights to the World Cup, but Univision had obtained those rights for the United States. So, I went to see the owner of Univision, Jerry Perenchio, whom I had known since he copromoted with Jack Kent Cooke the "Fight of the Century," the first Ali vs. Frazier fight. (Perenchio wangled control of Univision because Televisa had no choice and had to divest; foreign control of broadcast licenses was forbidden.

One Azcárraga Jean associate called it "the most lucrative green card in history," since it ultimately made Perenchio a multibillionaire). Perenchio told me he had no say on soccer programming; that was exclusively in the hands of Azcárraga Jean.

I had to fly down to Mexico City to try to persuade Azcárraga Jean, who (so it was said), had made, broken, and controlled many a Mexican president. I offered "El Tigre" half, or a cut of $40 million, if he would simply approve delaying the Spanish-language broadcast of eight World Cup matches. He heard me out.

"That is a lot of money, $40 million, but I cannot do it," he said. "They would kill me."

I'd known of Azcárraga Jean and had previous business dealing with him when Televisa bought the L.A. Aztecs from us. I also knew that with his near monopoly of the media, he allegedly controlled the president of the country. So, I thought I might be able to persuade him to agree.

"Señor Azcárraga Jean, a man of your standing and influence, a man who presidents turn to for advice, surely a little bad publicity would not be grounds for killing a lucrative deal."

He gave me a quick look.

"You don't understand," he said. "I said they would kill me. They would. Some crazed fan would shoot me."

That was that. Forty million dollars, gone.

Jumbotrons in stadiums were new to FIFA. I demanded that we show the telecasts of the games live in stadiums. FIFA agreed but forbade replays, fearful of inflaming fans and subjecting referees to second-guessing. I argued that the vast majority of times the officials' calls are correct, and a replay would quiet fans against whom a call had been made and support the referee. Current use of VAR supports that argument. Furthermore, why should people at home viewing the match for free have a better experience than fans in the stadium, who had paid a pretty penny? In any event, while agreeing that we wouldn't show the replays, we nonetheless showed the live feed including replays. Only once did FIFA complain, which we ignored without repercussions.

Another idea we had was to bring The Three Tenors together for a concert at Dodger Stadium to help drive interest in the World Cup Final. When Plácido Domingo, José Carreras, and Luciano Pavarotti first teamed up for a joint concert in Rome in July 1990, it was a huge success, so we decided to replicate it. We didn't have anything in Los Angeles to compare to the historic Baths of Caracalla, where the three had performed in Rome, but we did have Dodger Stadium, which brought its own kind of history—and 50,000 seats.

How did one go about trying to land The Three Tenors, each of whom had an ego as big as his massive talent? We were advised the only way was to work with Hungarian-born impresario Tibor Rudas, who had made a specialty of such extravaganzas. It wasn't easy. And it took forever. But Rudas controlled the Pavarotti rights, so without him, we were nowhere. Finally, after months of negotiations, we had an agreement.

Through all this time, I had not yet picked up the phone to reach out to Plácido Domingo, who lived in L.A. We were instructed to focus first on Rudas and Pavarotti. So, when I called Plácido and met him for lunch, I had a problem on my hands—a large problem. Of operatic proportions, you might say.

"How could you not talk to me?" Plácido complained as soon as we sat down at our table.

He was in high dudgeon. His artistic ego was injured, understandably so.

"Who is Pavarotti?" he continued. "I am Plácido Domingo! Do you not know that we book my schedule five years in advance? What made you believe I could possibly even be available on such short notice?"

I let him talk. I let him vent. He railed on and on, but finally calmed down. A lifetime fan from the time he was a boy growing up in the Retiro district of Madrid, he loved soccer and talking soccer too much to stay mad. He was no longer shouting by now.

"But of course my manager knows never to book me during the World Cup," he confided, "because I have to go and watch Spain wherever they are."

After that we were friends, to the point where we flew with him on his private jet during the World Cup when we needed to get from Boston to New York in a hurry to catch two games in one day, and he was going our way. Our youngest son, Danny, had been living in Buenos Aires, working as a photographer for *El Gráfico* magazine, Argentina's version of *Sports Illustrated.* They'd sent him to the United States to photograph the World Cup. He befriended Plácido, who invited him backstage for The Three Tenors concert at Dodger Stadium to spend the day photographing them.

That concert was a fabulous success, so much so that 20 years later they released a DVD of the performance. The three of them were really on. Zubin Mehta conducted the Los Angeles Philharmonic. We had the chorus of the Los Angeles Opera. And the night before the Final of the World Cup, an estimated 1.3 billion viewers worldwide tuned in live to watch the concert.

Georgina and I actually ended up voluntarily giving up our front row seats. Through some mix-up, my predecessor at U.S. Soccer, Werner Fricker, ended up with no seats, so we gladly offered him ours. I was happy to do it. Werner had done so much to get the World Cup to the United States, and he was on the outside looking in. I felt it was the least I could do considering all his contributions and sacrifices.

The final draw in Las Vegas in December 1993 helped set the big-event tone. It was clear to me from the beginning of our organizational effort that we had to make the World Cup a big event in every way imaginable. That was why we got as many celebrities as we could to liven up events that might otherwise have been staid. The night before the final draw, we had a big banquet with James Brown and Smokey Robinson as the featured entertainers. We also created the first-ever FIFA World Cup Expo.

Robin Williams emceeing the draw was just on fire. His routine still gets picked up on YouTube. He loved soccer and was excited to be there and he was having a great time joking with anyone and everyone. He kept calling Blatter "Sepp Bladder," making a little cupping motion for emphasis, even after Sepp scolded him, "This is not a comedy." We couldn't stop laughing. What a genius. We were backstage beforehand, and dignitaries from different countries would talk to Robin, and he would respond in a dialect that sounded like whatever language they were speaking, but was actually nonsensical, pure gibberish. It was amazing to see how fast his mind worked, and how talented he was.

Roger Bennett, one of the Men in Blazers, was still marveling over the glitz of the event 20 years later, writing for ESPN: "The star-studded event took place at Caesars Palace on the Las Vegas Strip. A cast of thousands including Barry Manilow, Julio Iglesias, Faye Dunaway, and Dick Clark"—whose company produced the event—"were involved in a fantastical affair that the great Bob Ley described being as if 'Salvador Dalí could produce a state lottery.' Fittingly for such a surreal occasion, it was Robin Williams who stole the spotlight."

Amid all the parties in Vegas we organized, we were under incredible pressure to have the draw come off as a spectacular success, but we had one big problem. Havelange, FIFA president, had some beef with his fellow Brazilian, Pelé, one of our biggest single assets—alongside Mohammed Ali, the best-known athlete in the world—despite being long since retired. Havelange forbade us from using Pelé as part of the draw. So, we got creative. We arranged for Pelé to be given a credential and make a dramatic entrance just as the draw was about to start. Havelange was fuming, but we got our Pelé moment.

Virtually everyone involved in the commercial side of sport was present in Las Vegas. So, we took the opportunity to make the first introduction of our planned professional league to potential investors, sponsors, and the media. Momentum for what became Major League Soccer began to build at that moment.

Even after we had hyped the World Cup every way we could for years leading up to June 1994, three weeks before the opening game a poll found that 71 percent of Americans were unaware it was going to be played on U.S. soil.

The one team we were fearful of coming out of the South American group was Colombia, which Pelé himself had predicted would win the whole tournament. Argentina and Brazil were both seeded No. 1, so we weren't going to have to face either of them in our group. The night before, they rehearsed how the draw would work. Ball in here, ball there, you pull it out. If they'd done it the way they rehearsed it, we would not have played Colombia. I was so happy. Then Blatter, on his own—I don't know if he had a brain freeze or he just changed his mind—he put Colombia in our group. I was angry beyond belief. We figured Colombia was going to kill us and spoil our party. How wrong I was.

"Alan was not happy," Cobi Jones remembers. "It was every curse word in the book that was coming out at the various people. Being placed in with Colombia, who just dominated within their region, was basically a death sentence for us—at least everybody thought it was. But, fortunately, it ended up working out in the end."

In spring 1994, I got a call from someone saying she was a secretary to President George H.W. Bush and had him on the phone for me. This was out of the blue and I had no idea if the call was legit. Was this Dana Carvey—"Wouldn't be prudent!"—doing a Bush impression, like he had so many times on *Saturday Night Live*? No, it was the real George H.W. Bush, the former president, asking me for tickets. Argentina would be playing at Foxboro Stadium and Bush wanted to host his friend, Carlos Menem, then the president of Argentina.

"Do you think you can help us?" the former president asked me.

Easy call: of course. Bush was relieved and talkative.

"I don't know if you know this," he told me, "but before I left office, I had a visit abroad, and I took a gift that you gave us to King Fahd."

I was wondering where he was going with this. Was he going to say the king was insulted by the 10-dollar toy Tim had found for him?

"He so appreciated my thoughtful gift that he reciprocated," Bush continued. "He sent me a solid gold replica of the Royal Palace in Riyadh." Not a bad exchange!

I remember when we were in Boston, President Bush was there sitting in the tribune with us with one of his grandsons. A server came to the tribune with an excellent assortment of food delicacies and drinks, but President Bush said, "No, no, no," and sent his grandson to the concession stand for hot dogs and ice cream. I'm a good Democrat, so it's hard to say, but: I really liked this guy! I sure wish we had more political figures like him leading our country today.

Early in 1991, we had a management retreat. The first order of business was to create our mission statement and our tag line. We agreed on the somewhat audacious statement that we would "present the greatest World Cup in history." Everyone was ready to leave, and I stopped them. It was not enough.

"I don't want this to be like the circus, where everyone has a good time and when it's over all you're left with is elephant dung to clean up. We have to leave a legacy." So, the tagline for the World Cup became "To put on the greatest World Cup in history—and leave a legacy for the sport." From then on, our focus was always twofold: to present the greatest World Cup in history, and equally if not more important, to leave a legacy for the sport of soccer. I couldn't be prouder than to say, “Mission Accomplished.” We also created the advertising tagline “Making Soccer History,” which we sure did.

The story of how Chicago won the right to host the first match of the World Cup fits with that perfectly.

“We know the Final’s going to be in Los Angeles,” Jay Pritzker, the prominent Chicago business leader who later joined our World Cup board, told me on the phone, “but Chicago would really like to have the opening match. What do we have to do to get it?”

I told Jay I’d think about it and get back to him, but I already had a pretty good idea. At the time I was elected, the U.S. Soccer Federation’s offices were a trailer in Colorado Springs. That was all they had, since they had no money, and the USOC made that facility available to all constituent members. It was time for us to do better. We wanted an office, not a trailer. We’d have to find a way to pay for it. We also wanted to be in a major metropolitan area, preferably centrally located, and as a matter of fact, Chicago fit that bill nicely.

“We’d love to move our offices to Chicago,” I told Jay.

We understood each other. His people went to work and got back to us in no time. They identified a mansion that was owned by a family trust on a street that had nothing but those kinds of houses, large family homes in various states of disrepair. We knew the area was about to be gentrified. In fact, Mayor Richard Daley Jr. had just bought a condominium on the next block, so we figured there would be good security there. Jay and his team arranged with that family trust to give us a lease way below the market value, with an option to buy way below market. Then they introduced us to a bank that gave us a loan at an interest rate way below market to finance the move from Colorado Springs to Chicago, and the bare minimum of refurbishing and decorating and furnishing we had to put in to set up our new offices in Chicago. Soon a production company filming a movie about a Catholic cardinal approached Hank Steinbrecher about using the office as the Pope's residence. Hank negotiated great terms, and the office was redone with wood paneling, lush carpeting, and exquisite wall coverings. That was how Chicago maneuvered to host the World Cup opener—and those offices ended up serving the Federation well for the next three decades, having been purchased pursuant to the option with funds provided by the Foundation from the World Cup surplus.

We wanted to engage as much of the country as we could and get them excited. We thought of using a famous American artist for the official World Cup '94 poster, like Frank Stella or Jasper Johns. But in the end, we settled on Peter Max, who might have been less renowned in the art world, but he certainly was kitschier. Max, born in Berlin but raised in Brooklyn, a pop artist known for his love of bright colors and for designing the posters for events like the "Be-In" for hippies in Central Park in 1967, loved soccer. He turned out to be an excellent choice for us and was very involved in promotion.

As a United Press International article reported from New York in March 1994, "With the financial rewards of the World Cup games looming, New York City officials are trying to infuse the citizenry with soccer fever. At a news conference in Manhattan Wednesday, the unlikely trio of New York Mayor Rudolph Giuliani, psychedelic artist Peter Max, and the World Cup USA mascot beagle, Striker, unveiled plans for two months of special events geared to the championship." Full disclosure: often inside the mascot Striker costume was our son, Richie, who volunteered to help, including that day in New York. "I flew out to NYC to join my older brother Brad, who was running the World Cup Legacy tour, for the unveiling of the Striker dog mascot for World Cup USA 1994," Richie remembers.

Richie wound up being driven to Radio City Music Hall in the back of a limo with Brad. They were joined by Tony Meola, U.S. starting goalkeeper at the time, famously a Jersey boy, who had made a few appearances on the popular nighttime soap *Melrose Place*, and *Melrose Place* regular Andrew Shue, who would later play several games for the L.A. Galaxy their first season, 1996.

"I get out of the limo and was acting my ass off, gesticulating wildly, and making soccer poses, kicking in line with the Rockettes while Tony and Andrew waved to fans and signed autographs," Richie remembers. "Back in the limo, Brad was high-fiving me and holding my Striker head. I was sweating bullets and Tony and Andrew were talking to each other and looking at me perplexed."

"Rich, I don't mean any disrespect, but we're wondering, you're the chairman's son…" Tony said. "What are you doing in the dog suit?"

"I came here to do this for Brad to help him launch Striker," Richie said.

"Rich, I get you wanted to come to NYC to hang out with your bro and watch him work, but you could have come here, rolled around with us, but you could hire someone downtown who would do this for ten bucks. You're the chairman's son. What are you doing in the dog suit?!"

Tony and Andrew couldn't stop laughing, but soon they'd reached their next stop, a soccer clinic where Richie kicked the soccer ball with Tony and Andrew and Bora Milutinović, who was there for the promotion.

We wanted to take a page from the Olympics, which had found success with a torch relay all over the country. Unfortunately, we didn't have an Olympic torch or anything comparable to that, but we did decide to set up what we called a Legacy Tour. We figured: go with our strongest asset, which was the World Cup trophy itself. Somehow, I don't quite know how, we persuaded ISL, FIFA's marketing company, to create a copy of the World Cup trophy—not a replica, but an actual copy—made of more than 13 pounds of 18-karat gold, just like the World Cup trophy. The Legacy Tour, managed by my son Brad, was really great in terms of creating the city-by-city interest and energizing the Host Committees in all nine of our venues. Obviously, we went through each of the venues where the World Cup was going to be played, but also with stops in between. The *Baltimore Sun* wrote about it, quoting Legacy Tour '94 national director Maris Segal Goodis: "This is a once-in-a-lifetime opportunity to be part of World Cup soccer." The *Chicago Tribune* also wrote about it, quoting me: "We're not waiting until the World Cup ends to establish a legacy."

Now, interestingly, in the chaos after the World Cup was all over, FIFA and everyone else seemed to forget we had this exact copy of the World Cup trophy. ISL had dissolved. I had it in my possession for some years, not knowing what to do with it. Nobody was asking for it. Nobody wanted it. So, we kept it in a thick protected glass case at the Premier office on Fourth Street right off Wilshire Boulevard in Santa Monica. The day of the demonstrations all over the country after the video circulated showing George Floyd's shocking death, some vandals unfortunately latched onto the protest and broke into our office. There was nothing of commercial value in there, no high-end sneakers or anything to loot, but the one thing that they did take was that trophy. They busted that huge heavy glass case and stole the World Cup trophy. Somewhere out there, either there's somebody having fun with a World Cup trophy, or they gave it to somebody to melt it down for the gold.

The other thing we did was stage a fan festival for 10 days at the L.A. Convention Center. We called it SoccerFest. Basically, we took a leaf from the NFL Experience, where they would always have something there for the people who couldn't get into the Super Bowl, but still wanted a connection with the Super Bowl. But our event outdrew any NFL Experience. It created a great atmosphere for the semifinal and the Finals that were in Los Angeles, a lot of fun for a lot of people.

A TREAT FOR FEET: SOCCERFEST OFFERS VICARIOUS THRILLS TO THE MANY SPECTATOR WANNA-BES was the *Los Angeles Times* headline on July 8, along with an article explaining: "SoccerFest is a 500,000-square-foot soccer celebration opening to the public today and running until the end of the World Cup on July 17. Its organizers say the event, modeled after other professional sports parks such as the NFL Experience, is a chance for those who couldn't get to the World Cup to get a taste of the international festival."

"This really allows people to participate in the sport," Peter Max told the *Times*. "They're able to collect pins, to see star players...to feel the real ambience of soccer."

The festival, the *Times* continued, "consists of more than 20 pavilions of soccer-related treats, plus three soccer arenas, an arcade, and live music from all the World Cup countries. Giant inflated soccer balls loom over displays on soccer history and soccer heroes while stands offer food from a variety of World Cup countries. Novices and lifelong fans can learn about the sport and test their skills at a variety of interactive booths and contests. … Clinics for all levels will be offered on the fields, some by such World Cup players as Paul Caligiuri of the United States and John Milla of Cameroon. Organizers say they expect other non-soccer celebrities to show up, from opera star Plácido Domingo to boxer Sugar Ray Leonard, who was on hand Thursday. Pelé, the Brazilian soccer legend, is also expected to make an appearance." Popular Hispanic boxing champion Oscar De La Hoya also participated.

Also quoted was "SoccerFest executive producer" Brad Rothenberg: "Public, grassroots events like this help build the tangible legacy the sport needs to continue after the World Cup is gone."

Brad actually loved doing that so much, afterward he started a grassroots soccer business, primarily promoting tournaments for Hispanic and Black kids who are not recruited properly by the organized soccer community under their whole pay-to-play concept. He's had a really successful and rewarding run with that. As part of that, he also created a nonprofit foundation. He puts some of the sponsorship revenue in the foundation, Access U, and they provide mentoring to these kids to get them scholarships to some really good colleges. They work with coaches to identify the players who are interested, as well as being good athletes and students. That's his passion. Access U has arranged scholarships for boys and girls from underserved communities to Ivy League schools, Duke, Stanford, UCLA, and UC Berkeley, among others, enabling these scholar-athletes to receive a college degree—and debt free!

We were always trying to think big, and for the World Cup opening ceremony in Chicago, we cycled through all kinds of ideas. Originally, we were going to have Disney produce the opening. I met with Michael Eisner, then Disney boss, and told him, "I understand you want to promote Disney. Mickey's okay, but no Chip and Dale, please." Their reputation was that anything they did, it would be all characters from Disney. Sure enough, they showed us the first script, and it was as I had feared. So, we terminated the contract and hired a production company to do the show.

One thing we cooked up was having beloved singer Diana Ross take a penalty kick, and the instant the ball entered the net, the goal would split in two. Sounds cool, right? There was only one problem. Diana was a singer, not a soccer player. Her kick was wide of the net. The goal still split in two.

For our master of ceremonies, we had the amazing Oprah Winfrey, who greeted everyone with such poise and graciousness, we couldn't have made a better choice. She was a total pro. For the stage, we had to put two stages together into one large platform, but I guess they weren't secured quite right, leaving a small gap. Oprah was walking on the stage, talking into her mic, when her foot caught in that gap—but she kept right on talking, didn't miss a beat, just a consummate professional.

It was hotter than 90 degrees that day in Chicago and as humid as you can imagine, a very uncomfortable combination. In the days leading up to the match, the Secret Service in Chicago had been working with our people going over all the protocols we would have to follow with President Bill Clinton attending, as well as German chancellor Helmut Kohl and the Bolivian president, Gonzalo Sánchez de Lozada. Then when

Clinton arrived, the DC-based Secret Service traveling with him overrode pretty much everything we'd been told by their counterparts in Chicago. They changed all the plans.

Suddenly, you had a situation where on a very hot day, tens of thousands of fans were stuck outside waiting in long lines to try to get inside Soldier Field. I saw one man who had sweated through his tie from the inside out. Moods were bad and rapidly getting worse. Somebody got a message to me that the president of American Airlines, one of our key sponsors, was stuck in line with one of his board members just blowing a gasket. He was urgently demanding that we find a way to pull him out of line and get him somewhere with air-conditioning, which we were able to do. Later I found out that one reason he was so upset was that this person in line with him was not only a board member, but also chairman of his compensation committee.

It got pretty bad for everyone; all of us in the tribune were wearing suits and ties. I remember in particular Helmut Kohl, who was a massive man, standing 6′4″ and weighing nearly 300 pounds. He was in a three-piece wool suit that day, and we were all overwhelmed by the extreme heat and kept waiting for him to take his jacket off so, per protocol, the rest of us could as well. Finally, the chancellor removed his jacket and unbuttoned his vest and that gave all of us license to take off our jackets. One of the people sitting with us was our board member, former U.S. Secretary of State Henry Kissinger, a huge soccer fan going back to his days as a boy in Germany. (He told me that growing up his ambition was to be the goalkeeper on the German national team. It was only when he realized he wasn't talented enough that he pursued a different field of work.) When Henry took his jacket off, he flipped his suspender straps down.

"Nancy doesn't like to see me with suspenders visible," he said, meaning his wife.

Then at halftime, he started to stand up, and of course, without the straps his pants were getting loose, and it looked like they might fall down.

"Henry," Bill Clinton said, twinkle in his eye, "that's the first thing I've seen you do that I approve of."

Clinton and Kohl were sitting right behind me at Soldier Field, in our spot at midfield, and I could hear them talking about the game. It soon became clear that when it came to soccer, Clinton was a total novice. Early on, Kohl had to explain everything to him. The two men had met about a year earlier for the first time, in Germany, and had established a good rapport. West Germany had won the previous World Cup and were now, joined by East Germany, playing as united Germany for the first time since 1938. By the second half Clinton had caught on. He was following the game closely and with interest. He didn't need Kohl to tell him what was going on. He got it. That's how much of a sports fan he was. The game was scoreless at the half, but Jürgen Klinsmann, who had played four years earlier on the West German team that won the World Cup, scored an easy goal in the 61st minute, getting an empty net when the keeper came out to challenge. That gave Germany a 1–0 win over Bolivia.

Also at the game were First Lady Hillary Rodham Clinton and daughter Chelsea Clinton, a big soccer fan, sitting in the row behind us. An impressive duo.

The first U.S. game would be in Detroit. It was a hot and humid day, so it was like being in a sauna. Before the matches, when we were scoping out what we had to do to move on in the tournament, we figured*: Okay, we'll beat Switzerland, lose to Colombia, and then a tie with Romania would get us enough points to make it through.* Then came game day, and we couldn't score against the Swiss! As we neared halftime it was 0–0. Then, in the 39th minute, Switzerland went ahead 1–0. And probably the most unique personality on our team, Eric Wynalda, curved in a beautiful free kick to score for us in the 45th minute and make it 1–1, which held up as the final score. "I love you, forever, Eric," I told him afterward. And I told him again in 1996 when he scored the first goal in the inaugural game for MLS.

Next up was Colombia, and I very much expected us to lose. It looked bleak. For that game, Georgina and I were going to be sitting with the Colombian president, Ernesto Samper. Before the game, there was a death threat against Samper, which I didn't hear about until we were actually seated, and I was right next to him, with Georgina next to me. So, for the whole game, we tried to be subtle about leaning away from him as much as we could, just in case some sharpshooter missed the target. Fortunately, it was a threat that was not carried through.

Going back to when we were putting together our final World Cup roster of 22 players, I had been told that Bora was going to use the last spot for Fernando Clavijo, our oldest player. Great guy and a great player. Bora's wife and Clavijo's wife were good friends, and they would keep each other company during the six weeks when the team was in training and then playing. I was thinking ahead to founding Major League Soccer and wanting to have homegrown stars from the national team we could promote in MLS. I figured Clavijo was at the end of his career and wasn't going to play anyway, so it didn't matter.

"Bora," I said, "Don't put Clavijo on the roster."

I told him we would pay to have his wife, Maria, and Clavijo's wife travel together.

"Put on Chris Henderson," I suggested instead.

Henderson was a good-looking 22-year-old out of UCLA we'd love to be able to showcase in MLS as a former national team player.

So, Bora, just as he always did, said: "Yes, Mr. President. Yes, Mr. President. Yes."

And then of course when I saw the final roster, Clavijo was on there and Henderson wasn't. Ah, Bora. I didn't think about it much after that—until the game against Colombia.

That was a highly dramatic game. We were all shocked in the 34th minute when on a U.S. cross, highly respected Colombian defender Andrés Escobar scored an own goal! We couldn't believe it. Then, after the halftime break, almost as unbelievably, Earnie Stewart, one of the immigrants we had recruited, scored to give us a 2–0 lead. Against a team we were sure would beat us! Colombia scored one late goal, in the 91st minute, and we had to sweat out stoppage time. Bora had actually started Clavijo that game. The player I was sure would never play! He was 38, but he was the fastest one on the team. Right near the end of game, as we were trying to protect our lead, Clavijo chased down a Colombian player on a breakaway and made a beautiful slide tackle to save the match. So much for me telling the coach what to do.

We'd pulled off an incredible upset. "For us," said Bora, "it was a perfect game." Added Lalas: "We all had that moment that kids dream about that you see with the flags and holding it up and screaming and yelling. When it finally happens, it's very surreal because there's no soundtrack. I just remember thinking: *There's no music right now. It feels wonderful but there's no music.*"

Even though we lost to Romania 1–0 in our next game, we still advanced, an incredible validation of our program. I'd always said that to truly succeed with the first World Cup in the United States, we needed the organization and execution to be a triumph—and we needed our team to more than hold its own. We knew that no matter how great the World Cup otherwise was, if the U.S. national team was a disappointment, it would put a huge damper on our mission. Having beaten powerful Colombia and moved out of the group stage was exactly what we needed to ensure total success of our venture.

The reviews were already coming in on the overall success of the event. "It's a sensation," Egidius Braun, president of the German soccer federation, told the *Los Angeles Times*. "It will be very difficult for any other country in the world to do it the same way in the future. It can't be done."

Now our boys, under Bora's magical leadership, had pulled it off. They would move on to a Fourth of July match against the best team in the world, Brazil, at Stanford Stadium in Palo Alto. The Brazil match was ugly. Shortly before the end of the first half, the Brazilian left back Leonardo Araújo unleashed one of the cheapest and most brutal fouls I've ever seen, swinging an elbow at Tab Ramos that was savage in its intensity, leaving him with a concussion and fractured skull. We lost one of our best players, an absolute key player in the middle, and still only lost by one goal.

I had mixed emotions about the loss. On the one hand, just by being there, in the knockout stage, and playing the world's most dominant soccer power close to even, the United States moved itself up incalculably in the eyes of the world. The blunt, ugly truth was the U.S. team played tough and strong enough to make the Brazilians look bad. Noted soccer authority Paul Wilson, writing in the London *Guardian*, was withering in his analysis: "Brazil were supposed to supply the fireworks for America's great Fourth of July soccer party but instead they turned up with a box of damp squibs including the dismissal of the full-back Leonardo for a vicious and unnecessary foul. Short on ideas and often embarrassingly inept in matters of distribution and control, Brazil were wholly unconvincing as aspiring champions."

More important was the atmosphere in and out of the stadium that Fourth of July. Tens of thousands of face-painted American fans singing, dancing, and chanting side by side with thousands of Brazilian fans. It was so exciting that a few of us jumped out of the car that was driving us to the stadium so we could join the fans as we danced our way into the stadium. That was the moment I knew that America had at last arrived as a passionate soccer nation. We had joined the international soccer world as a full-fledged member.

One terrible footnote on that World Cup came six days after Colombia's last game when Escobar, the defender whose own goal was so costly to his team, was murdered in Medellín. No one knew for sure what had happened, but in Colombia and elsewhere the widespread assumption was that he was killed for costing Colombia the match. I couldn't help but think about what Azcárraga Jean had told me in his Mexico City office about how he could not delay game broadcasts because someone would kill him.

It was 100 degrees the day of the Final at the Rose Bowl, Brazil and Italy, and I remember being down on the field before the game. ESPN reporter Jim Gray looked up at the sellout crowd, and asked me: "Did you really have to do all this hyping?"

"Probably not," I told him. "But I wasn't going to take any chances."

Looking back, we completely changed the way the World Cup was presented to the public. Until the United States became the host, the tournament was presented solely as the great sporting event it was. With the exception of The Three Tenors concert in 1990, there was little, if any, entertainment or celebrity participation to wrap the World Cup into a monthlong sports and entertainment spectacular. We utilized a veritable who's who of entertainers in and surrounding the World Cup: the aforementioned Oprah Winfrey, Diana Ross, and Jon Secada at the opening; Plácido Domingo, José Carreras, and Luciano Pavarotti—the Three Tenors—at Dodger Stadium; Robin Williams, Smokey Robinson, Liza Minnelli, Stevie Wonder, Bryan Adams, Daryl Hall, Enrique Iglesias, Barry Manilow, Willie Nelson, Vanessa Williams, Rod Stewart, Evander Holyfield, and John Williams.

I met with Mick Jagger trying to enlist the Rolling Stones, but he rejected our entreaties. We booked the famous Hollywood Bowl for a week of concerts showcasing various nationalities and ethnic performances; we enjoyed performances by acts as diverse as Van Cliburn, the Moscow Symphony Orchestra, the Red Hot Chili Peppers, Linda Ronstadt, Itzhak Perlman, Lou Rawls, and Garth Brooks. The Three Tenors concert was attended by President George H.W. Bush, Henry Kissinger, Arnold Schwarzenegger, Tom Cruise, Nicole Kidman, Faye

Dunaway, Maria Shriver, Frank Sinatra, and Bob Hope, among others. FIFA had never seen anything like it.

So new was our approach that FIFA squelched two great ideas. We proposed a star-studded opening spectacular the day before the first match instead of an abbreviated ceremony immediately prior to the match. It would have been a huge worldwide television event. I'm convinced it was nixed because Guillermo Cañedo, as head of the Spanish-language consortium, didn't want to have to pay a substantial fee for a separate opening. For the Final, we paid a humongous fee to Whitney Houston, then the biggest name in the popular music scene, and Kenny G, planning a halftime Super Bowl–style show. Havelange vetoed it, expressing fear of damaging the turf. We showed him statistics that there never had been measurable moisture on July 17 in the history of Southern California; so there was no fear of muddy conditions tearing up the pitch. We brought Cañedo to the 1993 Super Bowl at the Rose Bowl and showed him that, following the massive stage wheeled out for the Michael Jackson halftime show, there was not a blade of grass even bent when the stage was removed. Nonetheless FIFA said "no" and sadly, Whitney Houston performed from the sidelines barely visible, wedged in front of the crowd of fans. Very disappointing. (FIFA recently announced that in 2026 there will be a Super Bowl–type halftime show—42 years later.)

That Final was no classic, at least in the eyes of many. No goals were scored in regulation or overtime and Brazil ultimately won it on kicks. But for us, the score didn't matter, the larger result did: a Final matching two great soccer powers in the culmination of a World Cup tournament that had been a huge success. First, people doubted we could organize such an event. Then they saw we could and assumed we'd fall short in the passion and excitement department. Wrong again. During the years of hard work preparing for the World Cup, I'd instructed our staff that we had four primary separate audiences to please in order to be considered successful: the participating teams; the attending public; the media; and the FIFA officials, whose self-importance was such that if their often petty demands weren't met they'd complain to the media, which would then be critical of us. Thankfully, somehow, we had satisfied all four audiences, hard as that was.

I'd known *Los Angeles Times* Sports Editor Bill Dwyre for years, going back to my days working with the Lakers, and had an excellent relationship with him.

"Alan, I have to hand it to you," Dwyre told me in the press box during that World Cup Final. "You did a great job. I had reporters in all nine venues looking for something bad to write and they couldn't find anything."

"Bill!" I said with mock chagrin. "I appreciate the compliment, but do you realize what you said? You had reporters trying to find problems, not simply to report on the events?"

"That's our job!" he cheerfully replied.

That says it all!

Many speculated that, even if the World Cup overall was a success, our U.S. team would once again make us look bad—and instead our boys turned heads and earned worldwide respect. It was a signal moment for U.S. soccer. "There was no shame or embarrassment," said Lalas. "Our goal from the start was to get out of our group. Not just from a soccer perspective but what it meant for the country. We were under pressure to not embarrass ourselves and obviously to help grow soccer, and in order to do that, it was made very clear to us that we had to get out of the group."

We were no longer a soccer afterthought to the rest of the world. "We were a story, we were relevant," Wynalda said. "Regardless of the fact that we lost—and we did lose to the eventual champion—there was hope."

New York Times columnist George Vecsey, a deep lover of soccer who could at times be a little grumpy, celebrated the progress we had made. "Rothenberg, the impresario of soccer in this country," wrote Vecsey, "knew he lucked out because soccer officials tinkered with the rules to make the games more exciting and he lucked out with Brazil–Italy, but he and his associates deserved their success. They filled the stadiums with enthusiastic, well-heeled fans who brought ethnic excitement straight from 'the other side' with none of the dangerous flares and jostling and hooliganism of Europe."

Vecsey had a point. As much as I appreciated the compliment in the pages of the Paper of Record, I had to agree that as hard as we worked, as high as we set our sights, an element of luck clearly came through for us. Take the question of security, the single knottiest issue for any World Cup organizer.

In January 1993, Georgina and I were invited to the Clinton Inaugural Ball. While there I arranged a meeting with the FBI to discuss World Cup security. During that visit I heard vociferous complaints about the lack of cooperation and coordination between INS, the CIA, and the FBI. Specifically, they complained about a blind sheik whom they wanted to arrest as a terrorist but were prevented from doing so by INS. "You're so close to Clinton," I was told. (I had partners and friends who were, but I wasn't.) "Use your influence to get something done." I mentally dismissed it as typical venting by law enforcement. One month later, the first attempt to blow up the World Trade Center occurred. Sheik Omar Abdel-Rahmen, the "Blind Sheik," was at the center of the plot and was ultimately convicted of seditious conspiracy. That further drove home to me the very serious possibility of a terrorist attack targeting the World Cup and reinforced our preventive actions.

We insisted on a serious vetting process and had such a lengthy and detailed application form for all credential requests, the general counsel for the *New York Times* called to harangue me about invasion of privacy, the sacrosanct status of the Fourth Estate, and on and on. He threatened to sue us. I calmly told him about the potential terrorists we'd been able to identify, thanks to our extensive vetting, among them relatives of Saddam Hussein and Muammar Gaddafi. I added, "Please do sue us. I'd love that. Imagine the headlines about our extraordinary steps to keep out would-be terrorists."

England had failed to qualify, saving us the headache of dealing with untold numbers of UK hooligans streaming in through our airports, seeking to wreak havoc. At one point, it seemed plausible that Iran, Iraq, and North Korea—known later as the "axis of evil"—might qualify, costing us millions in added security costs and untold headaches. The day before the final Asian qualifiers, I expressed to Sepp Blatter my fear that one or more of them would qualify. All three fell short and had to stay home. I talked to him after Japan had failed to qualify following a controversial decision on added time, denying us a perennial fan favorite team in our draw. Blatter's dry reply when I complained: "Alan, you told me who you didn't want; you didn't tell me who you wanted."

Our success was not about us, it was about soccer, and the second we lost sight of that fact, our gains could feel like sand slipping through our fingers. I had always, from our first weeks working together, cautioned everyone never to take themselves seriously, since the moment the World Cup was over, nobody would particularly care about them—or, I could have added, about me.

The morning after the World Cup Final, I went to the Rose Bowl for a FIFA wrap-up press conference. As I was walking across the parking lot, a man with his young son holding a camera approached me. I started to put on my best smile, doing my best to graciously handle the demands of being in the public spotlight as front man for the World Cup. "Mister," the man said, addressing me, "would you mind taking a picture of my son and me with the Rose Bowl in the background?" I gladly complied, smiling to myself, and then kept walking.

Weeks later, it was already time for a vote on the next four-year term for president of U.S. Soccer. Given our amazing success in pulling off a universally acclaimed World Cup, stunning our many doubters, you might have thought I would be running unopposed. You would have been mistaken. I had opposition and had to go around the country to campaign for votes.

I arrived in Chicago, staying again at the Sheraton Hotel, one of our World Cup sponsors. Just a few weeks before, I stayed in the Sheraton's Presidential Suite, complete with a piano, fruit bowls, platters of cheese, flowers, and champagne. Now I was in a small single room. Having miscalculated how many days I'd be on the road when I was packing, I found myself at the sink washing my socks and underwear and then using the hair dryer to dry them. It was a loud and slow chore—even for an "impresario."

As I had cautioned, don't take yourself too seriously. Fame is fleeting.

CHAPTER 4

THE 1996 OLYMPICS CHANGED EVERYTHING FOR WOMEN'S SOCCER

THE ANNOUNCED CROWD AT SANFORD STADIUM, best known as the home of the University of Georgia football team, was calculated at 76,489, but down on the field after the U.S. women's 2–1 victory over China in the gold-medal game of the 1996 Summer Olympics it sounded even larger—and louder—than that. "U-S-A! U-S-A!" the crowd chanted over and over in a raucous eruption. It was a record crowd, and a historic occasion. Mia Hamm, the telegenic face of that team, a star hobbled that day by a lingering sprained ankle, alertly fed streaking defender Joy Fawcett in the 68th minute, with the Final knotted up at 1–1. Fawcett was unselfish enough to set up Tiffeny Milbrett in front for the game-winning goal into an empty net. Olympic gold for the U.S. women's team, and a golden moment for women's soccer, 2–1 winners of the first gold medals ever to be handed out in Olympic women's soccer. (In 1994 I sent a letter to Havelange asking him in his capacity as a member of the IOC to have it added, which he did.) They played before the largest crowd ever to watch a women's sporting event in history up until then, topping the old record of 65,000 set in 1991 in Guangzhou, China, at the first Women's World

Cup, also won by the American women—a record tainted by the fact that a large number of those were members of the Chinese military who were ordered to attend so China would look good.

"Just listen to the fans," Hamm said afterward after having a gold medal looped around her neck, beaming to the crowd. "That's what it means. They're excited about the game. It's electrifying to play in front of everyone out here and everyone enjoying themselves—that's what it's all about. We all believed in each other, we all believed in this day. We are a very confident group but that also must be because of the talent.... We always heard what it would be like to play in front of a crowd like this, but I never knew it could be like this.... Listen to them. This is perfect."

I don't remember what I said down on the field after the game that day to FIFA President João Havelange, whom I stood next to during the medal ceremony, but at that point, words didn't matter. The events of the day had made all the statement that needed making. So had the huge crowd. It was in a sense a replay of the 1984 Los Angeles Olympics in terms of what it meant for soccer. Back then, the overwhelming success of soccer at the L.A. Games showed skeptical FIFA stalwarts that the United States could be trusted to host a World Cup. Going into Atlanta, it was already known that we would be hosting the 1999 Women's World Cup tournament, but the giddy elation and record-setting attendance in Atlanta showed FIFA that we could afford to think big in '99, letting the women play in large stadiums.

"In the aftermath of the U.S. team's 2–1 victory over China, which some now call the greatest moment in American soccer history—even bigger than the U.S. men's upset of Colombia in the 1994 World Cup—players, organizers and fans wonder where it will go from here," wrote Ben Smith III in the *Atlanta Journal-Constitution*. "And how can you top a screaming world record crowd of nearly 80,000 for an Olympics gold medal Final?"

There would be time later to break down what it all meant—a crucial catalyst to set up the 1999 Women's World Cup as one of the great sporting events of our lifetime, but first, the U.S. women athletes who had trained so hard for so many months would get a break. They would get a chance to celebrate and let off a little steam. No one did that quite as memorably as U.S. goalkeeper Briana Scurry, who waited until after midnight and went for a naked run of celebration through the streets of Athens, Georgia.

"*Sports Illustrated* called and asked what I'd do if we won," she said at the time. "A lot of people say, 'Go to Disney World.' I wanted to do something different. So, I said I'd run through the streets naked. I did it at 2:00 in the morning. I ran about 20 to 30 feet down the road, back to my car. I took off my clothes in the car, put a towel on, got out of the car, threw the towel down, ran down the street and ran back with my medal on."

Trying to sum up what it all meant, Michael Farber wrote in *Sports Illustrated*: "This was a red-letter date on the time-line of U.S. women's soccer. Ten years ago, if these women had played on your lawn, you would have drawn the drapes. Six years ago, when Briana Scurry, the 1996 U.S. Olympic goaltender, was at the University of Massachusetts, she didn't know there was a women's national soccer team. Five years ago, after America won the first Women's World Cup, the family that knew and cared about the title hardly extended beyond the players' uncles and cousins."

After their gold-medal victory in Athens, Farber continued, "the team retired to the Kappa Alpha Theta house off the Georgia campus for a party with friends and family. A sorority house was the perfect setting for a celebration by a group of women who had become sisters. A month earlier the players had survived a day of team-bonding skills, including a wall climb that scared some of them witless. Between early-round Olympic matches they had carved cars out of squash, zucchini, and potatoes and pushed them down an incline in what they called the Fresh Produce 500, no doubt proving the theory that a team that races legumes together zooms together. Some of the players took the togetherness thing so far that they even discussed getting tattoos to commemorate their Olympic achievement. But judging by the adoring gazes of the girls who watched the U.S. team make history on a steamy night in Georgia, the indelible mark of this Olympic soccer tournament was left not only on the players but also on another generation."

Tony DiCicco, who had taken over from Anson as head coach of the women's team earlier in 1994, said after the gold-medal game, far more presciently than any of us understood at the time: "There are worldwide implications here. [A crowd of] 76,000 fans shows there's incredible interest in the women's game. This is something that should be taken very seriously. The women's sport is ready to explode."

It took a lot of hard work and a little luck to get us to that point. Following the women's 1991 World Cup victory in China, another indelibly important feel-good moment for

U.S. soccer, our focus at the Federation returned to preparing the men's national team, upgrading and professionalizing the Federation's management, and organizing the 1994 FIFA World Cup. The women, however, were not ignored. Instead, they were returned to the able hands of coaches Anson Dorrance and Tony DiCicco.

Tony may not have been the kind of larger-than-life presence and personality that Anson was, but he was a talented coach who had an amazingly good feel for the needs of his players. A youth soccer player growing up in Connecticut, he was an All-American goalkeeper at Springfield College in Massachusetts, and was always close to his mother, which instilled in him some key lessons. In fact, even as a 50-year-old man, coach of the women's national team, and father of four sons, he still lived in his hometown of Wethersfield, Connecticut, a mile from where his parents still lived.

"I got a lot of my motivation for women's athletics from my mother," DiCicco told the *New York Times* in 1999. "She used to shoot baskets with me in the driveway. She was a great swimmer. I always knew girls could play, because I played with her."

Tony was named assistant coach of the women's national team in 1991, the year of the first Women's World Cup, and learned some valuable, if painful, lessons early on: in short, coaches had other ways of connecting with players than the loud, harsh style of a Woody Hayes or Bobby Knight.

During a team meeting in 1991, reviewing game film, DiCicco openly criticized the play of midfielder Kris Lilly, a great player who would finish her long and distinguished career with 130 goals, third all-time in U.S. women's soccer history behind Abby Wambach (184) and Mia Hamm (158).

Tony didn't think twice about what seemed to him just a routine kind of game assessment. But he started to hear from other players that Kris was upset.

As defender Joy Fawcett explained this dynamic at the time to the *New York Times*, giving insight on her discussions with coach DiCicco, "With guys, you can yell in their face and they don't worry about it, but I think women take it more personally. The game is different to us. It's more about building relationships between ourselves and the coaching staff than just a game."

That describes perfectly the special chemistry behind that 1990s women's team. We arranged money to put them on a modest monthly salary of $3,000 to $4,000, which might not sound like much but was a lot better than what they had been getting before. They had an active schedule of matches, ultimately preparing for the 1995 FIFA World Cup in Sweden. But that was still a much different era. Public interest in the women's game had still not caught on. Games, including meaningful matches in CONCACAF Qualifying, drew paltry "crowds" that were far too often only in the hundreds, not the thousands.

We hoped it would be different for the first Algarve Cup, dubbed a kind of "Mini World Cup," which was held in Portugal in March 1994, featuring six women's national teams. Alas, more disappointment in terms of crowd size. The strong U.S. team advanced to the Finals with a 5–0 win against Portugal and a 1–0 thriller over Sweden, winning on a Mia Hamm goal—before a crowd of 450. The Final was against Norway, which the U.S. women had defeated in the 1991 World Cup, and the game in Faro, Portugal, was scoreless until the 83rd minute when Norway scored to win it 1–0.

Attendance for that game? A grand total of 1,152. It was sometimes hard to escape the feeling that no one really cared much. Even in the *Los Angeles Times*, that Final only warranted a five-line mention buried deep inside the sports section.

Despite that loss to Norway, the U.S. women headed into the 1995 World Cup as favorites. This was the first Women's World Cup that got to call itself a World Cup at the time, and yet, there was limited interest in the United States or around the world. Once again, as in 1991, there were 12 teams in the tournament, hosted this time by Sweden, and once again it came down to a critical match between Norway and the U.S.—this time in the semifinals.

The tournament, played in small stadiums, averaged a mere 4,315 in attendance. The U.S. team was plagued with injuries and misfortune. In its opening match in Group C competition, the U.S. took a 3–1 lead over China on a Mia Hamm strike in the 51st minute but ended up having to settle for a 3–3 tie. That set up a tense match with Denmark. Kristine Lilly opened scoring and Tiffeny Milbrett added a second goal to put the U.S. up 2–0, but late in the match our goalkeeper, Briana Scurry, received a very controversial—and, I might add, very questionable—red card.

As the Associated Press reported it, "Scurry was ejected with six minutes left after she stepped too far out of the 18-yard box, pounded the ball and carried it over the line on the follow. Referee Mamadouba Camara gave a red card." Even low-key Tony DiCicco was openly critical of Camara, and we filed a formal protest. "I don't agree with that call," the U.S. coach said afterward. "Maybe it's a hand ball. Maybe if the goalkeeper is trying to seek an unfair advantage it might be a yellow card, but I think it's really harsh that she got a red card. There is no way that an athlete should be put out of the championship for a ref's misinterpretation. It's not right." How's this for sportsmanship? Even the Danish coach agreed and offered to support the U.S. protest.

We had a problem. We were out of substitutions, so could not bring in a backup goalkeeper. Instead, Mia Hamm—yes, Mia Hamm, who had set up both U.S. goals—played goalkeeper for the final eight minutes of the match and was credited with one save. "I was terrified," she said later.

To advance, we ended up having to keep adding goals against Australia in our next match. Australia actually scored first and with only 21 minutes left in regulation was, incredibly enough, leading. "Astonishingly, Australia held a 1–0 lead after 55 minutes when 17-year-old Lisa Casagrande scored a superb headed goal that left American goalkeeper Saskia Webber, making her first world championship start, frozen on the line," Grahame L. Jones wrote in the *Los Angeles Times*. "The goal marked the first time in world championship history that the United States has trailed in a game. The Americans never fell behind while winning the title in China, or in the qualifying tournaments for China '91 and Sweden '95."

We were without top striker Michelle Akers, who had suffered a concussion and a knee injury, and Scurry was out because of the dubious red card from the previous game. DiCicco's hopes of resting his top players were out the window. Following the goal for Australia, he decided it was time to bring Julie Foudy into the game, replacing Amanda Cromwell.

"The effect was immediate," Jones wrote in the *L.A. Times*. "Two minutes after going in, Foudy leaped to head in a corner kick by Mia Hamm and tie the score 1–1. Eight minutes later, Joy Fawcett, the UCLA coach and another veteran of the China tournament, scored the game-winning goal."

But that wasn't enough. We had to worry about goal differential. If China racked up goals in its match with Denmark, the U.S. had to answer. "We checked the score again and China was leading 2–1, so I called out to the team, 'We need another goal,'" DiCicco said afterward. "They're an amazing group; they went out and got it. Now we were defending with like four or five minutes to go. We checked again; China had scored again. Now we needed that last goal. We yelled out again, 'We need one more goal.'"

As Jones described the action, "This time, Debbie Keller, a 20-year-old from suburban Chicago whom DiCicco had sent on as a substitute in the 77th minute, found the net, scoring her first world championship goal to make it 4–1."

In the knockout stage, Lilly again scored the opening goal in our 4–0 rout of Japan, advancing us to the semifinals and setting up another confrontation with our archrival Norway.

"Given the relative infancy of women's soccer, international rivalries haven't had much time to develop—with one glaring exception," Doug Cress reported from Sweden for the *Washington Post.* "The United States and Norway will meet here Thursday in the semifinals of the Women's World Cup, continuing a feud that began in 1987 and grows darker with each match."

A little dramatic maybe, but DiCicco backed up that spin. "It'll be a war," he said. "Their players don't like our players. Maybe they're jealous, who knows? But it's not a friendly match even when we play friendlies."

The Norwegians were known for a physical style, and apparently also for play-acting on the pitch, theatrically falling to fake having been fouled. "She's a diver," DiCicco said of Norway forward Hege Riise. "They scored two goals on us in Portugal on penalty kicks she set up with dives. You just can't tackle her—that's how good she is at diving. We thought about bringing her over to the U.S. for a clinic."

In the semifinal against Norway, the U.S. outplayed the eventual champion, but in addition to missing Akers at full strength and Carin Gabarra out entirely, they had two shots that looked like sure goals but unfortunately hit the post. As the *Los Angeles Times* wrote, "If world championships can be won on luck, they can be lost that way too. Even to the same team.... The U.S. team found that out the hard way." The lone Norwegian tally came on a corner kicked headed into the goal by Ann Kristin Aarønes. "I stood all alone and jumped and hoped for the best," she said afterward. "I closed my eyes, and when I opened them again, I saw the ball go inside."

Akers, playing on sheer will power, took the loss hard. "It's like your guts are kicked out of you," she said.

But Briana Scurry, who bounced back from her forced break to make some key saves late in the game to keep U.S. chances alive, spoke for many on the team when she took an upbeat attitude, pointing ahead to the Atlanta Olympics. "We'll be all right," she said. "This is a big disappointment for us, but as far as I'm concerned, the Olympics are more important. I think that we're going to be ready. It's a year away. We'll get over this."

That was how we saw it as well. This was a setback, but we saw what this U.S. women's team was building and could feel the future potential, especially if as Briana Scurry predicted, the Atlanta Games turned out well for the women's team. As soon as we returned to the United States after the World

Cup, Hank Steinbrecher and I talked about possibly hosting a Women's World Cup in the United States. The more we talked, the more excited we became. We contacted FIFA and expressed our interest.

FIFA wasn't as excited as we were, but we had their attention. While far from "all in" on the potential of the women's game, they'd been impressed by what we had delivered for them in the '84 Olympics, the '94 World Cup, and the launch of Major League Soccer. In no way did they discourage us on our prospects to host a Women's World Cup.

FIFA had not yet developed any application form for a Women's World Cup, so we simply sent a letter requesting the right to host the 1999 World Cup. That was all it took! FIFA granted the right. However, approval came with caveats—unacceptable caveats. FIFA told us they were limiting us to playing only in the Northeast, not nationally, and only in small stadiums (such as Holy Cross, Hofstra, and Boston University), although they reluctantly consented to the Final being at RFK Stadium in DC. We tried, unsuccessfully, to persuade them not to limit us geographically and with respect to stadium capacity. They sounded dug in, but we knew we would bring them around—we had to.

That was the context for why 1996 mattered so much. The 1996 Olympics in Atlanta were the first to include a women's soccer competition, and the stakes were high. As the Federation set up a training camp for the women at the Chula Vista California Olympic training site to prepare for the Games, it was faced with a crisis regarding equality for the women, a dispute that continued more than 25 years before being resolved in the historic contract between the Federation and the women's and men's teams in 2022. Nine members of the team—Michelle Akers, Carin Gabarra, Joy Fawcett, Julie Foudy, Mia Hamm, Kris Lilly, Carla Overbeck, Briana Scurry, and Tisha Venturini, the mainstay core of the team—being advised for the first time by a lawyer, boycotted the training site until they were granted the right to bonuses. The boycott ended when the Federation agreed to pay them a bonus if they won the gold medal. The men, however, were eligible for bonuses for gold, silver, and bronze. Progress, but not yet equality.

Our women's team was magnificent on and off the pitch. They played a beautiful, exciting style and were an intelligent, articulate, and personable group. And the crowd at the Final in the University of Georgia's massive football stadium, as I talked about back at the opening of this chapter, was a sellout of 76,489. This was a raucous celebration of our women's team and of soccer in general and women's soccer in particular with exuberant, face-painted U.S. fans waving the flag and on hand to see history being made as the U.S. women's national team won the gold medal in that exciting match against China.

As Michael Wilbon wrote at the time in his *Washington Post* column: "If anybody had told you 20 years ago that the U.S. men would fail to get a medal in the 100-meter dash, but the U.S. men or women would win a gold medal in soccer, the person would have been declared certifiably nuts. But the world turns and stuff happens. Or should we say, evolves."

The women's team earned their gold-medal bonuses, and we earned a new credibility, nationally and internationally. We immediately pressed FIFA to allow us to host the 1999 Women's World Cup nationwide and in larger stadiums—comparably sized stadiums to what we utilized in the 1994 World Cup. Finally, they listened!

Returning to Los Angeles, I tasked Marla Messing, our executive vice president and a former associate at Latham & Watkins, to prepare a business plan using 1994 as the model, which we presented to FIFA. They still didn't think we knew what we were doing. While they somewhat reluctantly agreed to our business plan, their expression was bemused. They all but shouted: "If you crazy Americans think you can do it, okay." They pledged support, but other than giving us that lip service, they and ISL, their longtime marketing arm, did nothing.

"Alan put his money where his mouth was, and that was important for us," Julie Foudy says now. "U.S. Soccer said it would assume liability for losses, if there were losses. FIFA would be off the hook. FIFA had essentially told Alan, *no, we're not going to assume so much risk.* U.S. Soccer needed to host the games in small stadiums and play it safe. Alan said: 'We're going big. We believe in this product. We believe it deserves equal marketing and equal support and all the things these women have been talking about for years.'"

We would have to earn success all on our own, but fortunately we had a secret weapon: Title IX, the landmark federal civil rights law enacted as part of the Education Amendments of 1972. There's no better example than women's soccer of the impact Title IX had. Almost from the outset in 1991, the U.S. women's team over the years has consistently been ranked No. 1 in the world, almost without exception. While the U.S. men have struggled to become a top team in international soccer, the women have been a powerhouse. Why? The men's team started almost a century after the world's great soccer powers and continues to play catch-up, definitely making progress, but still far from the pinnacle. Contrariwise, the women, because of Title IX, got a head start on most of the rest of the world, including many soccer powerhouse nations, whereas at the beginning of the '90s only a few Scandinavian and Western European teams, Japan, and China, all because of advanced liberal attitudes, had any commitment to the women's game. We didn't know at the time how much of a leg up that development would give us, but the 1999 Women's World Cup would show the world.

CHAPTER 5

FOUNDING A LEAGUE: MLS IN THE 1990s

REMEMBER, I ONLY RAN FOR U.S. SOCCER president to be able to run the World Cup. It wasn't even my idea to run! That suggestion—or instruction, if you will—came from Sepp Blatter of FIFA, delivered to me by Chuck Cale, a 1984 Olympics colleague who met with Blatter in Switzerland. Once the election was successful in August 1990, I was in for a series of surprises. Up until that moment, I had given virtually no thought to the seemingly obvious notion that as U.S. Soccer president I would have the responsibility for managing the Federation and overseeing the men's national team. The more I found out about what my new job actually entailed, the more onerous it looked.

Taking stock of what I had inherited, I was stunned. My predecessor as U.S. Soccer president and his CEO, Scott LeTellier—my colleague in the 1984 Olympics—had led a fantastic effort to secure the World Cup from FIFA, even mortgaging their homes to finance the bid. But in setting up the organization to manage the World Cup they faced serious difficulties. They were saddled with woefully inadequate personnel and financial support from U.S. Soccer—effectively nonexistent. They had no source of cash other than drawing against a small bank line of credit Scott had obtained that was running low. They had hired few staff members and were scrambling to get enough cities to bid to host World Cup games. They had farmed out marketing to an outside agency, which had yet to sell any sponsorships (and were anathema to FIFA). There weren't yet plans in place for the sale of tickets and merchandise, for booking of hotel rooms, or for transportation. There wasn't even a mission statement or logo. Clearly my hands would be full just organizing the World Cup, let alone presiding over the Federation and building our national teams.

In addition to dealing with all those messes, I was reminded, there was apparently another huge challenge to shoulder: in order to obtain World Cup rights, Werner Fricker and U.S. Soccer had promised FIFA that they would start a Division One professional league, there being none following the 1984 demise of the NASL, and—ready for this part?—FIFA expected this new league to be started *concurrently* with the organization of the World Cup. *Oh my God, what had I gotten myself into*?!

I immediately flew to Zurich and told Blatter and others at FIFA that things were even worse than they feared. There was absolutely no way we could create a professional league immediately. The only chance for success would be following the World Cup, and then only if the World Cup was an extraordinary success. In legal parlance, a condition subsequent, not a condition precedent. FIFA agreed to defer the creation of the professional league. What choice did they have?

For the time being I gave no further thought to starting a professional league. First things first. Whatever commitments had been made, it was clear to me that unless we got the World

Cup on track and pulled off organizing a successful event, there was no path forward for a serious professional soccer league in the United States. That would be dealt with later. My guess—or maybe it was a hope—was that if the World Cup was really successful, then perhaps a group of wealthy sports entrepreneurs would take it upon themselves to start a league, much as had occurred after the 1966 World Cup when the precursor to the NASL came into being. There was not an inkling, none at all, that I would end up playing a central role in the creation of a league.

I'll never forget my first visit to Colorado Springs to see the U.S. Soccer Federation's headquarters. That sounds somewhat grand, doesn't it? "Headquarters"? Actually, at that time, what the Federation had was a single trailer in Colorado, provided (rent free!) courtesy of the U.S. Olympic Committee. Its management at the time: General Secretary Keith Walker, a 60-year-old Englishman who was a career soccer referee up until he was named national administrator of U.S. Soccer in late 1984, the same year the headquarters was moved from New York to Colorado.

Walker played some professional soccer as goalkeeper for Lytham in Northern England, and in his twenties spent some time as an administrator for the Kent County Council, including a post as senior educational administrative officer, but up until he joined U.S. Soccer he'd mostly worked as a referee. He had no experience in marketing, sales, or accounting, nor in running an organization.

In 1990, former New York radio journalist Kevin Payne was handling some marketing and sales as administrator for U.S. Soccer, hired the year before by Werner Fricker. By 1991, Kevin left to become president of Soccer USA Partners (SUSAP), which as the *Washington Post* later explained it, was "a firm that owned the marketing and broadcast promotion rights to the U.S. Men's National Team in the buildup to the 1994 World Cup in the United States." Later Kevin and I became close colleagues, and he was instrumental in getting MLS launched successfully, but at that time the U.S. Soccer sponsorship cupboard was bare, mostly limited to sponsors paying primarily in kind—Adidas providing uniforms and cleats, Chiquita supplying bananas for player nourishment, etc.

Our success in organizing a U.S. Cup in June 1993 to test the readiness of both our organization and the U.S. men's national team leading up to the 1994 World Cup had been an important watershed. As explained earlier, when we beat the England national team 2–0, with goals from Dooley and Lalas, it was a stunner to many soccer fans around the world. To the *Los Angeles Times*, it was "the ultimate humiliation for the country that invented the game." If they were humiliated, we were validated—and so were the venues we'd be using during the World Cup: Foxboro Stadium in Boston, Soldier Field in Chicago, RFK Stadium in DC, and the Pontiac Silverdome in Detroit. If this was a shakedown cruise, we'd come through it more than intact. In fact, we were on a roll, excited to host the World Cup.

FIFA wasted little time in turning up the heat on us to get moving on the commitment we'd deferred. *Congratulations*! we were told. *Great job on the U.S. Cup! It's clear you're ready* to *stage a successful World Cup, and it's clear you're ready to start planning the professional league. NOW!*

I'd been hoping that as we built up toward the World Cup, entrepreneurs would step forward with the resources and commitment to start a new league. I was left hoping. No such figures emerged to lead the way. There was only one choice: I'd have to lead the charge to build a new league from the ground up.

Since Lamar Hunt formed the American Football League in 1959, no new sports league had been successfully formed. The NASL crashed and burned. Failing, the American Basketball Association was swallowed up by the NBA in 1976, after only nine seasons, leading to the adoption of the three-point shot in the NBA. Same for the World Hockey Association, founded in 1971, which lasted seven seasons before it folded, with four of its teams—including the Edmonton Oilers with 18-year-old star Wayne Gretzky—joining the NHL.

We had to start from scratch to build our new soccer league. That meant we would need to create a structure; develop a budget; raise sufficient capital; retain personnel; select cities and venues; sign players; sell sponsorships, tickets, and merchandise; obtain media partners; and determine rules of play and more. We had to do everything, right down to picking uniforms and nicknames for the teams. All while still organizing the World Cup!

Single Entity

To create a structure for our new league, I called upon my extensive legal and sports business experience and incorporated lessons learned in the NBA, the NASL, the Olympics, and now the World Cup. The result was a unique structure: organizing Major League Soccer as a single entity.

At our December 1993 U.S. Soccer board meeting in Chicago, we moved forward on single entity. "The board debates two philosophies: traditional NFL/NBA-style franchise ownership, represented by Salsa owner William De La Pena and the American Professional Soccer League; and single-entity, in which the league—its board of directors—owns and controls the franchise," Scott French reported for Knight Ridder. Single entity passed on a unanimous vote.

"It wasn't a foregone conclusion Alan's plan would win," board member Desmond Armstrong, a player on the national team, told Knight Ridder. "We were looking for the best option for soccer, not because the gentleman is president of the USSF or runs [the] World Cup."

As Clark Hunt, son of early investor Lamar Hunt, later told *Sports Illustrated*: "The single-entity structure was a big selling point for us and, frankly, everyone else who came in after the fact."

As a young lawyer for the Los Angeles Lakers, I was thrust into the Oscar Robertson case, the antitrust case brought by the NBA Players Association against the NBA, alleging that the league was guilty of violating the U.S. antitrust laws and was an illegal "conspiracy in restraint of trade." A conspiracy requires two or more parties; you can't conspire with yourself. Since the NBA—like the NFL, the NHL, and Major League Baseball—was formed as an agreement among the teams, by definition it was a conspiracy among competitors. (Although MLB was exempt from the antitrust laws as a result of an anachronistic, albeit unanimous, 1922 Supreme Court ruling, with an opinion authored by Oliver Wendell Holmes.)

Going back to my days in the 1970s serving on the NBA Board of Governors as Jack Kent Cooke's representative, I'd made friends with a bright young attorney working for the NBA by the name of David Stern. I can remember, while attending meetings with counsel for the teams and league, we would have side conversations discussing a 1940s Supreme Court case in which General Motors was found not to be in violation of the antitrust laws when it made an agreement on prices and markets with one of its wholly owned divisions. GM was deemed a "single entity," incapable of conspiring with itself.

"If only the NBA had been formed that way," we agreed, "it wouldn't be facing antitrust charges."

While never dreaming I would one day be starting a league, I did tuck away in the back of my brain a reminder that if ever called upon as a lawyer for a start-up league, I would urge the use of a single-entity organization in order to insulate the league from antitrust violations. Every time over the years another antitrust suit was brought against a sports organization, I'd say to myself, "If only they were a single entity."

Besides Major League Baseball's antitrust exemption, there are two legislative exemptions for sports leagues. One was granted in a bill sponsored by Senator Russell Long of Louisiana in 1961 shielding the NFL's national television contract from exposure. It permitted the league to divide rights fees equally among its teams. Without that exemption, it would have constituted a *per se* violation of the antitrust laws. Parity in the NFL was thus ensured: small market Green Bay would receive the identical amount of money as the giant markets, New York, Los Angeles, and Chicago. Equal distribution of television revenues, the brainchild of the NFL's legendary commissioner Pete Rozelle, remains the underpinning of the league's enormous financial success to this day.

When the AFL and NFL entered into their merger agreement, they would have been clearly in violation of the antitrust laws; they were eliminating a competitor and dividing markets, again *per se* violations. So, the NFL trotted down to Congress for another trip to the well. Again, Senator Long delivered. A law was passed permitting the merger. Between the 1961 and 1967 legislation, the NFL, NBA, and NHL had received broad antitrust protection. (Significantly, since there was not then a professional soccer league, soccer was not included in the exempting legislation; thus, the single entity was essential to protect a soccer league.) In November 1966, the NFL expanded into New Orleans, granting the new franchise to John Mecom Jr., a good friend of and major donor to Senator Long. Coincidence?

What had I learned from the NASL? Without legally enforceable rules, large markets and uber-wealthy teams will dominate a league, causing smaller, less-well-capitalized teams to fail. In the NASL, the New York Cosmos, owned by Warner Communications, went on a spending spree and signed some of the biggest names in soccer worldwide: Pelé, Beckenbauer, Carlos Alberto Torres, and Giorgio Chinaglia. There was no "salary cap," so the rest of the league couldn't keep up. For those and other reasons, eventually the league failed.

What did I learn from the Olympics and the World Cup? (And McDonald's, too?) Do not give up central control of your product. The IOC and FIFA only license their host committees, they never relinquish ownership, so they can dictate terms without legal liability. For example, they can—and do—retain sponsorship rights to major categories of products; the local organizing committee cannot seek sponsors in those categories. If Coca-Cola is the soft drink sponsor for the IOC or FIFA, the local organization cannot sell a sponsorship to Pepsi.

McDonald's had franchisees, licensees, running its stores. The franchisees owned the land and building, but never the name or product. Therefore, McDonald's could dictate prices to be charged and products to be used (again, Coke, not Pepsi) and could put geographic restrictions on its franchises, actions that otherwise would have been price-fixing and market divisions, both *per se* antitrust violations.

Sorry for the lengthy background, but it is crucial to understanding the vital importance of the use of the single entity in MLS, especially in its earlier years. We had no antitrust protection, but the single entity took care of that. So, the league, not the teams, signed the players and then allocated them to respective teams. At launch, MLS was able to sign the enormously popular Mexican star Jorge Campos and assign him to Los Angeles, with its large Hispanic fan base; in an open market, a team with a lesser Hispanic base could have signed him with a higher bid. Signing Campos was a big story, and we wanted to manage the announcement. To avoid a leak, Sunil and I met with Jorge to sign the contract in a passageway at the stadium in San Diego before a match. It was so dark and surreptitious looking, you'd have thought we were doing a drug deal.

MLS established exclusive league sponsorship categories and only allowed teams to sell to sponsors in other nonexclusive and noncompetitive categories. An elaborate plan was put in place by Randy Bernstein to protect MLS league sponsors. The league was lawfully able to establish a salary cap and have it stick. Years later, spurred by the opportunity to bring star player David Beckham to the league, MLS wisely created a "designated player" category, which permitted the signing of players over the salary cap, but still under league-controlled circumstances. It had to protect owners from themselves.

A great example: When we solicited John Kluge and his partner, Stuart Subotnick, to invest in MLS, Subotnick told me: "We've been shown virtually every possible professional sports investment opportunity, and this is the first one that makes business sense." No sooner was MLS up and running than Subotnick himself wanted to offer a player a salary exceeding the salary cap. When MLS rejected the move, he began yelling at us and cursed, "Damn it." We had to quietly remind him of what he had told us before he invested.

Another example: When we were forming MLS, William Simon had said that he and George Steinbrenner, the volatile, free-spending owner of the New York Yankees baseball team, wanted to obtain the New York team. When I met with Steinbrenner and reviewed the single-entity concept, he rejected it.

"This is communism!" he bellowed.

In the fall of 1994, Major League Baseball had to shut down, including the World Series, after a strike by players. One of Steinbrenner's sons received the same investment book his father had previously condemned as "communism!" and showed it to his dad during the strike. Seeing the enforceable restriction on salaries, Steinbrenner now shouted, "This is genius!" (Bob Nederlander, the theatrical impresario, was a limited partner of Steinbrenner's in the New York Yankees. I once asked him, "What's it like to be a limited partner of George Steinbrenner?" He replied, "It redefines the word 'limited.'")

After Major League Soccer started, a group of players did bring an antitrust case challenging the single entity (funded by the NFL Players Association, which was trying to become a union for all professional sports). The case sought to void the salary cap, among other things. After a two-week trial, during which I testified on nine days, a federal district court ruled that the single entity did not violate the antitrust laws. The decision was affirmed by the federal circuit court and the Supreme Court denied certiorari. The single entity was now unarguably validated. MLS was also able to establish in that lawsuit that there was no restriction on player movement, as there was an open worldwide market that MLS players could access if they didn't like the terms offered by the MLS. The NFL, NBA, and NHL cannot make the same claim.

In December 1993 when we announced the name of our league would be "Major League Soccer," Major League Baseball wrote demanding we cease and desist infringing on their name. Really?

"You don't own the words 'major league,'" I told MLB. "Sue me. I'd love the headline MAJOR LEAGUE BASEBALL FEARS MAJOR LEAGUE SOCCER." As with my similar retort to the *New York Times* during the World Cup, that line worked. We never heard from them again. In a similar situation, when DC United announced their name, Manchester United filed a protest. They had registered their name at the U.S. Copyright Office some years before, obviously thinking ahead about someday coming to the U.S. In any event, they were told they didn't own the word "United," and the matter dropped.

To brainstorm ideas for setting up the new league, once I accepted the mandate from FIFA, I called together my brain trust of Sunil Gulati, Randy Bernstein, Marla Messing, Scott LeTellier, and Hank Steinbrecher. It quickly became clear that we would need an incredible amount of legal documentation. We had to create the corporate structure, which, among other challenges, would be complicated because of the novel single-entity concept. We had to create the "book"—the document to be shown to potential investors, which had to be compliant with security laws. We had to prepare agreements between the league and the investor/operators as well as a form of player contract and many, many other legal documents.

While both Marla and I are lawyers, we were already overwhelmed with our other duties. Scott LeTellier, also a lawyer who oversaw our legal department, and the World Cup legal staff headed by Leah Tuffanelli were all overloaded as well, so I called a partner at Latham to ask for a referral. Coincidentally, in what turned out to be a historic moment for him and MLS, a young associate, Mark Abbott, was in the office and listened to the conversation.

"I want to do it," he told me.

"You're on," I said.

Mark had worked with me on a case, and I knew him to be very smart and a diligent worker with a pleasing personality. I also knew he, growing up in Minneapolis, had been a fan of the Minnesota Kicks of the NASL. Mark became MLS' first employee. (Technically, he was working for and being paid by the World Cup, since MLS had not yet even been formed). In addition to doing all the documentation, Mark served as liaison to our consultant, our outside lawyers, accountants, and investment bankers. He visited prospective cities to entice them to bid to be selected by the new league. (Mark would stay with MLS through 2022, becoming its deputy commissioner and president, before finally retiring at the end of 2022. He lived through all the ups, downs, and ultimate ups of the league. He should write a history of MLS. If he doesn't, we'll have to perform cryotherapy on his brain.)

At the outset, planning our league, we had to grapple with concerns that the average American sports fan—and particularly the media—wasn't sufficiently interested in soccer. We heard it all. "It's too low scoring," people said. Or: "It's boring!" So, we kicked around ideas of potential changes to make the game more wide open, with more scoring, not fully appreciating the beauty and drama of the "beautiful game" ourselves. Some ideas made sense, whereas others were off the wall. Ultimately the only ones we began the league with were that, in lieu of penalty kicks, ties would be resolved with the 35-yard shootout, used in the NASL, where the attacking player takes the ball 35 yards from the goal and goes on a breakaway with the goalkeeper able to move to stop him. Critics had panned penalty kicks as a way to end a game. "It was like ending a basketball game with a free throw contest," the unknowing naysayers claimed. We also instituted a countdown clock showing 90 minutes to zero to replace the standard clock, which just ticked off the elapsed minutes with no indication how much time was left, with the game ending only when the referee decided in his own good judgment to blow the whistle.

After two years, the league took a step back and accepted that the way to develop fans was not to try to convert non-soccer fans but to stay with the game as played worldwide and cater to traditional fans and grow that base. As a result, the shootout and countdown clock were abandoned. The soccer fan understood that because the games were low scoring it meant there was drama and tension for 90 minutes; one mistake, one fluke, one brilliant play resulting in a goal, or one spectacular save avoiding a goal was life or death for the match. Soccer fans never leave their seats to go to a concession stand for fear of missing that one pivotal moment. Contrast that with the claim that in an NBA game for the first 46 minutes you're entertained by extraordinary athletic feats, but you only have to pay real attention in the last two minutes. Ninety minutes of drama and tension versus two minutes of drama and tension. Take your pick.

"For the sport to take root in the United States as a spectator and television sport, the rules of the game must be changed to permit more goals," I wrote in a letter to FIFA President Havelange in late 1991. "The decline in goal scoring during the recent World Cup in Italy only reinforces this view."

Here are some of the other ideas we kicked around to make soccer more fan-friendly in the U.S.

Widen the Goals

The goal dimensions had been established in 1926 at a time when goalkeepers averaged 5′7″ and weren't necessarily great athletes. Now goalkeepers are over 6′ and very athletic (some, like Jorge Campos, actually move forward as attackers; many are used on corner kicks and to take penalty kicks.) FIFA actually authorized us to test larger goals in a lower league, which we did. The results showed more goals but not a dramatic enough increase to change the net size. While goalkeepers are taller and more agile, the ball is no longer a heavy leather sphere but a lighter, livelier synthetic ball that curves and slices, dips, and rises, making it much more challenging for goalkeepers. In rejecting the idea of wider goals, Blatter explained, "There are millions of goals throughout the world that would have to be replaced, many in poor countries who couldn't afford it."

Quarters

One other thought that I actually discussed with then-President Havelange was to divide the game into quarters. It would give players a break, and presumably cause them to pace themselves less during the match, and it would allow time for the coach to regroup and make tactical changes. Not insignificantly, of course, it would also enable the sale of more TV sponsorships, since commercials could be rolled during the break after the first and third quarters. Havelange rejected any consideration of the idea, not only because he was a hidebound traditionalist about the game, but also out of fear of being criticized for only caring about the opportunity to increase revenues. "Fútbol is a players' game," he said. "They have to make adjustments in the course of the game. Once they take the pitch the coach can do little: the game belongs to the players, not the coaches."

Tweaking Offsides

My favorite suggestion, which I still think should be considered, was to change the offside rule, taking a page from hockey. Once the ball crosses the penalty area onside, there can be no offside until the defending team takes possession. Other variations on play that were mentioned but not seriously considered included rule changes to allow players to play behind the goal, as in hockey (Wayne Gretzky's "office"), or to give players a choice between a kick-in or throw-in when the ball has gone out of touch.

Relegation/Promotion

The idea of promotion and relegation, prevalent in leagues around the world, was considered. One clear virtue of such a change would be that later in the season, when poorer-performing teams are out of contention, fan interest remains high in the fight not to be relegated to a lower division. And top teams in the lower divisions compete vigorously to be promoted. It works. It's exciting. Our fear was twofold. One, it was a concept totally foreign to American sports. More significantly, in a country such as England, for example, there are seven teams in and around London, so there never will be a situation where the largest TV market would not have a team. In the United States, the thought that a New York or a Los Angeles market could be supplanted by, say, Wichita or Abilene would be unthinkable.

Time of Season

The international calendar runs from late summer through winter into spring in the United States. That season would mean that teams in cold-weather midwestern and eastern cities would often be playing in the middle of harsh weather conditions. But being out of sync with the rest of the world would create problems on international transfers and on opportunities for matches on open dates. We opted for better weather and set the seasons from late February into late fall. That schedule also ducks head-to-head competition with the heart of the college and NFL football seasons. Instead, our season would largely be after the NBA and NHL seasons, in the midst of the long MLB season—as close to an open window in the crowded U.S. sports calendar as we could find.

The schedule is an ongoing problem. FIFA to this day keeps urging a change, even suggesting a midseason break to bypass the worst weather. MLS continues to study the issue, and with so many more warm-weather teams, it may one day be feasible. Both relegation/promotion and a move to the international calendar are as inevitable as tomorrow, but not so imminent.

We also had to overcome another FIFA hurdle, and avoid potential fan criticism, by handling the special considerations arising from having individuals owning two teams in the league. We had to establish clear-cut rules regarding trades, sponsorships, finances, and the like to avoid any possibility of even the perception of self-dealing. Here again the single entity came to the rescue. All transactions between teams owned by the same person had to be specifically approved by the league. FIFA gave silent assent. No fan criticism has ever occurred.

I made it clear that stadiums were a real issue. Our projections were that, to break even, we would need average attendance in the high teens (in hindsight, a substantial mistake; it would take more). But there were few, if any, stadiums in the United States that size. We'd have to play in huge American football stadiums, which would be terrible. If you put 18,000 fans in a 60,000-seat stadium, it looks awful and sounds awful, plus often we'd be playing with both football and soccer lines drawn on the field. We wouldn't control dates, nor concessions or parking revenues. At the other end of the spectrum there were smaller high school, junior college, and Division III stadiums, but it's hard to say you're a major league when fans have to sit on metal bleachers and go to port-a-potties.

We needed to have soccer-specific stadiums seating 20,000 to 30,000. We commissioned a consultant, the one used by the

NFL to evaluate new stadiums, to do a study. He showed it was financially feasible. In addition to soccer, there could be other tenants and the team as owner would enjoy rent and concession and parking revenue. So, the initial business plan, incorporated into the investment book, included the construction of soccer-specific stadiums.

Unfortunately, as I started to present the opportunity to would-be investors, their reaction was: *I may take a risk on investing in a new soccer league. Given the track record of failed soccer leagues, that's risky, but at least I can limit my liability in the event the league fails by just shutting down operations, losing only what I had already spent. But if I've built a single-purpose stadium that I still have to be financing and maintaining, that's too risky. I don't want a white elephant.* So, the final version of the investment book ultimately did not contain the requirement for a soccer-specific stadium. The concept remained front and center for us, but we downplayed it for the time being. It had been deferred, not abandoned.

We used the Final Draw in Las Vegas in December 1993 as an opportunity to introduce our concept for MLS to would-be investors, sponsors, and the media, holding a number of conferences as well as one-on-one discussions. We did the same at the time of the World Cup Final. In fact, I had invited Phil Anschutz to be my guest at the Final. Several years later, at a reception when he opened his soccer-specific stadium for the Los Angeles Galaxy, he kidded me about that.

"Alan, remember those free tickets you gave me to the 1994 World Cup Final?" he asked me. "So far they've cost me $300 million." And the amount continued to increase before MLS found its footing!

At one conference with potential sponsors, I found myself looking around the room and was taken aback when I realized I was the oldest person in the room. A first. I was a year ahead of my peers in school, achieved early career success, and seemingly was always the youngest in the room. Until that moment. Hopefully my age—mid-fifties at the time—only made me wiser.

Years later I had an analogous experience. CBS was about to launch the Stephen Colbert late-night show, housed in their Ed Sullivan Theater near Times Square. They wanted to sell naming rights to the theater. In a meeting with Randy, me, a number of my Premier Partnerships colleagues, and CBS President Les Moonves and his colleagues, we suggested it would be easier to sell naming rights without the Ed Sullivan name attached. Moonves was absolutely opposed.

"Ed Sullivan is a treasured part of CBS history!" he huffed at me.

"I understand, Les," I said, "but look around the room. You and I are the only people who have any idea who Ed Sullivan was."

Time flies by. Memories fade. I'm sure that most MLS fans today have no idea who Alan Rothenberg is.

When we had a complete first draft of the business plan, the first person I showed it to was Lamar Hunt, for obvious reasons. I met with him after he'd reviewed it and gone over it with a fine-tooth comb, making detailed marginal notes going into minute details, including even such minutiae as whether new stadiums should have players entering the field from the end or midfield. Lamar didn't have a preference between a midfield entrance or not, but he wanted us to think through both options before making a decision.

Lamar was there from the start. He also talked to potential investors, like Phil Anschutz and Robert Kraft. Their respect for him went a long way toward persuading them to invest. Hunt agreed with the need for soccer-specific stadiums and no sooner had the league been launched without those stadiums when he commenced construction of a stadium in Columbus, Ohio, that would demonstrate the value of building new facilities. When the stadium opened, Columbus—despite being the smallest market in the league—led MLS in attendance. Understandably, the original stadium was pretty "plain vanilla." But after seeing it and the results, Anschutz decided to be next. He sent his people to Europe to get design ideas and set about constructing what's now called Dignity Health Sports Park as a home for the L.A. Galaxy.

Ever since, MLS has been unbending in its requirement that any expansion team have a soccer-specific stadium or final, approved plans for one. The only exceptions have been Atlanta, Charlotte, and Seattle, where the NFL and MLS teams are owned by the same person and the large stadium is used. Those teams perennially lead MLS in attendance. In Boston, the Revolution have continued to play in the Patriot's Gillette Stadium while the Kraft family continues to search for a suitable site for a soccer-specific stadium.

I was sure we'd find enough investors, but as with all startups it's never easy to convince hard-headed businesspeople to make a leap of faith. As Kevin Payne told the *Los Angeles Times* in November 1994, "It's like many investments. Everybody's sort of looking around, saying, 'Well I'll jump in when you jump in.' At some point you have to get to the point where everybody's willing to hold hands and all jump in together. I think that's what Alan is working toward now." Investment in professional sports was not yet an asset class as it is now.

The involvement of Phil Anschutz is very interesting and of vital importance, as he later became the savior of MLS by financially supporting half of the teams in MLS as it survived its most treacherous years. He was a client of Latham. While I was not his lead lawyer, I was part of his team of lawyers when he bought the L.A. Kings and began plans for what is now Crypto.com Arena. I was reluctant to approach him directly because I was not his lead lawyer, and because for client relations as well as legal ethical reasons there is great reluctance to solicit a client for a personal investment.

I talked to Dave Rogers, my partner who was the lead lawyer. He decided he'd send the book to Anschutz, with a note reading: "My partner, Alan Rothenberg, is starting a professional soccer league. I didn't want you to find out about it later and wonder why I hadn't called it to your attention, so I'm enclosing the investment book." It contained no ask.

Thankfully, Anschutz was interested. He committed to buy one unit, which we valued at $5 million (in hindsight, incredibly way too low), as we planned to sell 10 such units for a league capitalization of $50 million. At a meeting in New York with the then committed investors, we were one unit short and had offered Phil an option for a second unit and a second team, an option Lamar Hunt had already committed to. During the meeting we received a call from Phil, who was co-chair of Bob Dole's finance committee in his 1996 presidential campaign. From his plane, flying to a Dole meeting in DC, he told us: "I'm in." It was as if the voice of God had spoken from above. We finally had our initial capitalization committed. Anschutz was in for Denver and an option for a second team (later Chicago). Hunt was in for Columbus and Kansas City; Kraft in for New England; Kluge and Subotnick in New York; and in DC a group, including George Soros, was led by SUSAP and Kevin Payne.

Los Angeles ended up being another example of fate, of being in the right place at the right time. The Los Angeles investor was a group led by Marc Rapaport. Marc had been an associate at my law firm but left to join Michael Milken's high-flying Drexel Burnham Lambert firm, where he made a lot of money. In 1990, he co-founded the capital division of Jefferies & Co.

One Saturday afternoon, Georgina and I were having lunch at Ivy at the Shore, a popular restaurant in Santa Monica. Marc, whom I hadn't seen in many years, came into the restaurant with his son, who had just finished a soccer game and was still in uniform. Talk about your ideal openings to talk soccer! Marc and I chatted, and I told him about the league being formed. I explained I had many likely investors in Los Angeles, but no one was stepping up to take the lead. A few conversations later, Marc Rapaport became the general partner of what became the investor/operator of the L.A. Galaxy. After the second year, Marc had to make a capital call on his partners, which he hated to do. Phil Anschutz stepped up and bought the Galaxy for $26 million. Rap and his partners were the first, and for a long time, the only investors who had made money from owning a professional soccer team.

At that time, I had been working with Eli Broad and Ed Roski trying to get the NFL to come back to L.A. Roski, who was a partner with Anschutz in the Kings, had asked Anschutz to be part of it. Phil wasn't interested. After the Galaxy acquisition closed, I had a question for Phil.

"You're willing to make a very risky investment with a start-up soccer team, but you're not willing to invest in an NFL team where you can sit down and with certainty calculate a great return on your investment," I said. "I'm curious, why?"

"In the NFL, I'd just be another rich guy sitting around the table," he said. "They don't need me. In soccer I think I can make a difference."

Boy has he ever!

In a classic case of risk versus reward, the initial investors who put up $5 million each now have an asset package valued in excess of $1 billion—and growing.

I was sure we needed a minimum of 10 teams to start the league, but we were unable to find investors for the last two, so at the outset we established Tampa Bay and San Jose as league-owned teams. San Jose would end up hosting the first game in MLS history, hosting DC United at Spartan Stadium on April 6, 1996, live on ESPN.

When we started seeking media partners, ESPN was an obvious choice for English-language rights, as its parent, ABC, had been our World Cup broadcaster, and Univision, which had done the Spanish-language rights, was also a natural choice. Since there was much uncertainty as to the success we would achieve, the deals were on a shared basis, where MLS was responsible for production costs, unlike the other established leagues, where the rights holder paid a rights fee and also paid production.

Working with Randy Bernstein, who would go from MLS vice president of marketing to chief revenue officer, we took the bold position that, on deals with media and sponsors, we would only do multiyear deals. Pretty gutsy for a start-up in a sport strewn with failed leagues. We wanted to avoid one-year contracts, which had the effect of being options. The sponsor or media partner would "take a look" before making a more permanent commitment. The problem with that is, that meant they wouldn't put much or anything behind the sponsorship. Contrariwise, if a long-term commitment is made, the sponsor will spend a lot of money, sometimes as much or more than the rights fee, behind activation and promotional programs, which benefit the league and clubs substantially.

Early in the process, I flew to Oregon to meet with Phil Knight at Nike headquarters in Beaverton. I urged Phil to consider Nike not just being a sponsor and uniform and equipment provider but also being an equity investor in MLS. (Another advantage of the single-entity structure: you didn't have to own a team to be an investor; in fact, Dentsu, the massive Japanese agency, was an initial investor in MLS.) Phil shot me down.

"I'm just not convinced about soccer in the United States," he told me.

Just a few months later, I got a call from Howard Slusher, Knight's longtime "consigliere," whom I had known for years going back to when he was an agent representing Paul Westphal, which is when he met Knight.

"Can you come to Beaverton?" Howard asked me. "We'd like to talk to you about soccer."

This time not only was Nike interested in sponsoring MLS, but they wanted to be the exclusive provider of uniforms and equipment for the league and U.S. Soccer. In yet another gutsy move, Randy and I rejected Nike's request for exclusivity. We limited Nike to half the teams. We wanted as many endemic soccer companies as possible to be part of the league. Randy was successful in bringing in Adidas, Reebok, and Puma as uniform suppliers; Umbro to uniform the referees; Mitre to supply the balls; and Kwik Goal to provide the goals. Randy even helped design the multicolored ball: the green representing the pitch, the blue the sky above. Never done previously, the uniform suppliers took the lead in efforts to prepare logos, uniform designs, and color selections and conducted the promotional rollout. Another first in American team sports: we sold sponsorships on the uniforms.

What caused Nike to change its mind about soccer? They had decided to go international. Thus, soccer. But to be credible as they went to foreign countries, they believed it would be important to be the supplier and kit provider to their home country's national team and league. When the U.S. Soccer rights were negotiated, Sunil, who had taken the lead, also got Nike to agree to house our youth players at the famed IMG/Nike facility in Bradenton, Florida.

Nike's international strategy worked. Germany was always going to be Adidas (note: in 2024, Nike finally wrested the German kit sponsorships away from Adidas), but the Brazilian national team rights were open, and Nike aggressively and successfully pursued them, and after that they were off to the races. They obtained the Italian rights with the help of our New York World Cup venue director, Charlie Stillitano, who through his Italian contacts was able to determine the right amount of money to put in the "blind bid" envelope called for by the Italian National Association.

With Nike, I also learned a very basic branding concept. When they signed the U.S. Soccer contract I said, "I understand the value of sponsoring basketball, as kids and adults can wear basketball shoes all the time, not just when they're playing. On the other hand, soccer cleats can only be used for playing."

Tom Clark, the former Nike vice president, responded: "We love to have the youth playing in our gear as young as possible. Once they start with Nike, they continue for the rest of the lives, not just for shoes, but caps, sweats, tees, everything. It becomes their default brand."

How right that was. I'd started drinking Coca-Cola as a youth. I'm not sure I'd pick out Coke in a blind tasting of colas today, but whenever I order a soft drink, it's always Coke.

Randy Bernstein, my close colleague and friend since 1982, has enjoyed an amazingly successful career. While finishing his responsibilities as our vice president, corporate partnerships for the World Cup, he was simultaneously working on MLS sponsorship, merchandising, and media rights. Incredibly, before we'd played a single match, he'd secured $100 million in sponsorships—double the capitalization of the league—with the help of his three-person team (one of whom was Kathy Carter, who went on the become president of MLS Properties—Soccer United Marketing, and the initial CEO of the 2028 L.A. Olympic Organizing Committee, and another of whom was Nick Sakiewicz, who went on to run three MLS teams over two decades). In one case, the ad agency for AT&T turned us down. Randy researched and found a different agency represented AT&T for Hispanic advertising. He secured a long-term sponsorship from AT&T through that agency. A few years later he sold an MLS sponsorship to Yahoo, a first. They were so impressed with him they hired him away from MLS.

While with Yahoo, Randy retained me as his lawyer and Yahoo became a FIFA sponsor, creating and managing the first FIFA website. I was in Zurich on that deal on 9/11, sitting frozen in front of a TV at FIFA House watching the horror unfold with people from various countries in the world. We were all speechless. I was stuck in Zurich for several days before I could find a flight home. It was so hard to be away from Georgina and the family and the United States during those emotionally fraught days. When I returned home after being isolated abroad, I realized just how devastating the emotional impact had been for my family and the whole country.

Initially, it was expected that MLS would be launched in the spring of 1995, immediately following the World Cup. We decided otherwise. Coming off the high of the World Cup, there would be undue expectations, and the public would be disappointed that the level of play and the extreme passion in the stands that they had witnessed in 1994 were severely diminished. We had to lower expectations. Time would help to do that. Additionally, we were still a work in progress and far from 100 percent ready. Not every sponsor and investor dollar was in the bank; we had many employees, most former World Cup staff, including in venue cities now working for the MLS team in that market, but we still weren't fully staffed. And really important, we'd signed a lot of players but more had to be recruited and signed.

Sunil Gulati had accomplished amazing success in signing up virtually all the Americans who had played for the national team both in the World Cup and other competitions. Names that had become well known to the soccer public were in the fold: the "Jersey Boys," Harkes, Meola and Ramos, plus Lalas, Cobi, Wynalda, and Jorge Campos. Sunil also was able to sign Carlos Valderrama, the Colombian superstar recognizable by his curly blond hair, and the talented Bolivian Marco Etcheverry. We'd made incredible progress, but there was still more to be done. So, I made the decision to wait a year and start play in 1996. Using another sport's metaphor, if we tripped out of the starting block, we might not get another chance.

We began play in San Jose in April 1996 before a sellout crowd of 31,683 at Spartan Stadium. Eric Wynalda saved the day when his fantastic curving free kick broke a 0–0 tie. When it was over after much hugging and hand slapping, I turned to Sunil and Hank.

"Mission accomplished," I said. "Now tell me how we can win a World Cup."

The answer to that question has yet to be given, but one day.... 2026?

After the first season, I was in the process of taking over the San Jose team from the league, in partnership with Peter Ueberroth and Dentsu—which was to provide most of the financing—when the Japanese economy crashed and Dentsu pulled out, so the deal never went ahead.

A decision on my continuing role with Major League Soccer had to be made. While totally in charge of putting the league together to the point of launch, I wasn't sure how involved I wanted to be moving forward. I had determined that, while we'd successfully run the World Cup out of Los Angeles, if we really wanted to be considered major league, MLS had to be headquartered in New York, where all the other major leagues, most major ad agencies and their corporate clients, and the media were headquartered. Several of my "brain trust" gathered and pleaded with me to move to New York to serve as MLS commissioner. Marc Rapaport came to my office on behalf of the owners to discuss the potential of an agreement.

"I don't think I want to do it," I told Marc.

"Why?" he asked.

"My guess is that there's a 5 to 10 percent chance that MLS will be a huge success right from the start, in which case I'll probably regret not being the commissioner," I said. "There's also an equal 5 to 10 percent chance it'll be an immediate bust and fold quickly. And there's the 80 to 90 percent likelihood that it'll be a long, hard struggle before we see the light of day, and I'm certain before not too many years, I'll be fed up and burned out and resign or, more likely, be removed by the owners. During the past several years I haven't spent as much time with my family and friends as I'd like to, nor have I been involved in the many community and philanthropic organizations in Los Angeles that I love supporting. I've been on the road constantly. As commissioner of a new league that will continue unabated, if I go to New York and after several years I have to return, I'll have exacerbated those lost relationships and, at close to 60 years old, I'll have to start my career all over again and try to bring back my lost friends and activities."

Marc took this all in.

"You're really risk-averse, Alan," he said.

"I guess so, Rap."

I settled instead for a board seat and a consulting contract for five years with a small equity position. And as it turned out, I had it scoped correctly. After a very positive first year, things turned bad, and it took many years to turn things around. The initial commissioner the owners hired didn't turn out well. The success of the first year made him think he had a sinecure, and little was done in the offseason to get ready for season two. After another very disappointing year, he was replaced. As the owners began a search for a commissioner, my son Brad suggested I talk to Don Garber, then the head of NFL International. In his previous role with the NFL, he had been in NFL Properties, where Brad had worked with him when he was running the NFL Experience On the Road. I'd met Don very briefly a couple of times but didn't really know him.

I scheduled a breakfast meeting at the Bull & Bear Prime Steakhouse on the Lexington side of the Waldorf Astoria, and I laid out the potential opportunity. He seemed interested. From there, Bob Kraft and Lamar Hunt, who as NFL owners were his bosses, took over and before long persuaded Don to become MLS commissioner. His visionary, creative, strong, steady leadership coupled with the firm backing of ownership enabled the league to ride through some very rough years and start what has been an inexorable climb.

With the breakthrough Apple TV contract; the addition of Lionel Messi, the GOAT; and the upcoming 2026 World Cup, MLS is truly "Major League!"

Looking back, I am pleased with my decision not to go to New York as MLS commissioner. After retirement from Latham & Watkins, I started a commercial bank, 1st Century Bank, which has enjoyed great success, and Randy Bernstein and I created Premier Partnerships and have enjoyed that successful 20-year endeavor, now as part of Playfly Sports, which acquired Premier. I have served as a board member of several publicly listed companies. And serving my beloved Los Angeles community, I have been president of the Los Angeles Airport Commission, which operates LAX; chairman of the Los Angeles Chamber of Commerce; and chairman of the Los

Angeles Tourism Board. I also resumed my active positions with the Los Angeles Sports & Entertainment Commission and the Los Angeles Sports Council and actively participated in the U.S. Soccer Foundation formed with the surplus from the 1994 World Cup.

But most importantly, I have been able to spend the time with Georgina, our three sons and their wives, friends, and our six grandchildren that I had missed so much during those several years when I was gone so often. We've taken long, wonderful family vacations. Georgina was quoted saying she "had bought an airline seat from our American Airline sponsor so Alan will feel right at home." I was able to join Georgina for our grandchildren's after-school activities, including soccer games. I was able to spend time with friends, old and new. None of that would have been possible had I gone to New York, a city that I love and where Georgina and I have a place we escape to occasionally.

In 1996, the owners unexpectedly honored me by placing my name on the league trophy given to the winner of the MLS Cup, the Alan I. Rothenberg Cup. There it remained for over 10 years, until it was renamed the Philip F. Anschutz Cup. I had to admit: While it hurt to have my name replaced, the name change made a lot of sense. I had created the league, but Phil Anschutz had saved it.

CHAPTER 6

RAPTURE: THE 1999 WOMEN'S WORLD CUP

ONCE WE HAD BEEN GIVEN the green light by FIFA on planning the 1999 Women's World Cup the way we wanted from the start, the onus was suddenly on us to get going and get organized and live up to the big promises we'd been making. The FIFA leadership was openly skeptical; they thought we were wildly overstating the potential audience for women's soccer, and if we didn't do the work, forge the partnerships, and do the planning, we would never get a chance to prove how wrong their doubts would turn out to be. It was a little scary, but I loved a good challenge and so did my team. We knew we had history on our side. So, we set about with our plans that resulted in the historic, record-setting 1999 Women's World Cup, which served as the event that launched not just women's soccer but women's team sports as an indispensable member of the sports community and society.

Past success was not going to be much help with this fresh challenge. Most of the great people we had working with us on the 1994 World Cup had moved on, including Scott LeTellier, who launched his successful "Big League Dreams" business. In one area that I'm so proud of, a good many of them began their own careers as soccer executives, going to work for Major League Soccer teams, the Federation, or other organizing committees. In a first, two actually went to Zurich to work for FIFA: Jim Brown, who got his start at 26 working for us during the 1994 World Cup as director of operations at Stanford Stadium; and Mary Harvey, the starting goalkeeper on the U.S. women's team that won the first World Cup in China, who eventually ended up being hired as FIFA's director of development, the first American hired to head a FIFA division. Richard Motzkin, another Latham associate whom I had brought in as the first general counsel of the U.S. Soccer Federation, has gone on to become the leading soccer agent in the United States. Ivan Gazidis, yet another Latham lawyer, has become an international soccer executive with stints as CEO of Arsenal and AC Milan. Cheche Vidal, who was the IT maven for us, has had a great career since in international soccer technology. Charlie Stillitano was our New York venue director and has become an international game promoter. Nelson Rodriguez was our New York deputy venue director and has enjoyed success as an executive on MLS teams. Tom King was our Detroit venue director and became the men's national team manager. Dan Flynn was our Chicago venue director and became the Federation's general secretary and then FIFA's U.S. consultant for '26. Doug Arnot was our chief venue director, overseeing all nine venues, and since has been the IOC's infrastructure officer. And many, many more. Nothing makes me prouder than to have helped so many people enjoy great careers.

So, in planning the first Women's World Cup on U.S. soil, we had to begin from scratch. While in the first instance we could rely on the core group—Sunil Gulati, Hank Steinbrecher,

Marla Messing, and Randy Bernstein—of that group only Marla was available full time. Hank had continued on as the U.S. Soccer General Secretary; Sunil was actively involved with MLS, teaching his class at Columbia, and still overseeing the men's national team; and Randy was MLS' chief revenue officer. A word about Hank, who was with me from the start: He was instrumental in building the U.S. Soccer Federation management. While I was preoccupied with my responsibilities for the World Cup, MLS, and the '99 Women's World Cup, Hank was 110 percent with U.S. Soccer and invaluable to the cause. Remember, I was the "outsider," but Hank was from the so-called "soccer family" and his rousing speechmaking at U.S. Soccer meetings and events earned him the nickname "Reverend Hank."

Our initial funding for the 1999 World Cup came from a $2.5 million loan from the U.S. Soccer Foundation, which had been created by the surplus of more than $50 million from the '94 World Cup.

I made the decision that, whereas I would be the chairman of the Organizing Committee, it was more appropriate that a woman should be the CEO. It was, after all, a *Women's* World Cup. We retained a search firm and hired a very qualified woman, a former university athletic director. She looked great on paper and came across very well in person, but it turned out she was a "fish out of water" in the job, so we had to start over.

Marla had been lobbying me heavily for the position all along, and I'd resisted her entreaties. I was well aware she was smart, capable, and hardworking, and I knew that with her experience in '94 (in particular her overseeing all the events surrounding the Final Draw) and with my oversight, she would be well equipped to handle many of the duties of the job, but I had concerns about her inexperience at the top of an organization. Since the position was also public facing, I was also concerned that she had very little experience with the public or press.

I contacted Donna de Varona, who had been on the '94 World Cup Board and also worked on the '84 Olympics. Donna was an Olympic gold medalist swimmer, was the first female TV sports commentator, and co-founded the Women's Sports Foundation with Billie Jean King. She agreed to serve as honorary chair with Marla as president/CEO, which worked out great. We could have a well-known and respected person, Donna, as our face to the public with Marla doing the day-to-day work out of our offices in Los Angeles. Marla's performance allayed any concerns I'd had. She showed great leadership and became an accomplished public speaker, magnificently managing the breakthrough women's sporting event.

Although we exuded supreme confidence that we'd sell out our large stadiums, as June McIvor began booking them for us, we were also blocking time and establishing a budget to have major concert performances before the games, just in case. Fortunately, once we began selling tickets, we knew we wouldn't need the concerts and could safely abandon that effort. We did plan to have a major concert before the opening match at Giants Stadium. (By this time FIFA—finally—did not object to a concert on the field.)

One day Marla called me all excited.

"I've booked *NSYNC for the opening," she blurted out, a little breathlessly.

That meant nothing to me.

"What's an *NSYNC?" I asked her.

I'd never heard of Justin Timberlake or *NSYNC at that point, given the generation gap and my sons no longer being at home to keep me "hip."

Marla also arranged for Jennifer Lopez, who was white-hot then with her debut album just out, to close out the World Cup by singing before the Final, again at midfield. She'd be performing her hit single "Let's Get Loud!," which was just the message we wanted to send to the huge crowd at the Rose Bowl.

It was the era of the "Soccer Mom" and much that was in the media linked our effort to the Soccer Mom mania. In truth, "Soccer Dads" may have been equally, if not more important. I had noted a phenomenon in walking the halls of my law firm. Male lawyers were on the phone talking to the girls on the soccer teams they were coaching. In contrast to how most boys' coaches acted by only communicating with the players at practice and games, the Soccer Dads were coaching their daughters' teams. It was a bonding experience, new to them, to share with their daughters and their teammates. They expressed concern about the girls' homework, how they were feeling, etc.—something unheard of with boys' team coaches, who never expressed concerns about "feelings." Marla's husband, Bret, had noticed the same phenomenon and urged her to pursue the Soccer Dads. So we went after the Soccer Dads, successfully.

There was one true Soccer Mom and another first, established by the '99ers: Joy Fawcett, a mainstay defender on the team, gave birth to a baby girl, quickly returned to play and star, and brought her daughter with her to practices, where she was "mothered" by the whole team and staff. Later, Joy had another child before the '99 World Cup and continued to play at peak level. (From 1993 to 1997, she'd served as the first head coach of the UCLA women's soccer team, and later she would join the ownership group behind Angel City FC of the NWSL. How's this for a remarkable distinction? Fawcett played the entire game for the USWNT not only in the 1995, 1999, and 2003 Women's World Cups, but also in the Olympics in 1996 and 2000—the only one who can make that claim.)

We embarked on an effort to set up group sales to girls' soccer teams through their coaches, almost all of whom were men—the Soccer Dads—to bring the players and their family and friends to matches. We also went to the soccer family, as we had in '94, to sell tickets in advance. And, as in '94, they quickly became "hot tickets," must haves: We started selling tickets in October 1997 and by April 1999 had sold more than 300,000; by June, we were up to half a million advance sales, setting a record for a women's sporting event, better even than for the NCAA women's basketball tournament.

Meantime, to spur interest and give our team game experience, the Federation working with the World Cup staff arranged matches for the team in cities where World Cup matches would be played. In some cases where matches weren't possible, we had the team have open practice sessions and media events. One launched a romance culminating in a marriage between two superstars.

On one date the team was going to be in Boston. We were asked if Nomar Garciaparra, the Red Sox All-Star shortstop, could be enticed to come to the team's practice. Great idea. I remembered reading several years before an article in *Sports Illustrated* about Nomar, in which he said that soccer was his favorite sport, and he only gave it up for baseball because there was more money available for players in baseball.

I looked up the schedule and found out the Red Sox would be in town at the same time our team would be practicing. I knew that Nomar was represented by Arn Tellem, whom I had mentored when he was a young lawyer at my law firm. I called Arn and asked if Nomar would like to go to the practice. He would! And did. There he met Mia Hamm, who later became his wife.

We knew we wanted to open the tournament in the New York area. We'd have done that in 1994 as well, but Chicago made us an offer we couldn't refuse, so Chicago it was. For us in 1999, Giants Stadium in East Rutherford, New Jersey, was the natural spot for the opening ceremonies and first match of the tournament. I also knew—of course I did—that the Final would have to be played at the Rose Bowl, where we'd had such amazing crowds in 1984 and 1994. Sorry, Thomas Wolfe, sometimes you *can* go home again.

As Grahame L. Jones of the *Los Angeles Times* wrote in announcing our plans, "It is August 11, 1984, a warm Saturday evening, and 101,799 fans pack the Rose Bowl in Pasadena to see France defeat Brazil 2–0 for the gold medal in Olympics soccer. It is a decade later, July 17, 1994, and 94,194 fans wend their way down the Arroyo Seco on a hot Sunday afternoon to see Brazil defeat Italy on penalty kicks to win the World Cup. It is July 10, 1999, and.... What?"

I had an answer to that: "I think L.A.'s record speaks for itself," I told Jones. "What we're going for is the soccer hat trick."

By the time the first game finally rolled around, the buildup had gone on so long, it was almost jarring to see the U.S. women stars out on the field at Giants Stadium. They'd done so many interviews, so many appearances drumming up interest, and had so much pressure on their shoulders given the high hopes they'd win the whole tournament, it looked at first as if the weight of that pressure was simply too much. Playing in front of 78,972 fans, again a record for a women's sporting event, the high-pitched cheers were deafening.

"You couldn't hear from one side of the field to the other," Mia Hamm said afterward. "This is what we always dreamed a World Cup should be. To see the emotion, I can't tell you how proud it makes you feel."

Denmark had the early jump, making the host Americans look flat-footed by comparison. "Denmark drilled a shot across the goal mouth in the second minute and the American goalkeeper Briana Scurry, still woozy from a freight-train collision in front of the net, smothered another ball in the 15th minute," Jeré Longman wrote in the *New York Times*. "The Danes were winning balls in the air at midfield and the American defense found itself in unaccustomed retreat. On attack, passes were being made too soon or were erratically placed. The United States needed a play, a goal, a galvanizing moment, to settle itself, and Hamm provided it."

In the 17th minute, Mia Hamm showed why she would go on to be named FIFA World Player of the Year in 2001 and 2002. She turned the tide of the game dramatically by collecting a pass from Brandi Chastain in the penalty area with her right foot, then drilling a left-footed shot past the surprised Danish goalkeeper for a 1–0 lead—and her record 110th goal in international competition.

"Are you kidding me?" Hamm commented later. "I don't score goals like that."

Hamm paced the U.S. to a 3–0 win in that game, with Julie Foudy and Kris Lilly adding goals as well, and they were on their way, next rolling over Nigeria 7–1 and North Korea 3–0. "Every time she touched the ball, Hamm did something wonderful and the cheering started again," Filip Bondy wrote in the *New York Daily News.* "Hamm is the sort of player the men's team doesn't have, somebody who can finish what she starts."

Once competition began it was magical. We caught lightening in a bottle. There were sold-out stadiums, brimming with excitement. Our team was awesome. Playing "the beautiful game" beautifully, and charming the media with their wonderful, intelligent, and articulate personalities. They were a perfect example of the importance of a team. If you were to look at the countries that have recently dominated the Men's World Cups, it was Germany, where most of the players were teammates at Bayern Munich; Spain, where most of the players were from Real Madrid and Barcelona; and France, where most of the players were graduates of the French national program at Clairefontaine. The core group of our '99 women's national team had been playing together under the tutelage of Anson Dorrance, Tony DiCicco, and Lauren Gregg since before the '91 World Cup: Michelle Akers, Joy Fawcett, Julie Foudy, Mia Hamm, Kris Lilly, and Carla Overbeck. They knew each other the way twin sisters know each other.

The U.S. match in the quarterfinal was played at Jack Kent Cooke Stadium in Landover, Maryland, attended by President Bill Clinton and First Lady Hillary Clinton, and had the air of an instant classic. "Never has women's soccer created such a stir in the United States as in the past two weeks, and last night the sport's surprising, movable feast arrived in the Washington area to another banner crowd and produced one the most riveting games of the Women's World Cup," the *Washington Post* wrote. "The likable and talented U.S. team, which is leading the recent surge of interest in the sport, overcame a crucial mistake and a strong showing by Germany for a 3–2 victory."

The crucial mistake was an early own goal by Brandi Chastain, after a breakdown in communication with goalkeeper Briana Scurry, but Chastain later scored to help fuel the U.S. comeback. Afterward, the president and first lady visited the U.S. locker room and posed for a group picture, as the team chanted, "Clinton! Clinton! Clinton!"

"He told us what an inspiration the team was, coming from behind," Julie Foudy said.

After all, he referred to himself as "The Comeback Kid."

The semifinal was on the Fourth of July at Stanford Stadium between U.S. and Brazil, as had been the case in '94. Again, there was a sellout crowd. Again, fans were joyous, singing, dancing, flag-waving, and face painted. The result, though, was different: USA 2, Brazil 0. (An interesting side note: one of the U.S. goals was scored by Cindy Parlow, who in 2020 would take over as president of U.S. Soccer and sign the historic equal pay agreement between the U.S. men's and women's national teams.)

The Final match remains to this day as one of the most memorable sporting events in history. It was the U.S. versus China on a steaming hot day before a sellout crowd of 90,185 fans at the Rose Bowl in Pasadena in a rematch of the '96 Olympic Final.

It was incredibly hard fought and ended in a scoreless draw, to be decided by a penalty shootout, perhaps the most dramatic way to end any sporting event. Along the way, the U.S. had lost Michelle Akers, for years the best player in the world. "The United States contained China in regulation time as the brave and aggressive old star, the 33-year-old Michelle Akers, dominated with her range and her will and her booming headers," George Vecsey wrote in the *New York Times*. "Akers, who has had how many surgeries ('I lost count') and suffers from chronic fatigue syndrome, went down after a collision at the goal line at the 90th minute and had to leave the game, and the United States barely hung on without her."

The first four Americans—Overbeck, Fawcett, Lilly, and Hamm—all converted their penalty kicks, and after Briana Scurry saved the fifth attempt by China (a save not without controversy, as she was accused of moving forward before the kick), Brandi Chastain stepped up with a chance to win it. Chastain, who in China in 1991 had pulled me out onto the dance floor (me!?) with a big smile to celebrate the U.S. women's victory in the first-ever World Cup, now calmly caught the ball and placed it down in preparation for her attempt. In one of the most iconic moments in sports history, captured on the front pages of newspapers throughout the world and the cover of *Sports Illustrated*, after netting the winning kick, Brandi celebrated exuberantly by running across the pitch and sliding on the grass after removing her uniform top, revealing her Nike sports bra and a "six pack" abdomen. What I'll always remember about that moment was the sheer exuberant joy of that big smile she flashed.

"I temporarily lost my mind," Chastain said afterward.

"Didn't we all?" columnist Bill Plaschke wrote in the *Los Angeles Times*. "Once again, they gave us the shirts off their backs," he wrote. "And what a marvelous and fitting gesture it was. Brandi Chastain ripping off her white jersey, throwing it into the air, then dancing into the arms of the largest crowd ever to watch a women's sports event. Once again, the U.S.

women's soccer team stripped athletics down to its barest passion. And once again, we cheered like we never thought we could cheer, for ponytailed and earringed wonders we never dreamed would be giants, in a world that is changing with every kick.... It was a triumph of character from a group of women who spent the last month carrying the hopes of all women's athletics on their thin shoulders, delightfully skipping under the weight."

It was a perfect moment, a perfect day, and in many ways a perfect tournament, all that we could have hoped for and more, but the immediate aftermath of the '99 World Cup triumph was spotty. The women planned a "Victory Tour" and began scheduling matches. U.S. Soccer had also been considering taking the team on an international tour and threatened litigation. To say things were testy is an understatement. My term as president of U.S. Soccer ended in 1998. I agreed not to run for another term with a promise from my successor, Dr. Bob Contiguglia, that I would continue to be in charge of the '99 Women's World Cup, which he honored.

As tensions between the women and the Federation escalated, at the request of the players, Dr. Bob asked me to try to mediate the dispute, which was also caught up in collective bargaining between the Federation and the women players. Ultimately an agreement was reached allowing the players to go on their Victory Tour with U.S. Soccer sponsors attached to the tour. But the deep antipathy between the players and U.S. Soccer remained for another 22 years.

"I look back, and I'm grateful Alan Rothenberg was the one in charge of U.S. Soccer in the 1990s," Julie Foudy says now. "We had our battles with U.S. Soccer, that goes without saying, but in Alan we had someone who was open-minded and flexible and willing to think for himself. You could talk to him. You could say: 'Look, this is why this matters. This is why this is important. Here is the big picture. This is what we see. Here is the vision. Maybe others don't see it, but it's there.' And Alan would hear us out. He would listen. He might not always have been fully on board with our requests or our vision. But often he would get it, he would understand, and then try and activate on that."

Julie and the others made a strong case—I'd have been a fool not to listen and listen closely.

"In the '90s, when we were fighting the Federation on contract stuff, demanding more equitable treatment, we would ask Alan to be in the room with us during negotiations because we knew he understood the potential," Julie continued. "He could understand that big picture. They didn't want to pay us what we were asking, which by today's standard was measly. But we were asking for equitable pay—and flash forward to today, the women's team pushed for equal pay and got it."

Feeling headstrong, the players decided the time was ripe to start a professional league, which they did: the Women's United Soccer Association (WUSA). They raised some money and received modest support from U.S. Soccer, but sadly the league was a financial disaster and folded after three years, losing an estimated $100 million. Interestingly, as it was being formed there was some discussion about a joint operation with MLS. The players were overconfident and feared that MLS, still struggling to get grounded, might not be beneficial to them. Looking back, I think it's clear that their decision to reject the opportunity to join with MLS may have saved MLS. Had the league suffered substantial additional losses from the women's league, it may have been the straw that broke MLS' back.

After a hiatus of several years, women's professional soccer tried again, this time with the full support of U.S. Soccer. Unfortunately, Women's Professional Soccer (WPS) also had a quick demise, lasting just three seasons, starting in 2009. Hopefully the third time is a charm. The National Women's Soccer League (NWSL) was launched in 2013 with major support from U.S. Soccer as well as private investors. It had modest success at best when in 2021 it was hit with major scandals involving alleged sexual harassment by coaches, known and tolerated by team owners and management. U.S. Soccer President Cindy Cone asked Marla Messing to step in and act as interim CEO to help stabilize the league, which she successfully did. Following two separate investigations, by the league and the players' association, a collective bargaining agreement was negotiated. League administration was totally overhauled, and new private investors were brought aboard. Stability was established with new, well-capitalized investors paying record prices for existing and expansion teams and new valuable media and sponsorship contracts. NWSL Commissioner Jessica Berman and the league itself received top honors at the *Sports Business Journal*'s 2024 annual awards event.

"We always said the potential was there, we could feel it," Julie remembers. "And yet our arguments were all anecdotal. We had no data to back it up. So, when we were able to pull it off, and we were able to attract those numbers, there was shared glee for sure. All those packed stadiums gave people a template. It gave other people the confidence that they could also pull this off, [that] they could do national footprints and think big and plan events on a large scale in big stadiums. If we could sell our sport the way we did in '99, others could sell big events as well. That really changed the landscape of sport for women, both nationally and internationally. It was crazy after that. From '99 on we were finally getting the recognition and support and impact that we had wanted for years. So much of what we had fought for wasn't about standing on the top of a podium, although of course as athletes that was vitally important to us. We had our eyes on bigger goals than winning."

The tag line for the '99 World Cup was "This is my game. This is my future. Watch me play." The team and the event lived up to that slogan. Attendance and TV ratings set records. The event is considered a watershed moment in women's sports. The attendance at the Final stood as a record for a women's sporting event until the fall of 2023, when it was broken by a University of Nebraska outdoor volleyball match.

"Alan stuck his neck out for women's soccer, and I'll always applaud him for that," Julie says now. "When he became president of U.S. Soccer in 1990, he could see the potential. He knew women's soccer would be big. And when he was organizing the 1999 Women's World Cup, he thought big. He insisted on large stadiums for that World Cup at a time when no one, least of all the old guard at FIFA, had any idea what kind of crowds to expect. Having Alan at the helm of soccer at that time was huge for us. Let's be blunt: there could have been a lot of different white guys in that position—it was always white guys in that job back then—who didn't really care about women's soccer and really didn't care what any of the players had to say about the future of our sport. Believe me, we had lived through that. So, for Alan to say, 'I hear you, I see you, I'm listening, I'm acting on it,' that was huge for us, and as we've seen, not just huge for us, but hugely transformational for the sport for a lot of women."

Marla Messing, talking to the *Washington Post* at the time, summed our hope to be, as Julie put it, "hugely transformational" over time. "We're not going to know the full legacy of the tournament until we're deep into the new millennium," Marla told the *Post*. "I firmly believe that registration numbers are going to go way up among girls and women this year and for years to come. Federations will continue to put resources behind their women's programs. This is going to fuel the growth of women's soccer all around the world."

Prescient!

CHAPTER 7

FIFA: THE GOOD, THE BAD, AND THE UGLY

1984 Olympics Soccer Commissioner Alan Rothenberg with '84 Olympics World Cup CEO Peter Ueberroth; record attendance for soccer matches led FIFA to grant the 1994 FIFA World Cup to the US. (Credit: Alan Rothenberg's collection)

Georgina Rothenberg meeting with Cuban President Fidel Castro to arrange a match between the L.A. Aztecs and the Cuban National Soccer Team at the Rose Bowl. (Credit: Alan Rothenberg's collection)

White House reception with President George H.W. Bush honoring the U.S. Women's National Team, champions of the 1991 FIFA Women's World Cup. (Credit: Alan Rothenberg's collection)

Alan Rothenberg with the GOAT, Pelé, at a gala in New York. (Rothenberg made Pelé send a check for $1,000, which he sent to all employees with the message: "If Pele pays, everyone pays; no complimentary tickets." His check was never cashed.) (Credit: Alan Rothenberg's collection)

Alan Rothenberg with legendary coach Bora Milutinović, celebrating a U.S. Men's National Team victory.

The 1994 Men's National World Cup Team with U.S. Soccer General Secretary Hank Steinbrecher and Alan Rothenberg.

Georgina Rothenberg talking with a Soviet tank driver outside the Kremlin during the attempted coup of Mikhail Gorbachev in 1991. (Credit: Alan Rothenberg's collection)

Former National Security Advisor and Secretary of State Henry Kissinger, Honorary Chairman of the 1994 FFA World Cup organizing committee, with Alan and Georgina Rothenberg.

President Bill Clinton with Alan and Georgina Rothenberg at White House State Dinner honoring the King of Morocco. (Credit: Alan Rothenberg's collection)

Diana Ross performing before the 1994 FIFA World Cup opening match in Chicago; she then missed an open net penalty kick.

Sunil Gulati, U.S. Soccer President after Alan Rothenberg and Alan Rothenberg enjoying a helicopter ride from a World Cup match in Boston to one in New York.

Former President George H.W. Bush (with then Senator John Kerry) and Alan Rothenberg at a World Cup match in Boston.

Brad Rothenberg at Nickerson Gardens in South Central Los Angeles as part of the Legacy Tour run by him.

Alan Rothenberg with Mexican fans celebrating Mexico's upset draw with ultimate World Cup finalist Italy in D.C.

Alexi Lalas and Alan Rothenberg with Metallica's James Hetfield and Lars Ulrich after a World Cup match.

Boxing Champion Oscar De La Hoya and Alan Rothenberg at the Soccer Fest in Los Angeles during the 1994 Finals week.

Frank and Barbara Sinatra with Pavarotti at The Three Tenors Concert at Dodger Stadium the night before the Final.

Tom Cruise, among many celebrities, at The Three Tenors Concert at Dodger Stadium the night before the Final.

There never was an actual Rick's Cafe as depicted in the movie *Casablanca* (it was a faux cafe produced in a Hollywood studio), but Kathy Kruger, pictured here, formed one and was joined at its opening in Casablanca by Alan Rothenberg. (Credit: Alan Rothenberg's collection)

WITH EXCITED ANTICIPATION I stood in the Rose Bowl press box looking down at the young boys playing soccer prior to the Los Angeles Wolves' opening match of the season. It was April 1968, and I was the 28-year-old general manager of a professional soccer team, never having played or coached the game and only having seen five games in my life at that point. The day before, I'd received a phone call from Hans Stierle, a German American from Torrance who in 1964 co-founded the American Youth Soccer Organization (AYSO) with nine teams. Stierle, who had been organizing youth soccer games for the Los Angeles Soccer Club, a team mostly of German immigrants, told me about his youth league and wondered if I'd like to have him bring boys to play pregame matches. I liked the idea right away. I knew the Lakers, long before the advent of the "Laker Girls" in the "Showtime" era, invited boys' teams on the court pregame and at halftime. It built fan interest, and since the boys (it was only boys at that time) all had friends and family, it added hundreds of spectators. It was a lifetime memory. Just ask my son Richie, whose team of

10-year-olds got to take the court before a Lakers game at the Forum in 1977.

"Great," I told Stierle. "Bring your teams."

As I was enjoying watching the boys play, I felt a tap on my shoulder. I turned to face a middle-aged man wearing a green blazer with a crest over the breast pocket with the logo of the United States Soccer Football Association, as it was called at the time.

"Get those boys off the field," he said.

I thought he was joking—or some kind of quack. Astonished, I asked who he was.

"John Best, and I am the soccer federation's regional director," he replied stiffly. "Those players are members of the American Youth Soccer Organization (AYSO), and they aren't affiliated with the federation. If you don't remove them from the field immediately, I will notify the federation, which in turn will notify FIFA, and the Wolves' certification will be revoked."

"You're kidding," I said.

Best, who I found out later had worked as a FIFA-certified referee for years, including at the 1948 Olympics in London, folded his arms and glared at me solemnly.

"I'm serious," he said. "Get them off the field immediately."

That was my introduction to the sometimes smug, petty, imperious governance of the U.S. Soccer Federation and the long powerful octopus arm of its parent, FIFA (pronounced "Feefa"), officially known as *Fédération Internationale de Football Association* in French, or International Association Football Federation in English, headquartered in Zurich, Switzerland. FIFA is the international governing body for the sport of soccer. Like the International Olympic Committee (IOC), it is a nonprofit entity that owns an asset of enormous value, the FIFA World Cup, whereas the IOC owns the asset of the Olympic Games. Both are intangible assets, simply intellectual property (IP), unique among huge multibillion-dollar enterprises in that they are not directly subject to any overseeing governmental authority. FIFA's membership consists of virtually every country throughout the world, each of which has a national football association. From a governing standpoint, each country has an equal vote, regardless of size, wealth, or prominence in the sport.

Prior to the 2015 "FIFA scandals," which broke wide open in May 2015 when seven FIFA officials were arrested on corruption charges at a Zurich hotel before the 65th FIFA Congress, operation of FIFA was overseen by a 24-member executive committee, whose membership was established in the FIFA bylaws. The committee, consisting of representation of FIFA's five continental confederations, was the classic old boys' club, dominated by members from UEFA (Union of European Football Associations), all of whom were men, of course, until one woman was added. (It still brings a smile to my face to think back on how shocked they must have been when, for one executive committee meeting in the 1990s, I brought my top 1994 organizing committee executives: two men and two women, two Jews and a Mormon. I doubt they'd ever seen women, Jews, *or* Mormons on an organizing committee before. Welcome to America!)

Following the furor over the FIFA scandals of 2015, governance was revised to a 36-member executive council, which for the first time also included several women. The selection of the president of FIFA, as with the IOC, is by a vote of the membership at large, not the executive committee. Historically, leadership of the World Cup and Olympics Games, through FIFA and the IOC, had long been dominated by Europeans. Starting in 1974 with the election of João Havelange, a Brazilian, that European chokehold was removed. Shortly thereafter, the IOC elected a Spaniard, Barcelona's Juan Samaranch. Key to both events was the emerging money derived from television and marketing rights in the 1970s.

Horst Dassler, whose family owned Adidas, is sometimes called the father of sports sponsorship. He acquired exclusive media and marketing rights from both the IOC and FIFA—for the Olympic Games and World Cup—and negotiated huge fees from a handful of major international businesses, first among them Coca-Cola, still a major backer. With so much money involved and an unregulated government controlling entity, it made FIFA and the IOC easily subject to corruption. In the case of the IOC, that corruption was highlighted with bribes given for votes to select a host city and, in some cases, to select favored sponsors and vendors, and with FIFA, a host country. (As recently as the 2020 Tokyo Olympics, a former Dentsu managing executive, Haruyuki Takahashi—with whom I worked closely during the 1994 World Cup and formation of MLS—was indicted for bribing Tokyo organizing committee officials to obtain lucrative licensing rights.)

The assumption of corruption throughout international soccer was so rampant that when the bonus I received following the 1994 World Cup was publicly announced, inferences were immediately made. (When I assumed the role of chairman and CEO, I had declined to take a salary since at that time there was still a fear that the endeavor would be a financial disaster; instead, I asked the board to decide on a bonus, if any, depending on results.) At least half a dozen FIFA executive committee members asked me, "How much did you *really* receive?" They all assumed I must have actually been paid much more, under the table. Not in the United States!

The 1966 World Cup in England was one of the first major sports events telecast by satellite back to the United States, pulling in a surprisingly large audience of more than a million, and catching the attention of American sports entrepreneurs, who saw soccer's growth potential. Two separate groups formed to start professional soccer leagues in the United States, and each sought FIFA sanctioning, though under FIFA and U.S. Soccer regulations, only one could be selected. FIFA gave the nod to a group named the United Soccer Association (USA), one of its members being Jack Kent Cooke, my original sports mentor, and other founders included Lamar Hunt, owner of the Kansas City Chiefs. Hunt, son of billionaire oilman H.L. Hunt, considered the second-richest man in the world behind J. Paul Getty, also owned the Dallas Tornado.

The USA planned to start play in 1968, giving it time to get properly organized. The other group, the National Professional Soccer League (NPSL), rather than disappearing, secured a TV contract with CBS and decided to go ahead immediately in 1967 without sanctioning from FIFA and its national association, the U.S. Soccer Federation (then officially known as the U.S. Soccer Football Association). Thus, the NPSL was an "outlaw league" and couldn't host or participate in international competitions, nor could any of its players, who were thus effectively permanently banned from ever playing for their national team or any top club.

The USA was not about to let the NPSL get a one-year head start. Soon the decision was made to start play in the USA a year earlier than planned. With very little time to get up and running, USA used its official status and relationships with all the important soccer bodies in the world to populate its first year with teams loaned from elsewhere. Thus, the Los Angeles Wolves were actually the Wolverhampton Wanderers from the English First Division, repurposed. (Jack Kent Cooke, being a former Canadian, was an unabashed Anglophile, always boasting of his fine fashion, the bespoke creation of the world's finest tailors from London's Bond Street.) Other teams in the league included the Boston Rovers (Shamrock Rovers), Chicago Mustangs (Cagliari Calcio), Detroit Cougars (Glentoran of Belfast), and Washington Whips (Aberdeen of Scotland).

When the Wolves started their first season in Los Angeles, it was the first time I'd ever seen a soccer game in my life. During the offseason, the two leagues merged and became the North American Soccer League (NASL). Though only 28, I was a member of the group that negotiated the merger, terminated the NPSL commissioner's contract, and entered into a contract with Dick Walsh, a former Dodgers executive, to be commissioner of the merged league.

The Wolves now had to develop an actual team, and Cooke put me in charge. No more team on loan. No more Wolverhampton Wanderers. We bought some players from defunct teams of the NPSL, and then Jack dispatched me to England to find a coach and sign the rest of the players to fill out the roster. I was connected with the English Football Association—the FA, the most prestigious soccer association in the world. They in turn put me in touch with

West Bromwich Albion, chaired by Bert Millichip, later the head of the FA and a member of the House of Lords.

This was my first foreign trip. I didn't even have a passport until then. West Brom, I learned, was located in the northern industrial city of Birmingham, which according to a travel book I read was described as a "grungy industrial city." The guidebook went on, in snarky fashion, to explain that "a visitor to England would want to visit Birmingham as much as a visitor to the United States would want to go to Detroit," my hometown.

Interestingly, when Georgina and I boarded our flight to England, league co-founder Lamar Hunt was there as well, seated in coach. When we checked into the Dorchester Hotel, we could hear Hunt, just ahead of us, asking for a small single room. The son of one of the richest men in the world, flying coach and booking a small single. I decided I'd better get us a smaller room!

Hunt's wife, Norma, later told *Sports Illustrated*, "We're the world's outstanding tourist-class travelers." Hunt was famously low key. "In a crowd, Lamar Hunt stands out like wallpaper," Jack Olsen wrote in *Sports Illustrated*. "Headwaiters consistently overlook him, and maîtres d'hôtel ask him to 'step aside, please,' while they admit celebrities like the vice-mayor of Hasbrouck Heights [New Jersey] and the chief dog warden of Gilpin County, Colorado. Hunt shrugs, and stands quietly. He absolutely refuses to use his name or his prestige."

In 1959, at age 26, Lamar Hunt had been a principal founder of the American Football League, which later merged into the NFL in 1970. In the AFL's first year of operations, Hunt's team lost over $1 million. When H.L. Hunt was asked how long his son could keep losing a million dollars a year on a football team, he is supposed to have said, "Well at that rate, he'll be finished in 150 years."

Lamar was a true sportsman, proud of having made the Southern Methodist University football team, albeit as a third stringer, and also a true gentleman. Besides being instrumental to the formation of the AFL and NASL, he was also an owner of the Chicago Bulls, a founder of World Championship Tennis, a member of my 1994 World Cup board, and a founding investor in Major League Soccer.

Before I left for England, Jack Kent Cooke had allotted me a budget to spend for the coach and the players—the magnificent sum of $500,000—sending me off with the admonition, "Remember, I'm a proud man, and these players better be good."

I was introduced to a young coach, Ray Wood, a former goalkeeper who was a surviving member of the Manchester United team that had suffered a tragic air crash trying to take off from the Munich airport in 1958, killing eight of its players (and 23 people total) and seriously injuring several of its other players, coaches, and administrators. What was then left of the budget, I turned over to Wood to sign up the players, leaving him with the admonition from Mr. Cooke: "Remember, I'm a proud man, and these players better be good."

To say that the introduction of big-time soccer in the United States at that time was premature is an understatement. Attendance was paltry, and there was no large media money. I knew our days were numbered when, at a midseason game against Lamar Hunt's Dallas Tornado team, Mr. Cooke—the richest man I knew at the time—looked down at the field and pointed to Lamar and said, "If I were a rich man like him, I'd stick it out." Wealth is relative.

The league would have gone belly up that year if not for Hunt. At the end of the 1968 season, the league shrunk down to only five teams and was kept afloat largely due to Hunt's largess, much as Phil Anschutz did later to save MLS. A new commissioner, the Welshman Phil Woosnam, a former inside forward, was hired in 1969 and enthusiastically regrew the league. By the mid-'70s, led by the New York Cosmos, the league began to soar, only to crash and burn, as I described earlier.

After the 1968 season, Jack Kent Cooke folded the Wolves, and that was pretty much it for my involvement with FIFA and U.S. Soccer until Peter Ueberroth brought me on as soccer commissioner of the 1984 Olympics, except for my brief involvement as co-owner of the L.A. Aztecs, which I described in Chapter 1. My work on the Olympics led me to meet three people who became prominent in soccer, for good and evil, and significant in my life in soccer: Sepp Blatter of Switzerland, general secretary of FIFA from 1981 to 1998 and then its president; João Havelange, the Brazilian president of FIFA; and Chuck Blazer, then a grassroots officer of the U.S. Soccer Federation, who later became general secretary of CONCACAF and a member of the FIFA executive committee. Both Blatter and Blazer were ultimately central figures in the FIFA scandals, exposed by the U.S. Justice Department in 2015, as was Havelange, though by then he was no longer FIFA president.

Leading up to the 1984 Games, I had a chance to visit Zurich and attend an executive committee meeting, where I was introduced to the beautiful autocracy of FIFA governance.

Havelange, imperiously presiding, spoke in French in deep, mellifluous voice, and a row of translators in the back of the room gave "instant" translation to members through earphones. However, there was a slight delay, and by the time anyone had heard the translation of "Any questions?" into their language, Havelange had already moved on to the next agenda item and could hardly be interrupted midsentence. Intimidating as it was to question Havelange's pronouncements, there was rarely any discussion, nor debate. Everything had been decided beforehand. It made it even more daunting to have to ask to have a prior matter reopened after it had already been approved.

My next (very telling) introduction to the money-driven politics of FIFA came when I attended my first Congress, at which Havelange was standing for reelection. While at the time FIFA did not remotely have the kind of money to distribute to its members it later would, even then they distributed money to every national association, supposedly granted to help develop soccer infrastructure and build the sport in the respective countries. To rich European soccer associations, the money was relatively insignificant, but to many countries in Africa and Asia and the Central American and Caribbean members of CONCACAF, as well as to some South American countries, the money was meaningful. As each member nation's delegate (almost always the president of the national association) was about to enter the stage where the balloting was taking place (there was no electronic voting yet), they were greeted by Blatter and Havelange and given an envelope with their distribution *in cash.* Your guess is as good as mine how much of that distribution made its way to the coffers of the national association and how much was pocketed by the association's president. (Notwithstanding the prevalence of electronic banking, the raw payment in cash stuffed into envelopes was still used by Mohammed bin Hammam in 2011 to bribe the members of the Caribbean Football Union in his quest for their vote for his presidential candidacy, ultimately leading to the 2015 FIFA scandals.)

When the 1984 Olympics were over, many in FIFA were impressed with the success of soccer in those Summer Games and were ready to bring the World Cup to the United States. Clearly at that time the U.S. Soccer Federation did not have the capability to organize a World Cup. As previously mentioned, that was my view, and it was the view of Blatter and FIFA. I had some discussions with Blatter about bypassing the U.S. Soccer Federation and organizing the World Cup with an independent, nonprofit entity. No question, he was tempted. It would have been easier in some ways. But the precedent would have been toxic. He risked undermining the whole FIFA governing structure if he went around a national association. So, FIFA proceeded with awarding the World Cup to the U.S. Soccer Federation. I had no involvement until, as described previously, dissatisfied with the status of preparation, they maneuvered in 1990 to get me elected president of U.S. Soccer.

FIFA's involvement in my hotly contested reelection in 1994 was even more direct, including President Havelange in attendance sporting a "Rothenberg for President" pin. That election was an example of the problems plaguing the governance of USSF. The election was barely a month after the 1994 World Cup. You would think that after such a hugely successful World Cup, the substantial upgrading of USSF's management, and the outstanding showing by the U.S. men's national team, I would have been reelected by acclamation with no opposition. But no. Just as the grassroots had abandoned Werner Fricker, notwithstanding the fact that he had brought the World Cup to the United States and presided over the national team's first World Cup appearance in 40 years, so too was I vigorously opposed. To the grassroots, I was still the "outsider" who had "kidnapped" their federation. To a would-be new professional league, I was the competitor who was behind MLS, and I got caught in the "shoe wars" between Adidas and Nike, one of which was backing the other league and the other MLS. My enemies accused me of having a conflict of interest; "No," I said, "it's a confluence of interest."

It took two votes. On the first vote, in a San Diego hotel ballroom, I pulled in 48.8 percent of the vote, just shy of the 50.1 percent I needed to win, and my main challenger, USSF treasurer Richard Groff, had 46.9 percent. It was tense. During a break before the second vote, U.S. coach Bora Milutinović told the *Los Angeles Times*, "Somebody told me that penalty kicks were bad. This is worse."

I prevailed by only the slightest of margins when a third candidate, Hank des Bordes from Louisiana, dropped out and supported me before the third vote, and I ended up with 53.4 percent. Later, in litigation involving an allegation that I had strong-armed des Bordes into receiving support, under oath he shot that down. In the deepest drawl, this burly Cajun testified, "I'm a United States Marine. I landed in Vietnam on the day of the Tet Offensive. You think I'm afraid of Alan Rothenberg? Are you out of your mind?"

The press noted FIFA's strong involvement on my behalf. "Havelange's unprecedented attendance here has angered some delegates who resent FIFA's interference in the election," the

L.A. Times reported. "At a banquet Friday night, Havelange spoke for several minutes and lavished praise on Rothenberg, mentioning him by name some 16 times. On an evening that was meant to celebrate the sport of soccer in the United States, Havelange's nomination speech seemed out of place. Even Rothenberg admitted that Havelange's dinner speech lacked subtlety and ran the risk of backfiring—USSF delegates might not have appreciated an international body meddling in the internal politics of a member federation."

It's true. I told the *Times*: "It was a little heavier handed than I would have written it. I was cringing."

My election in 1990 began a period of my deep involvement with FIFA at various times as a member of the FIFA World Cup organizing committee, the FIFA Women's World Cup committee, and the FIFA ethics committee (an oxymoron if there ever was one); as head of the inspection committee for the 2006 World Cup; and later retained by Morocco to organize their bid for the 2010 World Cup, a bid they lost due to a bribe later revealed by the 2015 U.S. criminal action alleged to have been engineered by Sepp Blatter between South Africa and Jack Warner, the president of CONCACAF.

Currently my involvement with FIFA is through my company, Playfly Premier Partnerships, representing a number of the cities that bid to and will host the 2026 World Cup. Our president, John Kristick, leads that effort, as well as working with CONMEBOL, the Premier League, and other organizations in the FIFA international web. Also personally, because of my long-standing relationship going back to 1994 with Jaime Byrom, longtime executive chairman of BEYOND Hospitality and its predecessor, MATCH hospitality, I was a partner in the marketing of hospitality packages in Qatar and

Australia/New Zealand, and was deeply involved with the 2025 and 2029 FIFA Club World Championships as well as accommodations and other activities during the 2026 FIFA World Cup. Additionally, our U.S. Soccer Foundation is implementing the legacy programs for many of the host cities.

Since USSF is part of CONCACAF, as president of USSF I was also part of the CONCACAF board. Interestingly, at that time CONCACAF was entitled to three seats on the 24-member FIFA executive committee, one from North America, one from Central America, and one from the Caribbean. They were voted on by the total membership of CONCACAF, not by the respective regions. At that time Jack Warner from Trinidad and Tobago, president of CONCACAF, effectively controlled all 30 of the Caribbean nations and thus completely controlled CONCACAF.

In 1997, when Guillermo Cañedo of Mexico died, a *New York Times* headline declared that his DEATH SHAKES UP SOCCER. Cañedo, former president of Atlético Zacatepec, was senior vice president of FIFA and longtime North American member of the executive committee. His death, Rob Hughes wrote in the *Times*, "deprives world soccer of its second most influential administrator."

Cañedo's death would surely lead to a power struggle. Havelange and Blatter approached me and asked me to fill his seat. Jack Warner had other plans. He wanted his general secretary and henchman, Chuck Blazer, in that seat and told Havelange and Blatter as much. At the time, FIFA's bylaws forbade any paid employee of a member organization from serving on the executive committee. Clearly, as the general secretary of CONCACAF, Blazer was ineligible. But given that Warner controlled the biggest single bloc of votes at any FIFA Congress and would control three of 24 executive committee seats, Blatter and Havelange looked the other way, totally violating their own bylaws, and allowed the appointment of Blazer. They briefly discussed a possible legal action but instead their political instincts carried the day.

As it turned out, up until the scandal that erupted in 2015, Blazer was an excellent executive committee member, maybe the smartest in the room. He was, in fairness, enormously helpful to Major League Soccer and U.S. Soccer. FIFA was on the verge of assigning U.S. TV rights to the 2006 World Cup directly to a network, NBC. Blazer blocked it, thereby allowing the joint venture of MLS, U.S. Soccer, and ESPN to obtain the rights, a move that was financially crucial to U.S. Soccer and MLS, which was still struggling financially.

Then came the scandal, and Blazer was removed. In May 2015, the U.S. Justice Department filed a criminal action in which five FIFA executive committee members were accused of accepting bribes in connection with the granting of the World Cup rights to Russia for 2018 and Qatar for 2022. Also indicted was Jack Warner for having accepted a bribe to vote for South Africa to host the 2010 World Cup, rather than Morocco, to which he had previously committed. Several people were also indicted who were not on the executive committee for paying and accepting bribes for TV and marketing rights in CONCACAF and the South American Football Confederation (CONMEBOL). Many of those indicted were men I had known and dealt with over the years. There had been constant rumors of bribes swirling around them, but they had never before been exposed.

While I was not in any way part of the FIFA scandals, I was directly affected by the disclosures. After having met Moroccan soccer and governmental officials during my inspection for 2006, they retained me to assist in their bid to host the 2010 World Cup. Before accepting the invitation, I met with Blatter, with whom I enjoyed an excellent relationship. I knew Blatter wanted South Africa to be selected, and I told him I would not accept the Morocco assignment if he objected. Looking back, he undoubtedly thought the selection of South Africa was a foregone conclusion. So, he blessed my assignment.

Over the ensuing two years, I assembled a top-notch team, put together an outstanding bid, and took the Moroccan officials around to FIFA events to meet with FIFA executive committee members. We had done so well in making a case for Morocco that when I had gone to bed the night before the vote, I was confident that Morocco would prevail over South Africa. I was stunned the next morning when the vote turned out to be for South Africa.

Two votes had flipped: Jack Warner and the representative from Costa Rica, whose vote Warner controlled. The criminal action years later disclosed that Warner had received the bribe that Blatter had engineered. At the time, I didn't know the details on what had happened, but I knew something was amiss. And for me it was doubly disappointing. I'd been looking forward to a Morocco World Cup and my contract to help the Moroccans organizing their World Cup was, of course, lost. On the bright side, I was untainted, an innocent bystander.

An interesting sidenote: While I was representing Morocco, a woman who worked in the State Department, Kathy Kriger, was extraordinarily helpful. She would not accept any gifts or gratuities I offered her. "I'm just doing my job," she said. As my work wound up, Kathy approached me. "You know that in the famous movie *Casablanca* there never really was a Rick's Café in Morocco?" she asked me. "It was a fictitious invention for the movie, which was made entirely in studios in Burbank, California." She had my interest! *Casablanca* is one of my favorite movies, along with *The Godfather*. "I have created an entity, The Usual Suspects, and I will be building a restaurant in Casablanca that will be a replica of the Rick's Café in the movie and I'm raising money for the enterprise." I was happy to help. I made an investment, which I considered a gift in lieu of what she had turned down. Amazingly, 20 years later Rick's Café in Casablanca is open and thriving, and I am a minority owner. Sadly, Kathy suffered a stroke and died in 2018—KATHY KRIGER, "MADAME RICK" AT HER CASABLANCA CAFÉ, IS DEAD AT 72 was the headline on her *New York Times* obituary—but at least she lived long enough to enjoy seeing Rick's Café in full bloom, including a pianist, Issam—not Sam—in the middle of the restaurant.

Interestingly, the facts surrounding the FIFA scandal all were revealed because of Chuck Blazer and the confluence of two otherwise unrelated events. Chuck was appalled at the openness of Bin Hammam's attempted bribery of the Caribbean members and had a falling out with Jack Warner as a result. Warner and Blazer had been so close, many of us privately called them the "Pirates of the Caribbean," little knowing how accurate that designation was.

Concurrently, Blazer was confronted by the FBI for failure to file or pay taxes for some 10 years. Unfathomable! All over the United States, people circle April 15 on their calendars and sweat out the tax deadline, not wanting to be an hour late, rushing down to the post office to get a postmark before midnight. Blazer blew off taxes for a good decade. It's an especially unbelievable lapse since Blazer was very smart and was legitimately—although highly criticized for it—making a huge amount of money as general secretary of CONCACAF. This was all publicly known.

When Blazer became the general secretary, CONCACAF was penniless. It had no regional tournament and no sponsors other than endemic in-kind sponsors. Blazer agreed to be compensated with 10 percent of whatever marketing money was brought in. He created the Gold Cup regional championship and otherwise generated tens of millions in licensing, sponsorship, and marketing money. There was no need to cheat, let alone fail to file or pay taxes. Blazer could afford to pay his fair share. But he was a tax cheat.

Caught red-handed, Blazer agreed to work for the Justice Department as it investigated the activities that culminated with the 2015 raid of FIFA's headquarters. He agreed to carry a wire. More accurately, he agreed to have a chip put in his key ring and proceeded to gather a treasure trove of information about nefarious acts for the Justice Department by having casual conversations with his colleagues.

Among the targets the FBI wanted Blazer to approach, as it turned out, was none other than me. Because I had been deeply involved in the 2010 bidding, working for Morocco, and apparently there were rumors that Morocco, too, had been involved in some questionable payments, the FBI wanted Blazer to get information from me. Chuck and I had always had a very cordial relationship, although I was always wary of him and Jack Warner and their boundless avarice. Hence the name "Pirates of the Caribbean."

One example: to court his favor, Havelange had arranged for a huge payment for a CONCACAF "center of excellence" to be built in Jack Warner's home country of Trinidad and Tobago but supposedly available for all of CONCACAF. Indeed, it was carried on CONCACAF's books as an asset. Only later, when all the exposures came, was it disclosed that it had always been in Jack Warner's name, undoubtedly known to Blazer, who maintained all the books and records of CONCACAF.

When Chuck would come to L.A., he would often ask Georgina and me to dinner. Before the London Olympics in the summer of 2012, he called to set up a lunch together while there. As it turned out, I didn't go to London. I found out later his intention was to record me for the Justice Department, hoping for something incriminating. Interestingly, in the book *Red Card: How the U.S. Blew the Whistle on the World's Biggest Sports Scandal* exposing Blazer's activities, author Ken Bensinger said I'd refused to meet with Chuck. Sure, it made me look good, but truthfully, I had no idea what Chuck was up to and found there to be nothing unusual about meeting him for lunch.

Many months later, he came to L.A. again and invited just me to dinner this time, during which, while not letting me know he was working undercover for the FBI, he started telling me everything that had happened surrounding the 2010 vote. Though I had my own assumptions and there was lots of talk, it was the first time I'd heard definitively that Blatter had arranged to have FIFA give South Africa "an advance on its legacy program," which was then paid to Warner to secure his and Costa Rica's vote. In retrospect, I realize Chuck was trying to draw me out regarding any wrongdoing by Morocco. Fortunately, he couldn't because I was not aware of anything. I had no knowledge of any wrongdoing by Morocco—and still don't.

I later was visited at my home by two FBI agents who showed up unannounced and then was interviewed twice in

New York by the U.S. Attorney's office, still trying to get damaging information from me. It turned out that when Chuck and I were having dinner, the FBI was sitting at the next table, recording our entire conversation. "The goal of the meeting, which the agents had rehearsed with Blazer beforehand, was to talk about Morocco's failed bid for the 2010 World Cup," Bensinger wrote in *Red Card*. "Rothenberg had been a consultant for the North African country's bid team, which, according to Blazer, had attempted to bribe him and Warner for their votes. But when [the agents] reviewed the recording their cooperator had secretly made during the dinner, they were disappointed. Rothenberg had said nothing of particular interest." I sure am happy I had not done anything wrong and knew of nothing my client, Morocco, had done wrong.

Four years earlier, when I chaired the inspection group for the 2006 World Cup, the bidders were Brazil, England, Germany, Morocco, and South Africa. I spent one week in each of the countries and was shown the best that each country had to offer. Among others, in South Africa I spent time with Nelson Mandela, who asked me to "say hello to Bill." I visited Soweto, which contains the only street in the world on which two Nobel Peace Prize winners lived, Nelson Mandela and Bishop Desmond Tutu. In England, I met Prince Charles (now King), who was very formal, but was a gracious host at a lunch he gave at Highgrove. I was also treated with a banquet at Windsor Castle, where I brought the house down with the following friendly barb.

"One of our tasks was to test the indigenous support for soccer in each country," I said. "Yesterday, I attended a classic London derby, Arsenal versus Chelsea, at Stamford Bridge. There I saw one team coached by an Italian play another team coached by a Frenchman with 22 players on the pitch, none of whom were English. Some indigenous support."

In Morocco, I met with the young king and visited two of his magnificent castles and met with government and federation officials, which led to my subsequent representation of Morocco in its bid to host the 2010 World Cup. In Germany, I was shepherded around by "The Kaiser," Franz Beckenbauer, considered by most Germans to be their best soccer player ever, and more popular at that time than anyone in Germany, including the chancellor, Gerhard Schröder, whom I also met. Beckenbauer's reputation was subsequently tarnished somewhat, as he was caught up in some of the suspicious activities surrounding Germany's 2006 World Cup when Swiss investigators targeted him and three other Germans working with the organizing committee, although no final legal action was ever concluded against him.

Actually, for one day, Franz Beckenbauer had been the putative U.S. men's national team coach. One month after I was elected president of U.S. Soccer, I met with Beckenbauer, and he agreed to coach our men's national team. We shook hands on it and had a deal. This was just after Beckenbauer had coached West Germany to victory in the 1990 World Cup, so we knew there would be other suitors. Olympique de Marseille, owned by Robert Louis-Dreyfus (cousin of *Seinfeld* actress Julia Louis-Dreyfus), had been after Beckenbauer. Sure enough, the day after "The Kaiser" and I shook hands, Beckenbauer reached a deal with Marseille, though he would not last the season.

In Brazil, I met with President Fernando Cardoso and was shown the beauty of that vast country and also experienced a match at the huge famous Maracanã Stadium, which had a capacity of more than 173,000 but was then quite dilapidated. (It was subsequently renovated extensively for the 2014 World Cup.)

I knew that Sepp Blatter really wanted South Africa to host the 2006 World Cup, hoping it would put him in the running for a Nobel Peace Prize (he even admitted later to having met with representatives of the Nobel committee, hoping to win the prize for FIFA to elevate soccer). Although the South African bid that year was credible, it would have been unrealistic to rank them above Germany, or, in the eyes of many, England and Brazil. So, I adapted a rating system we had used in California when evaluating prospective judges: well qualified, qualified, and unqualified. The latter rating was easy for Morocco, since at that time they had no well-thought-out plan, and hardly any stadiums; instead, we were taken to sandy areas under a tent, served Moroccan tea, and shown artistic renderings of stadiums. It was all far too vague, with assurances that if Morocco were selected, that was where a stadium would be built, but not supported with any architectural, engineering, or financial plans.

To the anger and chagrin of Brazil and England, I only ranked them "qualified," not "well qualified." In Brazil's case, they were completely disorganized and hadn't complied with some of the technical requirements and basic requisite government guarantees. England also failed to respond in detail to many of the technical requirements. Their attitude seemed to be: *Why do we have to answer all these silly questions? We're England! We invented the game, and we're commercially the most successful soccer country, so obviously we can host a World Cup.* They were right, of course. Obviously, they could. But the requirements were clear and not followed.

We then ranked Germany and South Africa both "well qualified." They had dotted every i and crossed every t. Though it seemed clear that Germany was more ready than South Africa, the ratings gave Blatter justification for pushing for South Africa. Going into the vote it looked like the executive committee would be evenly split, 12 each for Germany and South Africa. Under the rules, Blatter owned the tie-breaking vote and would, in that scenario, get his wish to have South Africa host.

In the end, in what later was disclosed as another unscrupulous if not illegal act, Germany won when the representative from New Zealand, Charlie Dempsey, whose confederation had directed him to vote for South Africa, walked out of the room before the vote, enabling Germany to prevail 12–11 and depriving Blatter of the opportunity to use his tiebreaking vote.

Later, of course, South Africa did get to host in 2010 and Brazil in 2014. England, as it has been since 1966, will continue to be shut out in the foreseeable future. There were rampant rumors of wrongdoing in the granting of the 2018 World Cup to Russia and of 2022 to Qatar. England was bypassed again, as was the United States, actions that bewildered the world and led to many stories of vote-swapping and payoffs and indeed became the subject of bribery allegations in the Justice Department's suit.

One thing that stands out regarding the United States in bidding for World Cups and the Olympics is that our government is reluctant to get seriously involved in support of bids. Indeed, the 2026 FIFA Congress before the opening World Cup match will be in Mexico City rather than the United States, in part because of the United States' rigid visa rules, which wouldn't be waived for the event. Beyond giving its blessing, we don't lobby at high diplomatic levels. We don't broker legitimate business deals. How could our great allies France and Germany have voted for Qatar rather than us?

Did all the expensive construction work and shipping that Qatar contracted for with French and German companies have any impact? Is the story true that the emir of Qatar promised French President Nicolas Sarkozy that if France voted for their bid, Qatar would rescue the heavily indebted—and storied—Paris Saint-Germain team, the most revered in France (and Sarkozy's favorite), from bankruptcy? Note who owns PSG today and what company's name (Qatar Airways) is on the team jersey. No way to know, but one thing is certain: the U.S. in contrast never gets into extracurricular but completely legal dealing. The Olympics and World Cups continue to come to the United States not because of aggressive activity by our government, but because of our state-of-the-art existing infrastructure and the wealth of our country. In the words of MLS commissioner Don Garber, "There's no question now that America has become the ATM for the soccer world." Based on the meeting between FIFA President Infantino and U.S. President Trump, and the creation of a Trump-led World Cup Task Force, perhaps we're seeing a change.

When FIFA executive committees and World Cup committees would convene, they would hold meetings throughout the world, allowing me to visit many iconic international venues, as often as possible bringing Georgina with me. We were given the opportunity to enjoy unique experiences. I had an audience with the Pope when we were meeting in Rome. The brother of Italy's FIFA executive committee member was general counsel of the Vatican and arranged it. The group of us waited for a long time as the then very frail Pope was napping. Eventually he was escorted into the room with attendants on either arm holding him up. It was quite amazing to see the coarse, hard, and tough FIFA men break down in tears as they paraded by the Pope and kissed his ring. I was moved by the incredibly deep-seated faith I witnessed.

In Seoul, the FIFA women were taken on a tour of the Hyundai factory. Hyundai was owned by the family of Chung Mong-joon, who was a FIFA executive committee member. At the factory in 2002, Georgina saw cars being produced totally robotically. That's how advanced Hyundai was that long ago.

We had an interesting experience in Tokyo. We attended a luncheon with the chairman of Toyota, who was accompanied by his wife. During the luncheon, she said nothing despite many attempts to engage her in conversation. We assumed she didn't speak or understand English. Toward the end of the luncheon, I asked the chairman where his U.S. plants were located. He rattled off the names of six of the seven cities but couldn't remember the seventh, at which point his wife gave him a jab in the ribs and stage whispered, "Louisville." After lunch we were talking to Naoko, a woman educated in the United States whom Dentsu had seconded to us through the World Cup and with whom we had forged a close friendship. In a different culture and a different time, she would have been an executive at Dentsu, not our escort.

"I bet his wife is going to hear from the chairman for embarrassing him," I said.

"No, just the opposite," Naoko said. "He's going to hear from her, berating him for not remembering his business."

As the world of soccer has become increasingly lucrative, long-simmering rivalries have become more problematic. UEFA has always felt more important than FIFA. They have almost all the major soccer countries in their membership. They believe their championship is more important than the World Cup, which they believe is diminished because it includes many lesser teams. At the same time, the major European clubs believe they're more important than either UEFA or the World Cup. They have the best players under contract, regardless of nationality. Furthermore, they're paying the players huge salaries, whereas when those same players appear for their national team they receive a fraction of that compensation, and their valuable assets, their star players, are risking injury while not playing for their club. They've attempted to create a "super league." Initial efforts were thwarted by serious objections from FIFA, UEFA, and European national associations as well as a fan uprising. However, a recent ruling by the European Union's highest court has opened the door for a potential super league and a new battle will undoubtedly emerge. Similarly, U.S. Soccer has prohibited other countries' official league matches in the United States, which has been challenged in U.S. courts. It seems that inevitably many of the existing barriers will be loosened and significant changes in the world soccer landscape will occur, undoubtedly benefiting soccer fans, professional clubs, and leagues but causing disruption within the international soccer governing structures. Restructuring and disruption, not unlike what we're observing in U.S. intercollegiate athletics due to court decisions against the NCAA, are likely to occur.

I previously mentioned ISL. After Horst Dassler died in 1987, his son-in-law Christoph Malms succeeded him and a few years later terminated Jürgen Lenz and Klaus Hempel, who had been the sales and marketing heads of ISL. They promptly defected to UEFA and led the creation of the Champions League, which now rivals both the UEFA championship and the World Cup in popularity.

In May 2015, the U.S. Justice Department swooped into Zurich and arrested FIFA officials, charging them with bribery, corruption, RICO violations, and wire fraud. To say it was like an earthquake had hit FIFA is an understatement. Initially it was met with outrage by those arrested as well as many of their countries.

How could the U.S. arrest people on foreign soil?

How could transactions that didn't take place in the United States be a crime prosecutable in the United States?

And isn't the United States hypocritical? Business in the United States is conducted similarly, yet it's considered perfectly legal.

First, there is no question that the cash payment to Jack Warner to "buy" his vote is a crime, everywhere in the world.

Second, the legal basis for jurisdiction in the United States for transactions taking place offshore is based on the mechanisms of international currency transfers. With the U.S. dollar the dominant currency in the world, the use of the U.S. Federal Reserve wire transfer system is utilized in most transactions. Thus, for legal purposes, the transactions had occurred in the United States.

Third, the claim of hypocrisy is not totally without merit. Excluding the direct bribe of Warner and others, the other underlying transactions targeted payments made to insiders to deliver valuable marketing and television contracts. The claim was that to receive permission to do business in the United States, you have to hire the right connected lawyers and lobbyists, who direct you to make contributions to the correct elected officials so that you will receive the desired approval, which is analogous to the transactions that were the basis of the criminal charges.

Notwithstanding the foregoing, the Department of Justice has received successful guilty pleas from many FIFA, CONCACAF, and CONMEBOL members. A number of FIFA Executive Committee members were removed. Some, including Havelange, have died. Sepp Blatter resigned, and FIFA underwent a thorough government reorganization. Unfortunately, to date Jack Warner remains in Trinidad and Tobago; the United States has not been able to extradite him.

While I have discussed some of the negative aspects of FIFA, there have been some fantastic developments that occurred under the leadership of Havelange and Blatter. Always recognized as the world's most popular game, soccer at the highest level had not been exposed to the whole world. From its inception in 1930 to 1970, the World Cup had only been hosted in Western Europe and South America. Mexico was chosen to host in 1970, the first World Cup in North America, but then it was back to Europe and South America: West Germany in 1974, Argentina in 1978, and Spain in 1982. Then in 1986 Colombia was awarded the World Cup, but ended up giving up its bid, unable to meet the criteria for preparation, and Mexico again hosted.

Under the Havelange and Blatter leadership, the World Cup was truly taken to the world. First, of course, was the United States in 1994, then South Korea–Japan in 2002. It had been Havelange's commitment to bring the World Cup to Japan, home country of several FIFA sponsors and FIFA's partner Dentsu. At virtually the last minute Seoul, led by Chung Mong-joon, the billionaire member of the Hyundai family, began to raise steam as a rival. To avoid the loss of prestige if South Korea prevailed over Japan, Havelange arranged the joint effort. An unintended benefit was proving that a World

Cup could be co-hosted, even by two countries with a long-standing antipathy toward each other. That opened the door for many more countries to bid. As the event becomes larger and larger, there will be fewer countries capable of hosting a World Cup on their own, so joint bids are now welcome.

After opening North America and Asia, FIFA then went to Africa for the 2010 World Cup, in South Africa, and soon Morocco in north Africa will co-host a World Cup. From there FIFA went to eastern Europe, Russia, for the first time and lastly, by going to Qatar in 2022, they opened the Middle East.

It truly now is a *World Cup*! Kudos to the much-maligned Sepp Blatter and João Havelange. Much as both have been the subject of accusations of wrongdoing, until now neither has been convicted of any crime. Havelange was accused by the DOJ, but died before any action was taken. Blatter was charged in Switzerland but acquitted. He was banned by FIFA, but that was an offshoot of an alleged unauthorized contract between FIFA and UEFA president Michel Platini, not part of the "FIFA scandals." In my experience and observation of Blatter, my conclusion is that his goal was obtaining and retaining power. His financial wrongs, if any, were in directing FIFA money to achieve his objectives, not necessarily to line his pockets, and undoubtedly looking the other way when nefarious activities were occurring.

My conclusion: Warts and all, FIFA and the past leadership I have dealt with since 1968 have been a force for good in increasing the participation and support for the game of soccer worldwide, while putting an unfortunate indelible stain on FIFA itself.

As loose as FIFA leadership was regarding financial issues, they were aggressive in protecting the integrity and good image of the game. They rejected ideas that were set forth before 1994: no replay in the event of a tie for fear of allegations of a "fix," since FIFA would have to reserve the TV time in advance; no high-priced tickets for the Final (leading to our creation of the premium packages) to protect the public; no halftime show on the field at the Final for fear of damaging the turf; insistence on grass, not artificial turf; rejecting in-stadium Jumbotron replays of close calls to protect referees from criticism; rejecting the idea of dividing the games into quarters in order to give players a rest and discourage players pacing themselves and allowing coaches time to revise tactics because they'd be charged with being motivated by the desire to sell more TV time.

Before 2002, Ladbrokes, a then dominant gaming company in England, proposed to sponsor the World Cup, paying for it by giving FIFA a generous percentage of the handle. FIFA feared being accused of participating in fixed matches, even though they would be compensated based on the total amount of money being bet without regard to who won or lost. The money that would have come to FIFA from that sponsorship in the ensuing six World Cups would have been in the hundreds of millions of dollars. Right or wrong, the decisions to forgo were taken to protect the image of the integrity of the game and concern for the fans.

As a result of the 2015 scandal, FIFA has revised its governance and established new leadership. There are more countries represented on the executive council, including women council members. The expansion of the World Cup has accelerated. More countries are participating with more joint hosting (United States, Canada, and Mexico in 2026; multiple countries and continents in the 2030 centennial World Cup, including Uruguay, Paraguay, Argentina, Morocco, Portugal, and Spain; Saudi Arabia in 2034; no doubt China at some point). We've seen aggressive support for an expanded world club championship, additional support for the women's game, and a Women's World Cup coming back to the United States in 2031.

Most important, so far, no hint of corruption under the aggressive leadership of its president, Gianni Infantino!

The "beautiful game" is better than ever.

CHAPTER 8

WOMEN'S WORLD CUP 2023: A BLIP OR THE END OF A DYNASTY?

THE U.S. WOMEN'S NATIONAL TEAM headed into the 2023 Women's World Cup in Australia and New Zealand with history so close at hand, they could almost taste it. No team—in men's or women's soccer—had ever pulled off the elusive three-peat, winning three consecutive World Cups, and if ever there were a team with the swagger and confidence to do it, the American women's team sure seemed to be a strong candidate. It wasn't just that this core group of players had won the two previous World Cups; they'd done it in style, unforgettably, winning 5–2 over Japan to win the 2015 World Cup, earning a ticker tape parade through New York City—the first ever for a women's sports team—and a White House visit with President Obama. Four years later, carried by flamboyant star Megan Rapinoe, who was essentially being heckled throughout the tournament by President Donald Trump, the U.S. women made it back to the Final and defeated the Netherlands 2–0 to win their second in a row.

That victory had a deeper cultural importance we'd seen building for years. Women's soccer had broken through beyond what any of us who were there when the sport was taking its first baby steps ever imagined. As a *New Yorker* headline put it following the victory, THE U.S. WOMEN'S TEAM WINS AND LEAVES THE STAGE AS A NEW KIND OF AMERICAN ROLE MODEL. "During the tournament, Rapinoe has become more than a star athlete," Louisa Thomas wrote in the accompanying article. "She has become a kind of beacon, the Statue of Liberty reimagined as a purple-haired social activist with strong feet and a flair for free kicks."

Dominance on the pitch is one thing, and in the 2019 Women's World Cup the U.S. team never trailed, leading the tournament in both shots per game and goals per game. They found a way to score within the first 12 minutes of every game up until the Final. None of that, however, quite explained the furor over the team back home, any more than the sheet music to "Penny Lane" explained Beatlemania.

"Some of the adulation—and, not incidentally, criticism—that the team has attracted, at home and abroad, has less to do with the stats and scorelines, and more to do with what the team represents: the United States of America," Thomas wrote. "As a group, the members of the national team are brash, idealistic, outspoken, thoughtful, disciplined, aware of their power and willing to use it, confident, and unapologetic. They have both inherited their claim to excellence and earned it, and they are unafraid to acknowledge their position. They are also, of course, women. Some of them are women of color. Some of them are gay. They are all underpaid and underappreciated—certainly by their international federation, FIFA, and arguably by their national one, U.S. Soccer, which they sued on the eve of the tournament. They see themselves as role models and revolutionaries, but they are also something more complicated to describe. They offer a new model on how to be an American citizen, one rooted at once in idealism and pragmatism. (It wasn't enough to be morally good; the players also knew they had to win.) By their existence and their conduct, they offer an alternative to the nationalism of men who claim a monopoly on the meaning of country and flag."

I'm not sure I quite agree with the use of "underappreciated" in any context as applied to the U.S. women's national team, but the overall analysis is both poetic and accurate—and conveys the massive weight of expectation that hung over these teams. That was a lot for any team to carry, a lot for any individuals to carry, and over the next few years it was clear they couldn't go on forever performing at such remarkably high levels under such intense pressure.

One story that broke after the 2019 World Cup concerned the departure of head coach Jill Ellis, one of only two coaches in the history of the World Cup, men or women, to win back-to-back World Cups, along with Vittorio Pozzo, who coached Italy to consecutive World Cup wins in 1934 and 1938. I'll repeat that: Only two soccer coaches in the history of the sport have pulled off that feat. The last time it happened was the 1930s, basically a century ago. No matter how easy Jill Ellis had at times made her job look, as if letting talent run loose on its own were a simple matter, if you've been on the inside, watching a national team deal with the pressures of preparation, you know how much happens out of public view that could easily have gone wrong.

Before Ellis started her successful run with the team, the players were asked what kind of coach they wanted, and team captain Christie Rampone told the AP: "A coach that would continue to grow this team. A coach who will have good leadership qualities, because there are so many successful people on this team."

As the AP explained, giving context circa October 2012: "Indeed, the women's team has come a long way from the days when they played, essentially, part-time, with only a few hundred people turning out for their games. The U.S. is on a first-name basis with Wambach, Hope Solo, and Alex Morgan, and they get the rock-star treatment pretty much everywhere they go. Almost 500 people showed up just to watch Friday's training session." Given the increasing demands players had on their time, with endorsements and media appearances, "the new coach will have to be strong enough to command accountability, on and off the field."

Ellis, in her quiet way, never flashy, seldom the center of attention, did indeed find a way to be a strong enough figure to command accountability, and her successor, Vlatko Andonovski, highly respected and well-liked by the players, never quite had the chance to match her record, or maybe events just dealt him a more difficult hand.

Leading up to the 2023 World Cup, the U.S. women were the favorites—not overwhelming favorites, but nonetheless favorites. Of nine experts Fox Sports asked to make predictions, five of nine predicted the U.S. women's team would win. "There's something about this team and making history, whether it's achieving equal pay or holding the record for the most World Cups," said journalist Laken Litman, author of *Strong Like a Woman: 100 Game-Changing Female Athletes*. "Winning three straight World Cup titles is unprecedented in both men's and women's soccer, but this squad has a chance to do it. And not with a super veteran group, either. Of the 23 players on the roster, 14 are playing in their first World

Cup. Yes, there are more threats this year, especially in teams like England, Germany, Spain, and Australia. But it would be foolish to think the USWNT won't find a way to win because that's what they do. Plus, the team has to send Megan Rapinoe off into retirement with another championship."

Then again, former USWNT star Carli Lloyd threw cold water on that feel-good scenario, accurately predicting Spain would win it all. "They disappointed at the 2019 World Cup by losing to the U.S. in the round of 16," she said. "Four years later, the women's game in Spain has grown, and this golden generation could finally be the one that lifts the trophy. But I also think France, Australia, USA, Germany, England, and Brazil could potentially contest for the trophy."

The U.S. women opened play on July 22 with a match against uncompetitive Vietnam, and won 3–0, which was not as good as it might sound. I thought the media criticism afterward was overblown, but the fact was, USA had so many scoring chances, they could easily have doubled their scoring output—and goals matter with goal differential sometimes deciding who advances and who doesn't. Lindsey Horan had a goal, but said afterward, "I could have scored maybe three or four more." Added Alex Morgan: "I definitely had a couple I should have put away, for sure." Out of 27 shots the team took, six were blocked and 13 were off target.

Next up was a match with the Netherlands, and the U.S. had to play well to come back to tie it 1–1. "When the United States was desperate for a spark," wrote the AP, "Lindsey Horan channeled her anger into a much-needed goal to keep the Americans unbeaten at the Women's World Cup."

Five days later against Portugal came another tie, this one 0–0. As the back cover of the *New York Daily News* succinctly put it: TIE PUTS U.S. WOMEN IN TOUGH SPOT. "The U.S. women slogged and eked their way to a dangerous, scoreless draw Tuesday against Portugal, while losing a soft path to the quarterfinal round," wrote columnist Filip Bondy. "The World Cup favorites advanced by a matter of inches, literally, to the knockout stage. But the team can't seem to find its way into the attacking box, where Alex Morgan has failed to score a goal, and the Americans just look completely out of whack. Portugal very nearly eliminated the desperate Americans in added time, when substitute Ana Capeta struck an open right-foot shot that fortunately went off the right post. A nation of spoiled-rotten American women's soccer fans held its breath, as the ball caromed safely away."

I was at home watching TV like the rest of the country's sports fans. I had no formal role this time around, unlike in earlier years. My only official connection to the 2023 Women's World Cup was in my capacity as a partner in the company that provided the official, FIFA-approved hospitality at the tournament. The following observations and analysis of the 2023 tournament are presented merely as one fan's notes, albeit a knowledgeable fan with more than 50 years of deep involvement with soccer and sports management in general.

The U.S. women advanced, which was the most important thing, but there were warning signs. Given the team's lackluster play, it was surprising to see many on the U.S. team looking utterly unconcerned afterward. "Former star Carli Lloyd became infuriated watching the U.S. players celebrating the draw with fans," wrote Bondy. "She blamed the U.S. Soccer Federation and the attitude of today's generation of U.S. players." An exasperated Lloyd said on the air: "To be dancing, to be smiling? [...] The player of that match was the post."

Again, in the knockout stage, the U.S. team would make it through regulation without scoring, knotted up 0–0 with Sweden. This time it went to penalty kicks, always a sad and unsatisfying way to be eliminated. Rapinoe came out to take one of the penalty kicks and looked a shadow of the dominant player she had been at the World Cup four years earlier. Even so, it was a shock when her kick sailed high. Talented young Sophia Smith, given a chance to win it for the U.S., also missed high. Veteran Kelley O'Hara hit the post—opening the door to Sweden to close it out.

"Just devastated," said Alex Morgan. "It feels like a bad dream. The team put everything out there tonight, I feel like we dominated, but it doesn't matter. We're going home, and it's the highs and lows of soccer."

Coach Andonovski was heartbroken, but proud of his team. "I think we came out today and showed the grit, the resilience, the fight," he said afterward. "The bravery showed we did everything we could to win the game. And unfortunately, soccer can be cruel sometime."

For the first time since the initial FIFA Women's World Cup was launched in 1991, the U.S. women failed to make it to the quarterfinals. Does that mark the end of an era? Does it spell the demise of a run of 30 years of domination for a team perennially ranked No. 1 in the world and never lower than No. 3? A team that had previously won four World Cups as well as four Olympic gold medals since the initial competition in 1996? Or does it simply represent a transition from a group of veteran players to a talented younger group that will ultimately carry the dynasty forward? Was the fate of the 2023 team, as in 1995, when the team finished third, largely determined by the absence of key players due to injuries and others just coming back from injuries?

My verdict, for what it's worth (and I hope I'm right), is that the 2023 result merely reflects a transition. I think the U.S. women's national team can deliver many more exciting positive results in the years ahead, as evidenced by their gold medal in the '24 Olympics, but I'm not saying it's going to be easy. It never is when sports dynasties try to maintain themselves, as a look at other sports can help demonstrate.

Recently we're looking at the crumbling of the New England Patriots of the National Football League. After the departure of the Patriot GOAT, Tom Brady, it's been nothing short of a disaster. Why? No meaningful steps were taken to be ready for that inevitable day. Replacing Brady's talent and leadership with one player would be impossible, but accumulating other talent to create an excellent team that a decent quarterback could at least make credible wasn't done.

Contrast that with perhaps the longest historic sports dynasty, the New York Yankees, from 1923 through post–World War II. When the GOAT, Babe Ruth, was ready to retire, waiting in the wings to pick up the cudgel both on the field and in the locker room was Joe DiMaggio. Again, talent and leadership, plus a complete team, stood ready. In a later era, the New York Yankees thrived again when George Steinbrenner exploited new free agency rules by gobbling up "Mr. October," Reggie Jackson, and other high-priced talent. But Steinbrenner, too, didn't plan for the future and was caught flat-footed, especially when baseball established a luxury tax to limit excessive free spending and competition was equalized. Ultimately after many dry years, the Yankees did it right by building a farm system so that they could again be dominant between 1996 and 2001, with four mainstays who had come up through the system together, Derek Jeter and Mariano Rivera, both future Hall of Famers, along with Andy Pettitte and Jorge Posada, to whom they added supporting players. Again, talent as well as steady leadership were essential.

One further example of leadership from the top that I cite is the case of the Los Angeles Lakers. First their success came under my mentor, team owner Jack Kent Cooke, initially with Elgin Baylor and Jerry West, then with Wilt Chamberlain added and Kareem Abdul-Jabbar replacing Chamberlain. Under Jerry Buss, the Lakers added Magic Johnson to the mix, and the "Showtime" era was off and running, followed almost immediately with the Kobe and Shaq O'Neal era. The Lakers' record under Dr. Buss: between 1979 and his death in 2013, they won 10 NBA championships and made an incredible 16 appearances in the NBA Finals. Since his death, notwithstanding the acquisition of all-time great LeBron James, the Lakers have recorded just one championship, and that tainted because it was during the shortened and bubbled pandemic season, plus only three other playoff appearances. The Lakers under Cooke and Buss are a great example of strong, forward-thinking ownership.

As a Lakers fan, I will be understandably brief in talking about the Celtics, who under the leadership of Red Auerbach had two almost back-to-back dynasties: from 1957 to 1969, led by USF star Bill Russell's talent and leadership, and, after an up-and-down decade 1979–89, a reign from 1979 to 1987 built around Larry Bird.

Lessons from those examples: all good things come to an end, so it's important to plan ahead and be ready, in the words of JFK during his 1961 inaugural address, "to pass the torch to a new generation." That requires forward thinking and planning leadership off the field from management and on the field from talented players.

I believe that's where the U.S. women's national team now finds itself. They've obtained a world-renowned coach and have an abundance of talented young players. Who among them will emerge as the kind of quiet leader who makes a difference away from the klieg lights, in the quiet of a nearly empty locker room, has yet to be determined. A key to past success was the leadership of Michelle Akers, Carin Jennings, and April Heinrichs in the early years, then the quiet leadership provided by Mia Hamm, Carla Overbeck, Joy Fawcett, and Kris Lilly and not-so-quiet leadership of Julie Foudy, succeeded by Carli Lloyd, Megan Rapinoe, and Lindsey Horan. Undoubtedly one or more of the bevy of young, talented players will fill that role. At this writing, she has yet to be identified. Based on their stellar performance at the Paris Olympics, undoubtedly the exciting front line of Mallory Swanson, Sophia Smith, and Trinity Rodman (the "Triple Espresso") and the rock-solid defender Naomi Girma will emerge as leaders. Additionally, the '99ers and the 2015–19 teams each had a mission that strengthened their bonds. For the '99ers it was to prove to the world the acceptance of the women's game.

"We were very cognizant of the impact we could have on that next generation of kids, girls and boys," Julie Foudy says. "We wanted to inspire them, that's what was so cool about that group. It was important for girls to see what we were doing but it was also very important for boys to see women doing these things in front of large crowds and also playing professionally and showing our value. We felt good about that. It wasn't like: we're finally making money! We were all about impacting the game in a really meaningful way. That was what meant a lot to us as players, especially given how hard—and how long—we had to fight for every advance we made for the sport."

For the 2015–19 team it was the drive for equality, with Megan Rapinoe front and center leading the charge on and off the pitch. What will this talented group adopt as its bonding mission?

Regardless of the mission, the talent is there and the on-the-field leadership, particularly of Naomi Girma, and the off-the-field leadership of Emma Hayes make me very optimistic that, notwithstanding the enhanced competitiveness of women's soccer worldwide, our women's national team will be a force to be reckoned with for the foreseeable future, even if not dynastic.

I know that coach Vlatko Andonovski has been criticized for the 2023 result. He faced a difficult set of circumstances that would have also represented a grave challenge to any coach, including Jill Ellis, his predecessor. Some key players were unavailable due to injury, notably longtime captain Becky Sauerbrunn and Mal Pugh Swanson, Catarina Macario, Samantha Mewis, and Christen Press. And coming back from long absences due to injuries and/or childbirth were Rose Lavelle, Megan Rapinoe, and Julie Ertz. The injuries and the uncertainty they brought compounded the challenge of merging starting veteran talent—five players over 30—with young players—three under 25—without ample time to play together.

Was Andonovski too conservative at times? For example, in not playing other young, raw talent like Trinity Rodman (yes, the 22-year-old daughter of former NBA All-Star and unforgettable character Dennis Rodman) or 18-year-old

Alyssa Thompson, the fastest player on the team (whereas Anson Dorrance played 19-year-old Mia Hamm in 1991)? Did he play a conservative style, unlike the more aggressive offensive style we'd grown accustomed to with our women's national team? Perhaps, but in most sports it's not unusual for conservative defensive play to dominate once you get to playoffs. We'll never know, and frankly it doesn't matter. Looking backward won't help.

Accepting the current challenge is what's important. In that regard, we need to accept that, while our women's national team can remain excellent, the likelihood of a dynastic run on par with what the USWNT has already enjoyed is highly unlikely. Because of Title IX, we got a jump on the rest of the world. Our only competition in the early years was from Scandinavian countries, as well as Germany, Japan, China, and Brazil.

Because of historical cultural reasons, England, France, Italy, Spain, Argentina, and other soccer powerhouse nations came to the women's game belatedly. Now many are supporting women's soccer in a big way. European powerhouse soccer clubs are going all in: Barcelona Man U, Man City, Real Madrid, Arsenal, Chelsea, Paris Saint-Germain, Bayern Munich, Liverpool, and many others in England, Spain, France, and Italy are putting huge resources behind their women's teams. National associations in those countries are committing abundant resources to their national teams as well. The highly respected Deloitte Football Money League *Report* states that there was a 61 percent growth in European women's teams' revenue in the past year. Spain seems to be emulating the incredibly successful French national camp at Clairefontaine, as they not only won the 2023 World Cup, but they were also reigning champions of both U17 and U20. It was a trifecta. The amazing success of the 1999 World Cup served as a proof of concept. Countries and clubs that had been slow in seriously backing the women's game started putting more and more resources in their women's team, which has led to the very competitive environment existing today.

The emergence of big-time support for women's soccer by the giant European clubs and nations is also a challenge for NWSL. Just as our domestic league is breaking out and is on a sharp upward trajectory, it will face difficulties in keeping the best American talent. As MLS has painfully learned, the money available in Europe may be far too tempting for young domestic talent to ignore. Naomi Girma was recently transferred to Chelsea for a record $1 million; a clear example of the commitment of the big European clubs to women's soccer, good for the sport but a challenge to NWSL. This also will affect the women's national team because players will be less available to prepare for or participate in international matches and will have less familiarity with one another. I hope the impact of the 2026 World Cup will result in greater financial returns for our clubs, enabling them to compete for talent on a more equal basis.

Then again, as journalist Lindsay Crouse wrote in the *New York Times* in August 2023, "The American women's team has built a legacy of thriving amid challenge, representing American optimism at its best. And when has the landscape been better for female athletes than now? They know what many of us believe: The best is still ahead. But we have to work for it."

We have leadership at the coaching level with USWNT head coach Emma Hayes, formerly the coach of Chelsea's women's team and considered the best in the business. We also presently have capable and stable leadership in president

Cindy Parlow Cone and general secretary JT Batson at the Federation level, fully committed to the women's national team, although due to the terrible governance structure of U.S. Soccer—in which grassroots volunteers and professional teams and players share equal voting strength but completely different objectives and values—it may or may not be lasting.

My conclusion: we can no longer realistically expect dominance as we've known it for the last 30-plus years, but we're certainly poised to stay a top-notch competitive force permanently. And in soccer, as in life, you never know what you can accomplish until you go out and earn it.

There's a very interesting parallel pattern of growth of men's and women's soccer in the United States. For the men, a successful 1984 Olympics led to a record-breaking 1994 World Cup; which led to a professional league, MLS; which after some incredibly difficult early years has taken hold and continues to grow dramatically. Similarly for the women, a successful 1996 Olympics, followed by a record-setting 1999 World Cup, has led to a professional league, NWSL, taking hold and beginning to experience "hockey stick" growth, following years of difficulties for it and its failed predecessors.

One last parallel, or so I hope: the U.S. men's national team endured the heartbreak of heading to Trinidad and Tobago in October 2017 needing only a tie to advance to the World Cup, then, in a nightmare for U.S. soccer, losing 2–1 and failing to qualify—only to bounce back four years later with a strong showing in the 2022 World Cup, setting the stage for 2026. So by my calculations, following these patterns, the U.S. women's national team is poised to rebound from the disappointment of 2023 with a strong showing in the 2027 Women's World Cup. I can hardly wait.

CHAPTER 9

LEAVING A LEGACY: THE UNITED STATES SOCCER FOUNDATION

Our 1994 World Cup mission was: "Stage the greatest World Cup in history and leave a legacy for the sport of soccer." Clearly, we had succeeded in staging the greatest World Cup in history: we had the largest attendance in history, 3,587,538, which stands till today (although it's sure to be surpassed in 2026), and a more than $50 million surplus. Those results spoke for themselves. But what exactly was the legacy for the sport of soccer in the United States? Unquestionably, there was heightened interest in soccer in the United States overall, quantifiable in the number of participants, more sponsorships, more television, more sales of merchandise, and greater attendance at men's and women's national team matches.

More specifically, here's what followed: Major League Soccer; the '99 Women's World Cup; a new headquarters for U.S. Soccer, "Soccer House"; a solvent American Youth Soccer Organization (AYSO); a player development fund; hundreds of new soccer fields throughout the country; and the beginning of a national trainer center. All made possible because of the creation of the U.S. Soccer Foundation, which acted effectively as the "Soccer Bank" for all of the above—thanks to funding from a surplus of more than $50 million left over from the '94 World Cup.

Let me explain. As I previously mentioned, shortly after becoming president of U.S. Soccer, I put forward a motion to the U.S. Soccer Board that any surplus from the World Cup would be put into a nonprofit foundation. My motion breezed through to adoption because at that time all the board members were utterly fixated on their fears that our World Cup could run up huge losses. In fact, they were so consumed with worries about that scenario that they'd created a separate corporation to run the World Cup, because they were afraid that a huge loss might drive the Federation—already on shaky financial grounds—into bankruptcy oblivion.

What luck! Undoubtedly if they'd thought there was any chance at all that there would be a surplus, let alone the substantial sum we earned, they'd have carved it up in the traditional style—"one for you, one for me, one for you, one for me"—among the multiplicity of grassroots organizations that at that time controlled a majority of the board. The money would have disappeared with precious little lasting benefit to anyone in soccer. Instead, we had the vision to invest longer term and create the U.S. Soccer Foundation.

Right at the outset, the Foundation faced a seminal decision. Would the Foundation, led by a board that was about half from the U.S. Soccer Federation and about half independents, focus on a longer-term strategy for effecting change and having an impact or would it employ a "big bang" philosophy, spending all the principal on, for example, a national training center and stadium, and then go out of business? This was one of the few times in our decades-long alliance within soccer in the United States that Sunil Gulati and I disagreed. He led the "big bang" advocates, supported by, among others, my successor as president, Dr. Bob Contiguglia. The Foundation exists and is flourishing today, over 30 years later, because fortunately those of us advocating for a perpetual Foundation prevailed.

Another decision essential to the ultimate and continuing success of the Foundation was where to house it. Customarily when a not-for-profit is started by another entity, the offices are side by side, considered sister and brother organizations, sharing personnel, office space, and administrative overhead. Adopting that approach with the Federation would have meant locating the Foundation at Soccer House in Chicago. I didn't think that was a good idea and pushed for an alternative.

I made the decision to locate it instead in Washington, DC, for two reasons. First was the continuing apprehension that proximity to the Federation would inevitably subject the Foundation to undue domination by the Federation. As is clear, I feared that under those circumstances the money would be spent with little meaningful to show for it in the end. Second, in addition to ensuring its independence, a DC location would put the Foundation in the midst of many other not-for-profits, some of which would be synergistic with our Foundation. Further, locating in the nation's capital would give us access to government agencies, possibly enabling us to receive grants.

The decision paid off. The Foundation has operated independently of the Federation, though always supportive. And it has received grants from both government agencies and other not-for-profits. Initially, the focus of the Foundation was 100 percent to support the Federation and its affiliates. We developed a detailed grant system. In almost all cases, the grants were made on a multiyear basis, requiring recipients to give annual updates. That ensured that, as much as possible, we could be satisfied that the grant money was being properly spent.

In its early years, the Foundation made the following vital investments.

Soccer Fields

In the first years of our existence, the Foundation granted financial assistance to help build soccer fields throughout the United States. The Foundation supported the development of some 600 full-sized soccer fields in all 50 states before shifting its focus to smaller spaces better suited to support growth of the game in more urban communities.

$5 Million Seed Money to Create MLS

During the 1992–94 period, almost all the revenue coming into soccer was from World Cup ticket sales, sponsorships, and licensing. We had stepped up sponsorships at the Federation, and they received ticket revenue from men's national team friendly matches. However, inasmuch as we were simultaneously professionalizing Federation management and underwriting the men's national team's lengthy residency camp as well as supporting all the other men's and women's national teams, the Federation was at best breaking even.

Things were happening so fast we were using the World Cup effectively as the bank for everything, without concurrently accounting for it. We cleaned up the accounting after the fact. While it was unorthodox, I don't believe we violated any laws (if we did, the statute of limitations would insulate us from liability, so I feel unrestrained in admitting to our bit of "sloppiness"). Undoubtedly, we didn't strictly follow generally accepted accounting practices, but I'm 100 percent confident no money "disappeared."

I'm giving this background because the Foundation didn't hand over a check for $5 million to MLS for its seed money. Rather, the bulk of the money was paid for accounting and legal services, fees to the stadium consultant, investment banker fees, travel expenses as Mark Abbott went to cities to solicit interest in having an MLS team, office start-up costs, meetings with potential investors, the media and sponsors, etc. When the dust settled, we totaled everything up and that was $5 million.

A challenge: Once we had the Foundation and MLS entities, how would we treat the $5 million? We contemplated having the Foundation deem it as an investment in MLS and take an equity piece. While it's unusual to have a nonprofit own a for-profit business, it's not unheard of. But we didn't want to push the envelope. Instead, we decided to treat it as a loan. That led to the obvious question: How would it be repaid? MLS barely had enough capital to get up and running and couldn't be saddled with a $5 million repayment, which would represent 10 percent of its initial capital. An agreement was reached. The loan would be repaid primarily in kind, through Foundation advertising on the field boards and other MLS assets as well as fine money collected by MLS. An independent advertising expert gave us an opinion as to the extent of advertising necessary to pay in kind for the $5 million and the loan was thusly repaid over five years.

Soccer House

When we negotiated with Mayor Daley and Jay Pritzker for Chicago to have the opening game in 1994, they arranged an option on a very attractive loan for us to buy Soccer House. The Foundation provided the Federation with the money to exercise that option. Soccer House was home for U.S. Soccer for 30 years until it was outgrown. The Federation is on its way to Atlanta, where Arthur Blank has been enormously generous and is building a new headquarters and training facilities in Georgia. U.S. Soccer is now selling Soccer House for a profit of several million dollars.

The '99 Women's World Cup

The Foundation advanced $2.5 million for the planning of the 1999 Women's World Cup once we'd received FIFA's okay to play in large stadiums nationwide.

American Youth Soccer Organization

AYSO was hit with a $1 million judgment against it and faced imminent bankruptcy. The Foundation gave AYSO the money to pay the judgment and stay in business.

Player Development

The Foundation provided the Federation with $5 million for its player development fund, the first time it ever had such a fund.

National Training Site

When Phil Anschutz was contemplating building his stadium, he asked for a commitment from U.S. Soccer to be a part of the project. In response, the Foundation provided $5 million to develop soccer fields on the property to serve as a training site for our national teams as well as be the site for youth and adult team matches. Additional funds were given to Dallas for training sites and a Soccer Hall of Fame.

Scholarships

Anticipating parents' concerns that when MLS tried to recruit young talent they might be giving up college scholarship opportunities, the Foundation agreed to provide those scholarships if the player signed and then within five years decided to go to college. Interestingly, while it was a great recruiting pitch to placate parents, not a single person ever asked for it. The young men either were successful players or, if not, stayed on in soccer at academies in administration or coaching.

Over time the mission of the Foundation has changed. It became clear that most of the organizations that applied for grants to build fields while being assisted by the Foundation grant were really capable of raising the money necessary to build the fields. It might take a bit more time and effort, but it could be done. On the other hand, in discussions with the Federation it became clear that underserved communities, primarily inner-city communities almost entirely of people of color, were completely underserved by the "pay to play" system prevalent at the grassroots.

The Foundation totally changed its emphasis. The grant program continued, but on a much-decreased basis, utilized only for special situations. Focusing on the underserved urban areas, the Foundation has developed a series of very successful programs, including Soccer for Success, Safe Places to Play, and Just Ball League.

By 2026, it will have built over 1,000 mini pitches and will serve over 1 million youth annually. Most inner cities lack large, open spaces, so it would be difficult if not impossible to build many full-sized soccer fields. The mini pitches can be put down on virtually any playground or small open space for a cost of $100,000, a fraction of what a full soccer field would cost.

The Foundation has developed programs, manuals, and training materials for coaches. Musco Lighting provides lighting enabling nighttime play, Kwik Goal provides soccer goals, Adidas and Nike have provided the pitches and equipment. The Foundation partners with MLS and USL teams and now NWSL teams, city recreation departments, and Boys and Girls Clubs in the various cities to develop and operate the programs.

The Soccer for Success program has provided youth in under-resourced communities access to free soccer programs led by trained coach-mentors who teach fundamentals of the game along with critical life skills. Besides being provided safe places to play, the participants learn nutritional and other life and health pointers and are assisted in learning skills. The programs have been independently evaluated by recognized valuation agencies and have received the highest ratings. The Just Ball League has been developed so that participants can enjoy competition in their own communities, as in most cases the cost and burden of out-of-area travel to compete would be prohibitive, thus depriving more players of that competitive experience.

"The legacy that was created through the U.S. Soccer Foundation goes so much deeper than just growing the sport. Our current emphasis is on the under-resourced communities, where far too many families are priced out of the sport or don't have accessible programs or fields," says Ed Foster-Simeon, the Foundation's CEO.

He continues, "Why is that important? Providing access to soccer is about much more than just fun and games. Youth who have the opportunity to participate have access to a non-traditional learning platform that can help shape their future. Through our game, youth develop critical life skills like leadership, teamwork, and perseverance. Even more, participation in soccer and the associated physical activity are essential to maintaining and improving the health and well-being of children. That's why the work of the Foundation is so important. It's about using our sport—soccer—to make a positive impact that extends well beyond the playing field. It's really about improving the lives of an entire generation through the game we all love."

To our good fortune, Foster-Simeon, a former *USA Today* executive, has been the inspirational and dynamic CEO of the U.S. Soccer Foundation for the past decade and a half. The makeup of the board has also evolved, with a majority of independent directors. While there is still representation by U.S. Soccer people, a diverse group of successful businesspeople (non–U.S. Soccer directors) have been added. The membership includes former national team players; MLS, NWSL, and Federation executives; professionals (doctors and lawyers); consultants; corporate executives in various fields; youth recreational organizations; and banking, private equity, and hedge fund principals. They have a common trait: they all love soccer. Most have played in college or professionally, many afterward; many have kids that play, others still coach, and everyone is committed to help youth. They are fully dedicated to the mission: “We transform children’s lives. We provide underserved communities access to innovative play spaces and evidence-based soccer programs that instill hope, foster well-being, and help youth achieve their fullest potential.” To ensure “fresh blood,” the Foundation has established term limits with one exception: in my honor, the board has designated me as a Life Member, for which I feel very proud and grateful.

I do think it’s sometimes worth taking a step back and acknowledging the steps taken in the past to achieve success today, and it was very gratifying when Charles (Cully) Stimson, wrapping up his term as chairman of the board of the Foundation in 2022, had some very nice things to say about the steps we’d taken. “We owe the very existence of this foundation to Alan Rothenberg,” he said in his speech at the time. “It was his vision in 1994, on the cusp of the World Cup, that *if* the organizing committee made money—which had never happened—that the net profits would be used to create a charitable foundation to grow and enhance the game of soccer here in the USA. Most people pooh-poohed the idea, but he didn’t.... Again, without Alan, none of us would be here today, and we wouldn’t be in the place we’re in.” And in closing, he added: “We were born out of the World Cup. How fitting it is that we are now gearing up to play a major role in the 2026 World Cup.”

Whereas previously the Foundation was funded exclusively by the return on investments from the '94 World Cup surplus, plus some corporate cash and in-kind support, recently it has begun to actively pursue philanthropic contributions with some great success. It has received multi-million-dollar support from major corporate entities, nonprofit foundations, and individuals, which together with the return on investments have enabled dramatic growth.

In the bid to host the 2026 World Cup, the United States designated the Foundation to be the organization providing the requisite legacy programs.

It's fair to conclude that:

- But for the Foundation, probably no MLS
- But for the Foundation, perhaps no '99 Women's World Cup
- But for the Foundation, no Soccer House
- But for the Foundation, possibly no AYSO
- But for the Foundation, hundreds fewer soccer fields throughout the country
- But for the Foundation, no initial U.S. Soccer player development fund
- But for the Foundation, no training fields at Dignity Health Sports Park
- But for the Foundation, no 1,000 mini pitches in urban areas
- But for the Foundation, no Soccer for Success programs for 1 million youth annually in under-resourced communities

With enormous pride I can say about 1994: it was both the greatest World Cup in history (to date) *and* the creation of a legacy for soccer in the United States!

EPILOGUE

THE BIG BOUNCE: THE EXCITING, UNIQUE PROMISE OF THE 2026 WORLD CUP

BASED ON THE EXPERIENCE I've had over the years working in sports and the sports business, I want to wrap up by making some observations of what I hope to see during the 2026 World Cup and what its legacy for soccer in the United States could turn out to be—and where future developments in soccer are going.

For starters, the 2026 World Cup in North America, with matches in Canada, Mexico, and the United States, will represent a step forward in an evolution of the event toward more creative arrangements that allow multiple countries to host, broadening the possibilities for the future. Earlier I described how in the run-up to the 2002 World Cup, FIFA president João Havelange had made a commitment to bring the event to Japan, then started worrying as the South Korean bid looked stronger and stronger; so Havelange got creative and arranged a joint effort with Japan and South Korea co-hosting.

It worked out surprisingly well, and everybody was happy. Previous thinking had been that joint bids were unwieldy and too challenging logistically, but after 2002 the idea gained currency.

Looking ahead to a possible 2026 bid for another World Cup in the United States, then U.S. Soccer president Sunil Gulati was weighing options and knew that Mexico and Canada were both also planning to bid to host 2026. To avoid a battle among the three countries, and also to strengthen the bid, he persuaded Mexico and Canada to join the U.S. in a joint bid. As Sunil said in April 2017, announcing the groundbreaking Canada-Mexico-U.S. bid, the plan made business sense, it was pragmatic, and it would also be a lot of fun and get people excited: “We think it’s terrific for soccer in the region—for Canada, Mexico, and the U.S.—given the close relationships we have already.”

Since the number of teams participating has increased from 24 to 48, the U.S. will be hosting more matches in 2026 than they did in 1994. The additional matches will be divided between Canada and Mexico, both of which would have been seriously challenged to host the entire competition on their own. Let’s call that a win-win—or maybe a win-win-win. Clearly, joint hosting is the wave of the future and will become commonplace. The event is so massive that there are only a handful of countries with the infrastructure and capacity to host it by themselves. It means greater opportunity for more countries to participate.

Look at 2030 and how that bid unfolded. In October 2020, the soccer federations of Spain and Portugal announced that the two neighboring countries were joining forces to bid on 2030. Then in March 2023, two and a half years later, came the additional announcement that Morocco would be joining the bid (Morocco is closer to the European continent than England is). So, the three countries will be co-hosts, and since it's the centennial of the first World Cup, in 2030 the opening ceremony and first match will be played in Uruguay, where the first World Cup was held in 1930, at Estadio Centenario in Montevideo. Argentina will host the second game and Paraguay the third, then the action will move back to Morocco, Portugal, and Spain. This three-continent World Cup will truly be a world celebration of the "beautiful game."

I feel especially pleased that Morocco will finally be a host. It's a fabulous country I grew to love during all the time I spent there trying to help them obtain the rights to host the 2010 World Cup, only to be thwarted by the Jack Warner bribery episode. And the Moroccan national team's electric performance in the 2022 World Cup, when they became the first team from an African or Arab country to reach the semifinals, captured the hearts of people worldwide. Host cities for Morocco will include Casablanca, Fez, Marrakesh, and Tangier, exotic backdrops all.

When FIFA increased the number of teams in the World Cup tournament to 48, many soccer fans feared the larger pool would dilute the quality of the competition by letting lesser-quality national teams participate. Morocco's performance in 2022 should have silenced the naysayers. Giving more opportunities to more countries advances the game worldwide.

In fact, I had suggested many years ago—and still think it's a great idea—that FIFA emulate the NCAA Final Four and increase participation to a field of 64 nations and instead of group play have single elimination throughout the tournament. Doesn't that sound exciting? While more dominant teams would usually prevail over lesser teams in the first round, there would be the occasional upset and many close calls, both of which enhance fan interest. Every now and then a "Cinderella team" would advance and capture the world's interest. As the Final Four has proven, that unpredictability generates widespread appeal. For the World Cup, it would also open up the opportunity to more countries to participate, stimulating interest in the sport in those countries.

Both internationally and domestically, we can anticipate much disruption in the current structure of competition. The European Court has opened the door to a European Super League, which has been perennially discussed. Its advent will have a major impact on national leagues, continental championships, and other competitions. Existing cross-border restrictions will be breached. Those precedents and potential antitrust decisions will lead to similar disruptions in the United States. What will be the impact of the recently announced USL1? Will the Saudis and Emirates decide to invest in the United States? All of these will be good for soccer, as the changes will open new competitions, but also will cause difficulties and in some cases challenging transitions that will have to be dealt with by existing national teams, leagues, clubs, and players as well as confederations and FIFA.

Speaking of disruption, there's one I wish would take place, although I view it as unlikely in the foreseeable future. The United States Soccer Federation should be split in two. One organization should oversee grassroots soccer. The other should focus on professional and Olympic competitive soccer. The current hybrid serves neither group maximally. Local "mom and pop" volunteer participants should not have any say over governance of multi-billion-dollar assets, nor should wealthy and powerful investors be in a position to tell local amateur participants how to operate. While competing at various ages, amateur soccer focuses more on "It's not whether you win or lose, it's how you play the game"—whereas at the professional and Olympic level, it's more like Vince Lombardi's saying, "Winning isn't everything, it's the only thing." Or as the former Man U manager Bill Shankly famously said, "Some people think football is a matter of life and death. I assure you, it's much more serious than that."

Both groups are vital to soccer, but they have different interests. Currently we are blessed with outstanding leadership. Cindy Cone, a world-class soccer player and an excellent youth coach but with no management experience, was thrust into the presidency of U.S. Soccer due to the sudden resignation of her predecessor. Under her leadership the historic "equal pay" agreement was reached; a lawsuit with the Foundation was settled; the crisis in NWSL was resolved; a new national training center and Federation headquarters are being built; sponsorships have been soaring, leading to a strong financial position for the Federation; and new world-class coaches for the national teams have been hired: Emma Hayes for the women and Mauricio Pochettino for the men. Yet the first time she ran for reelection she barely survived a challenge (not unlike my fate in 1994); who knows what she may face in 2026? (I am writing this book before the 2026 Soccer Federation AGM, where hopefully Cindy will be reelected by acclamation.)

Because of existing legislation—the Ted Stevens Olympic and Amateur Sports Act—it would literally take an act of Congress to accomplish my objective. It would be great for soccer but I'm not betting on that happening any time soon. Like the NFL, we just have to find our Senator Long.

We have more soccer fans in the United States every year. With MLS and MLS Next; USL Championship; and two other leagues (the pioneering efforts of Francisco Marcos and his successor Alec Papadakis cannot be overstated), NWSL and USL W League, there is hardly a town in America without its own home team. The U.S. Soccer Federation men's and women's national teams, as well as various youth teams, blanket the country with top-flight soccer. And traveling throughout the United States, everywhere you go you see kids and adults playing soccer, organized and pickup. It reminds me of what Georgina and I observed when we first traveled through Europe at the time of the 1982 World Cup. Kids and adults are playing in empty lots, in parks, in alleys on any surface, cement, dirt, sand, gravel, or grass. Recently I was in Ann Arbor for a Michigan football game and drove by fields where students used to be tossing a football around and were now kicking a soccer ball.

The U.S. market is very competitive, and sports fans have a lot of options, but sometimes you just feel a surge of energy—and, in a word, fun—infusing a sport with fresh momentum, and that's what we're seeing with soccer right now. The creative financial package that brought Lionel Messi to MLS was innovative and brilliant, and Messi's impact has been off the charts—not only for his hometown Inter Miami fans, but all over the country, where fans plan ahead to see when Messi will be in their city, working his magic and bringing the exuberance of a kid first kicking a ball around. Messi's contract runs through the end of the 2025 season and he's going to continue to bring new converts to the game.

Think back to 1988, when FIFA awarded the 1994 World Cup to the United States, holding their breath as to whether it would succeed. They had such grave doubts that they kept the notion of moving it to Germany or some other European soccer mecca in their back pocket, just in case things weren't working out. In 1990 no World Cup match was shown live on English-language TV in the United States. On a recent Saturday four Euro 2024 matches and three Copa 2024 matches were shown live on network TV, every MLS match was available live on Apple TV, and every NWSL match was live on CBS. We've come a long way, baby!

It's fair to say that for the time being our country has to be considered the world capital for major international soccer. Building on the interest generated by the United States hosting Copa América in 2024, with teams from South America and the Final played in Hard Rock Stadium in Miami, the U.S. also hosted the FIFA Club World Cup in 2025 as a prelude to the World Cup in 2026. As we saw leading up to 1994, we can count on numerous high-profile national team friendlies as other countries come to acclimate themselves to the market before the World Cup. Then, after the World Cup, it will be time to look forward to the 2028 Los Angeles Olympic Games, where this time we head into the competition knowing that soccer will be a huge draw on both the women's and men's side, unlike in 1984, when it was an afterthought that succeeded beyond all expectations—and then to the 2031 Women's World Cup, coming back to the United States.

The world will look to us and more U.S. fans will have more in common with soccer fans worldwide. Not unlike in the aftermath of the 1994 World Cup, undoubtedly there will be yet another surge in interest in soccer in the United States, elevating the sport even closer in equal popularity to the current big three in American sports—baseball, basketball, and football—potentially even surpassing baseball over time, in part because of demographic trends, such as the continuing growth of the U.S. Latino population. That will mean closer parity in popularity of the MLS to the NBA and MLB and, to a certain extent, the NFL. As in the aftermath of 1994, participation, media coverage, sponsorships, television, merchandise sales, and attendance at matches will soar. I'm sure Apple TV and MLS will see a dramatic upsurge in viewership on their path-breaking streaming contract. Similarly, the CBS viewership of NWSL will soar.

Clearly, the attendance records set in 1994 will be broken since there'll be more matches. On the other hand, there will be limited direct financial benefit to the host cities or the national associations, unlike the surplus from 1994, because FIFA has kept total control of the World Cup assets, bypassing the U.S. Soccer Federation. So, our record of a $50 million-plus surplus may remain intact. In fact, host cities will be hard pressed not to incur substantial losses, as they have few assets—sponsorships and tickets—to sell, while incurring huge costs to deliver the matches. The cities will offset those costs as much as possible by whatever revenues they are able to secure from the sale of local sponsorships and a modest inventory of tickets to be sold. Hospitality packages and local individual and corporate donations, motivated largely by civic pride, will realize additional revenue. The collection of tourism taxes from visitors will also offset public-service costs. Finally, hosting the world's greatest single sports event will allow host cities to showcase themselves to the world, presumably resulting in a substantial boon in future tourism. The overall direct financial profit from the event, however, will be FIFA's.

I foresee continuing improvement in the quality of our men's and women's national teams as well as the MLS and NWSL. Today they're a bit hamstrung because the better players are scattered around the globe, as we find it very difficult to compete financially with European clubs. Assembling them for international matches is difficult, as is creating an "American" style of play. Keeping them in our domestic leagues is challenging because of the economic disparity with the major European clubs.

The opening of Arthur M. Blank U.S. Soccer National Training Center in Atlanta with the new U.S. Soccer Headquarters will give us the opportunity to create our "Clairfontaine" and hopefully realize the success France and Spain have realized from theirs.

If, as I expect, one aftermath of 2026 will be to increase the TV, sponsorship, and ticket revenues for our clubs, MLS and NWSL teams will be able to afford to keep more young American talent at home, which will advance the leagues and the national teams. No doubt women's soccer and particularly the NWSL will get a substantial boost in popularity, especially with the 2031 Women's World Cup coming back to the United States. Will MLS teams consider adding capacity to their soccer-specific stadiums, to 30,000–40,000 seats? And will the NWSL teams follow Kansas City in building soccer-specific stadiums? I think so in both cases.

I've been bullish on soccer's continuing growth potential in the United States so long, Lionel Messi was a four-year-old joining his first team, Grandoli, in Argentina when I'd already started my tenure as U.S. Soccer president, and I continue to be bullish. Stepping back and comparing the soccer landscape in the United States in 1990 to what it will be in 2026 and beyond is breathtaking.

In bringing soccer from the hinterlands in 1990 to its status today, let alone what it will be after 2026 (at one point I was concurrently in charge of the U.S. Soccer Federation, the 1994

Men's World Cup, the U.S. Soccer Foundation, Major League Soccer, and the 1999 Women's World Cup). Some thought it was a conflict of interest. "No," I replied, "It's a *confluence of interest*."

Centralized management of U.S. Soccer, the 1994 Men's World Cup, the launch of Major League Soccer, the 1999 Women's World Cup, and the U.S. Soccer Foundation at that moment in time was essential to their success. Run separately and independently, they risked cannibalizing each other. Without the 1994 World Cup funds, the other projects would have been crippled financially. A confluence of interests was necessary.

Today the United States is truly a Soccer Nation because of what started in the 1990s. Mostly, however, it was the efforts of thousands of volunteers and staff and millions of soccer fans, who in growing numbers enthusiastically supported the beautiful game. Undoubtedly that growth will increase exponentially because of the 2026 World Cup. It was my extremely good fortune to have been thrust into the midst of the seminal events in the '90s, and I am ever grateful for that.

ACKNOWLEDGMENTS

I'VE TRIED TO ACKNOWLEDGE throughout *The Big Bounce* the contributions of so many individuals who have been vital participants in the journey taking soccer from the backwoods to the forefront of the American sports scene. While I was tempted to list the hundreds, truly thousands, of people who have done this for the "beautiful game," I feared I'd inadvertently overlook some important contributors, so instead let me express my deeply sincere thanks to all who have been part of this incredible journey, not just those on the foregoing pages, but also the millions of soccer fans without whose enthusiastic support the successes discussed in *The Big Bounce* wouldn't have been possible.

I'm incredibly fortunate and grateful to have been in the right position at the right time to have benefited from that support. Thank you, thank you, thank you!

A special thanks to my extraordinary wife, Georgina, and my three amazing sons, Brad, Richie, and Danny, who not only gave me loving support but rolled up their sleeves and actively participated in virtually every part of the journey. Brad ran the '94 Legacy Tour and Soccer Fest. Richie worked the '84 locker room and assisted Brad with the Legacy Tour, and Danny was our photographer for '94; many of his pictures are part of this book.

A special thanks to Steve Kettmann, a talented writer and now a good friend, who helped me write this book.

One final word: GOOOOOAL!

ABOUT THE AUTHOR

HOW DID A MIDDLE-AGED LAWYER who had never coached soccer, never played soccer—never even been a fan of soccer!—end up as a "Soccer Czar" who brought the sport from the backwaters to the forefront of American sports? More or less by accident. Alan Rothenberg oversaw the historic soccer tournament at the 1984 L.A. Olympics; organized the 1994 World Cup, which set records that still stand for attendance and profit; chaired the 1999 Women's World Cup, the most successful women's sporting event in history, universally considered the breakthrough event for women's team sports; and launched Major League Soccer, which few thought would survive beyond a year or two and which recently celebrated its 30th anniversary as a league. Alan Rothenberg, namesake of the trophy awarded to the MLS champion every year from 1996 to 2007, is a former president of the California State Bar Association and partner at Latham & Watkins and the Manatt firm whose seven-decade career in sports spans his days working with Los Angeles Lakers owner Jack Kent Cooke starting in 1967 to his continuing involvement with sports marketing company Premier Partnerships, a division of Playfly Sports, and work on various boards. Rothenberg lives in Los Angeles with his wife, Georgina, a sculptor and jewelry designer. They, their three sons, their daughters-in-law, and their six grandchildren are avid soccer fans.